Cleanroom Software Engineering: A Reader

CLEANROOM SOFTWARE ENGINEERING: A READER

EDITED BY
Jesse H. Poore and
Carmen J. Trammell

This collection copyright © Jesse H. Poore and Carmen J. Trammell, 1996

First published 1996

NCC Blackwell
108 Cowley Road, Oxford OX4 1JF, UK

Blackwell Publishers Inc.
238 Main Street, Cambridge MA 02142, USA

British Library Cataloguing in Publication Data

A CIP catalogue record for this book is available from the British Library.

Library of Congress Cataloging-in-Publication Data

Cleanroom software engineering: A Reader/edited by Jesse H. Poore and Carmen J. Trammell.
p. cm.
ISBN 1-85554-654-X (pbk. : alk. paper)
  1. Software engineering. 2. Computer software—Quality control.
I. Poore, Jesse H., 1942– II. Trammell, Carmen J., 1952–
QA76.758.R43 1996
005.1'4—dc20   95-4872
        CIP

Typeset in 10 on 12 pt Times by Wearset, Boldon, Tyne and Wear.

This book is printed on acid-free paper

Contents

**The following case studies can be downloaded as files from the World
Wide Web at;** http://www.blackwellpublishers.co.uk/ncc/cleanroom
1   A Case Study in Cleanroom Software Engineering:
     the IBM COBOL Structuring Facility   *R. C. Linger*
2   A Successful Cleanroom Project – os32   *L.-G. Tann*
3   Software Process Evolution at the SEL   *V. R. Basili and
     S. E. Green*
4   Phased Implementation of Cleanroom on the AOEXPERT/MVS
     Project   *P. A. Hausler, R. C. Linger, and C. J. Trammell*
5   The Application of Cleanroom Software Engineering to the
     Development of Embedded Control Systems Software
     M. Brewer, P. Fisher, D. A. Fuhrer, K. Nielsen, and J. H. Poore
6   A Case Study in Software Reliability Measurement
     J. A. Whittaker and K. Agrawal
7   Experience Using Cleanroom Software Engineering in the
     us Army   *S. W. Sherer, P. G. Arnold, and A. Kouchakdjian*

Dedication

This book is dedicated to the founder of Cleanroom software engineering, Dr Harlan D. Mills (1919–1996).

Dr Mills' contributions to computer science had a profound and enduring effect on theory, education, and industrial practice, and his service to the profession and the nation magnified the impact of his contributions manyfold. After earning his Ph.D. in Mathematics at Iowa State University in 1952, Dr Mills led a distinguished career.

Dr Mills' explication of the mathematical foundations of software had a signal influence on the discipline. His understanding that a program is a mathematical function enabled the application of a host of function-theoretic principles to software development and verification. His view of software testing as a statistical experiment enabled a scientific approach to software evaluation and certification. He contributed his ideas to the profession in six books and over fifty refereed articles in technical journals. His function-theoretic approach to program verification was presented in *Structured Programming: Theory and Practice* (1979), co-authored by Linger and Witt. A collection of his seminal papers on chief programmer teams, top-down design, structured programming, program correctness, and other fundamental ideas in software engineering was published in *Software Productivity* (1983). His reduction of the mathematics of specification and design to practice was published in *Principles of Information Systems Analysis and Design* (1986), co-authored by Linger and Hevner.

Dr Mills served on the faculties of Iowa State, Princeton, New York, and Johns Hopkins Universities, the Universities of Maryland and Florida, and Florida Institute of Technology. At Johns Hopkins and Maryland, he initiated one of the first American university courses in structured programming. At Maryland, he developed a new two-semester freshman introduction to computer science and the textbook *Principles of Computer*

Programming: A Mathematical Approach, co-authored by Basili, Gannon, and Hamlet. At FIT, he developed a new freshman and sophomore curriculum for software engineering using Ada with colleagues Engle and Newman.

Dr Mills was an IBM Fellow and Member of the Corporate Technical Committee at the IBM Corporation, a Technical Staff Member at GE and RCA, and President of Mathematica and Software Engineering Technology. At GE, he developed a three-month curriculum in management science attended by hundreds of GE executives. At IBM, he was the primary architect of the IBM Software Engineering Institute, where thousands of IBM software personnel were trained in the mathematical foundations of software. He later embodied the mathematical and statistical principles for software in the Cleanroom software engineering process. As founder of Software Engineering Technology, Inc., he created an enterprise for Cleanroom technology transfer.

Dr Mills had an abiding interest in fostering sound software engineering practices through federal programs. During the formative period of the DoD ARPA STARS Program in the 1980s, he provided fundamental concepts for development of high-quality software at high productivity.

In 1986, he served as Chairman of the Computer Science Panel for the US Air Force Scientific Advisory Board. During 1974–77, he was Chairman of the NSF Computer Science Research Panel on Software Methodology.

Dr Mills was a program committee member and invited speaker for many professional conferences, and a referee for many mathematics and computer science journals. From 1980 to 1983, he was Governor of the IEEE Computer Society. In 1981, he was the Chairman for the IEEE Fall CompCon. During 1975–81, he served as Editor for *IEEE Transactions on Software Engineering*. In 1977, he was the US Representative for Software at the IFIP Congress. In 1975, he was the Chairman of the First National Conference on Software Engineering.

Because of his work, thousands of software engineers are approaching and achieving near-zero-defects in software development. It is with deep admiration and affection that we dedicate this book to Dr Mills. All royalties from the book will go to the Harlan D. Mills Scholarship Fund at the University of Tennessee.

List of Contributors

K. K. Agrawal, StrataCom, Inc., 1400 Parkmoor Avenue, San Jose, CA 95126, USA

P. G. Arnold, Loral Federal Systems, 700 North Frederick Avenue, Gaithersburg, MD 20879, USA

V. R. Basili, Department of Computer Science and Institute for Advanced Computer Studies, A. V. Williams Building, University of Maryland, College Park, MD 20742, USA

M. A. Brewer, IBM Storage Systems Division, Department 74M/031, Tucson, AZ 85744, USA

M. Dyer, 7201 Wisconsin Avenue, Suite 780, Bethesda, MD 20814, USA

P. H. Fisher, National Applied Computer Technologies, 744 South 400 East, Orem, UT 84058, USA

D. A. Fuhrer, Software Engineering Technology, Inc., 2770 Indian River Boulevard, Vero Beach, FL 32960, USA

S. E. Green, NASA Goddard Space Flight Center, Code 552.1, Greenbelt, MD 20771, USA

P. A. Hausler, IBM Corporation, 6710 Rockledge Drive, Bethesda, MD 20817, USA

G. E. Head, Hewlett-Packard Company, 1501 Page Mill Road, MS 4L-4, Palo Alto, CA 94304, USA

A. R. Hevner, Department of Information Systems and Decision Sciences, College of Business Administration, University of South Florida, 4202 East Fowler Avenue, CIS1040, Tampa, FL 33620, USA

E.-A. Karlsson, Quality Laboratories Sweden AB, IDEON Research Park, S-223 70 Lund, Sweden

A. Kouchakdjian, Software Engineering Technology, Inc., 2770 Indian River Boulevard, Vero Beach, FL 32960, USA

R. C. Linger, Software Engineering Institute, Carnegie Mellon University, Pittsburgh, PA 15213, USA

B. A. Miller, Cleanroom Software Technology Center, IBM Corporation, 6710 Rockledge Drive, Bethesda, MD 20817, USA

H. D. Mills, Software Engineering Technology, Inc., 2770 Indian River Boulevard, Vero Beach, FL 32960, USA

D. Mutchler, Department of Computer Science, Rose-Hulman Institute of Technology, 5500 Wabash Avenue, Terre Haute, IN 47803, USA

K. A. Nielsen, IBM Storage Systems Division, Department 74M/031, Tucson, AZ 85744, USA

M. D. Pleszkoch, Cleanroom Software Technology Center, IBM Corporation, 6710 Rockledge Drive, Bethesda, MD 20817, USA

J. H. Poore, Department of Computer Science, 107 Ayres Hall, University of Tennessee, Knoxville, TN 37996, USA

P. Runeson, Quality Laboratories Sweden AB, IDEON Research Park, S-223 70 Lund, Sweden

S. W. Sherer, US Army ARDEC, Picatinny Arsenal, NJ 07806, USA

L.-G. Tann, Ellemtel Telecommunications Systems Laboratories, Box 1505, S-125 25 Älvsjö, Sweden

M. G. Thomason, Department of Computer Science, 107 Ayres Hall, University of Tennessee, Knoxville, TN 37996, USA

C. J. Trammell, Department of Computer Science, 107 Ayres Hall, University of Tennessee, Knoxville, TN 37996, USA

G. H. Walton, Department of Electrical and Computer Engineering, University of Central Florida, Orlando, FL 32816, USA

J. A. Whittaker, Software Engineering Technology, Inc., Mills Building Suite 304, 2200 Sutherland Ave., Knoxville, TN 37919, USA

C. Wohlin, Department of Communication Systems, Lund Institute of Technology, Lund University, Box 118, S-221 00 Lund, Sweden

PART 1

An Overview of Cleanroom Software Engineering

Introduction

Harlan Mills introduced an approach to software engineering based on fundamental ideas in mathematics, statistics, and engineering. He developed the theory, reduced the theory to practice, and demonstrated the practice. After highly successful application of the ideas in large demonstration projects, Mills offered them to the industry at large under the masthead "Cleanroom" – a term borrowed from the semiconductor industry to reflect his central emphasis on defect prevention rather than defect removal.

Many in the software engineering community have been inspired to build on the ideas Mills proposed as the foundation of sound software practice. His legacy at IBM, the Cleanroom Software Technology Center, has adapted the ideas to a wide variety of application and computing environments. His company founded to promote Cleanroom, Software Engineering Technology, has adapted the ideas to support the strategic plans of the world's largest software customer, the US Department of Defense. His admirers in Q-Labs of Sweden have made tremendous strides in introducing Cleanroom ideas in European industry. The Universities of Florida, Maryland, and Tennessee and the Florida Institute of Technology have advanced the ideas through continuing research and development.

Mills' original Cleanroom ideas can be found in two works. *Software Productivity* (Little, Brown, 1983) is a collection of Mills' early papers that were the seeds of Cleanroom. *The Cleanroom Approach to Quality Software Development* by Michael Dyer (John Wiley, 1992) is a description of the Cleanroom process by a colleague of Mills during Mills' tenure as an IBM Fellow, when the Cleanroom ideas were developed and demonstrated.

The evolution in Cleanroom ideas can be seen in three conference proceedings. The 25th Annual IEEE Hawaii International Conference on

Systems Sciences, held in January 1992, included a Cleanrooom track, where a variety of theoretical advances and field experiences were reported. The European International Symposium on Cleanroom Software Engineering (EISCSE), first held in 1993 in Copenhagen, was the first major gathering of Cleanroom practitioners. The second EISCSE was held in March 1995 in Berlin.

Many other theoretical papers and field reports have circulated in the open literature, in university theses, in corporate publications, and in private communications. The motivation for this book was the need for a convenient source of information about Cleanroom practice and experience.

- "Adopting Cleanroom software engineering with a phased approach" (Hausler, Linger, and Trammell, 1994) provides a well-rounded overview of Cleanroom practice today. The chapter presents theoretical foundations, a process model, a summary of experience, and a plan for introducing Cleanroom technology. A case study of the largest Cleanroom project undertaken in IBM to date – formerly part of the original paper – is now presented separately in case study 4 (available on the Internet).

1 Adopting Cleanroom Software Engineering with a Phased Approach

P. A. HAUSLER, R. C. LINGER, AND C. J. TRAMMELL

INTRODUCTION

Zero or near zero defect software may seem like an impossible goal. After all, the experience in the first generation of software development has reinforced the seeming inevitability of errors and persistence of human fallibility. Today, however, a new reality in software development belies the first-generation experience. Cleanroom software engineering teams are able to develop software at a level of quality and reliability that would have seemed impossible a few years ago, and are doing so with high productivity.

Cleanroom software engineering is a managerial and technical process for the development of software approaching zero defects with certified reliability.[1,2] The Cleanroom process spans the entire software life cycle; it provides a complete discipline within which software teams can plan, specify, design, verify, code, test, and certify software. The Cleanroom approach treats software development as an engineering process based on mathematical foundations, rather than as a trial-and-error programming process,[3–7] and is intended to produce software with error-free designs and failure-free executions.

In traditional, craft-based software development, errors were accepted as inevitable, and programmers were encouraged to get software into testing quickly in order to begin debugging. Programs were subjected to unit testing and debugging by their authors, then integrated into components, subsystems, and systems for more debugging. Product use by customers resulted in still more debugging to correct errors discovered in operational use. The most virulent errors were often the result of fixes to other errors,[8] and it was not unusual for software products to reach a steady-state error population, with new errors introduced as fast as old ones were fixed. Today, however, craft-based processes that depend on testing and debugging to improve reliability are understood to be inefficient and ineffective. Experience has shown that craft-based processes often fail to achieve the level of reliability essential to a society dependent on software for the conduct of human affairs.

In the Cleanroom process, correctness is built into the software by development teams through a rigorous engineering process of specification, design, and verification. The more powerful process of team correctness verification replaces unit testing and debugging, and software enters system testing directly, with no execution by development teams. All errors are accounted for from first execution on, with no private unit testing necessary or permitted. Experience shows that Cleanroom software typically enters system testing approaching zero defects and occasionally no defects are found in all testing.

Certification (test) teams are not responsible for "testing in" quality, which is an impossible task, but rather for certifying the quality of software with respect to its specification. Certification is performed by statistical usage testing that produces objective assessments of product quality. Errors, if any, found in testing are returned to the development team for correction. If the quality is not acceptable, the software is removed from testing and returned to the development team for reverification.

The process of Cleanroom development and certification is carried out in an incremental manner. System functionality grows with the addition of successive code increments in a stepwise integration process. When the final increment is added, the system is complete. Because successive increments are elaborating the top-down design of increments already in execution, interface and design errors are rare.

This chapter describes key Cleanroom technologies and summarizes quality results achieved by Cleanroom teams. It presents a phased approach to Cleanroom implementation based on the software maturity level of an organization. The results of a substantial IBM Cleanroom project (AOEXPERT/MVS*) that successfully applied a phased approach are given in the separate case study.

* Trademark or registered trademark of International Business Machines Corporation.

CLEANROOM PERSPECTIVES

The Cleanroom software engineering process evolved from concepts developed and demonstrated over the past 15 years by Harlan Mills and colleagues.[3-5,9] Cleanroom practices such as stepwise refinement of procedure and object hierarchies, team verification of correctness, and statistical usage testing, have been successfully applied in commercial and governmental software projects over the past decade. Such practices may not be the rule in software development today, but their use is growing as evidence of their value continues to accumulate. In many cases, software organizations considering a transition to the Cleanroom process have operational practices in place, such as incremental development, structured programming, and team reviews, that support Cleanroom concepts. There are only a few key concepts that must be understood and accepted in a transition to the Cleanroom approach.[10]

Practice based on theory

To be effective, any engineering discipline must be based on sound theoretical foundations. Cleanroom specification, design, and correctness verification practices are based on function theory, whereby programs are treated as rules for mathematical functions subject to stepwise refinement and verification.[4,5] Cleanroom testing and quality certification practices are based on statistical theory, whereby program executions are treated as populations subject to usage-based, stochastic sampling in formal statistical designs.[3,6,11] These theoretical foundations form the basis of a comprehensive engineering process that has been reduced to practice for commercial software development. A growing number of successful, real-world Cleanroom projects have demonstrated the practicality of these methods.

Experienced Cleanroom practitioners and educators have developed comprehensive technology transfer programs based on readily teachable, time-efficient approaches to such Cleanroom technologies as correctness verification and statistical testing. New practitioners will find that processes and tools exist that make the use of these Cleanroom methods highly practical.[12]

Right the first time

A primary objective of the Cleanroom process is to prevent errors, rather than accepting and accommodating errors through institutionalized debugging and rework. For this reason, Cleanroom development teams do not unit test and debug their code. Instead, they rely on rigorous methods of specification and design combined with team correctness verification. These Cleanroom development practices, based on mathematical foundations, yield quality approaching zero defects prior to first execution by certification teams. The purpose of testing in Cleanroom is the certification of software quality with respect to specifications, not the attempt to "debug in" quality.

Management understanding and acceptance of this essential point – that quality will be achieved by design and verification rather than by testing – must be reflected in the development schedule. Time spent in specification and design phases of a Cleanroom development is greater than in traditional projects. Time spent in testing, however, is likely to be less than traditionally required. The manager who wanted to start coding immediately because of the large amount of debugging expected was usually right, but would have difficulty becoming part of a Cleanroom team.

Quality costs less

A principal justification for the Cleanroom process is that built-in quality lowers the overall cost to produce and maintain a product. The exponential growth in the cost of error correction in successive life-cycle phases is well known. Errors found in operational use by customers are typically several orders of magnitude more costly to correct than errors found in the specification phase.[13] The Cleanroom name, taken from the semiconductor industry where a literal cleanroom exists to prevent introduction of defects during hardware fabrication, is a metaphor that reflects this understanding of the cost-effectiveness of error prevention. In the Cleanroom process, incremental development and extensive team review and verification permit errors to be detected as early as possible in the life cycle. By reducing the cost of errors during development and the incidence of failures during operation, the overall life-cycle cost of Cleanroom software can be expected to be far lower than industry averages. For example, the IBM COBOL Structuring Facility product, developed using Cleanroom techniques, has required only a small fraction of its maintenance budget to be consumed during years of field use.

Cleanroom project schedules have equaled or improved upon traditional development schedules.[14–16] In fact, productivity improvements of factors ranging from one and one-half to five over traditional practices have been observed.[15–18] Experienced Cleanroom teams become remarkably efficient at writing clear specifications, simplifying and restricting designs to easily verifiable patterns, and performing correctness verification. Cleanroom is not a more time-consuming development process, but it does place greater emphasis on design and verification to avoid waste of resources in debugging and rework.

CLEANROOM QUALITY RESULTS

As summarized in table 1.1, first-time Cleanroom teams in IBM and other industrial and governmental organizations have reported data on close to a million lines of Cleanroom-developed software. The code exhibits a weighted average of 2.3 errors per thousand lines of code (errors/KLOC) in testing.[2,15-19] This error rate represents all errors found in all testing, measured from first-ever execution through test completion. That is, it is a measure of residual errors remaining following correctness verification by development teams, who do not execute the software. The projects represent a variety of environments, including batch, distributed, cooperative, and real-time systems and system parts, and a variety of languages, including microcode, C, C++, JOVIAL, FORTRAN, and PL/I.

Traditionally developed software does not undergo correctness verification, but rather enters unit testing and debugging directly, followed by more debugging in function and system testing. Measured from first execution, traditional software typically exhibits 25 to 35 or more errors per thousand lines of code.[20] First-time Cleanroom development teams can produce software with quality levels at test entry at least an order of magnitude better than traditionally developed software. The following summaries of three selected projects from table 1.1 illustrate the results achieved.

IBM COBOL Structuring Facility

The COBOL Structuring Facility, which consisted of 85 KLOC of PL/I code, was the first Cleanroom product in IBM. It employs proprietary, graph-theoretic algorithms to automatically transform unstructured COBOL programs into a functionally equivalent, structured form for improved maintainability. Relentless design simplification in the Cleanroom process often results in systems that are small for their functionality. For example, the Cleanroom-developed prototype of the COBOL Structuring Facility, independently estimated at 100 KLOC, was developed using just 20 KLOC.

Comparable to a COBOL compiler in complexity, the product experienced 3.4 errors/KLOC in all statistical testing, measured from the first execution. Six months of intensive beta testing at a major aerospace corporation resulted in no functional equivalence errors ever found.[21] Just seven minor errors were reported in the first three years of field use, requiring only a

Table 1.1 Cleanroom project results

Year	Project	Quality and productivity
1987	IBM Flight Control: Helicopter Avionics System Component 33 KLOC (JOVIAL)	Certification testing failure rate: 2.3 errors/KLOC Error-fix reduced 5× Completed ahead of schedule
1988	IBM Cobol Structuring Facility: product for automatically restructuring COBOL programs 85 KLOC (PL/I)	IBM's first Cleanroom product Certification testing failure rate: 3.4 errors/KLOC Productivity 740 LOC/PM, 5× improvement Seven errors in first 3 years of use: all simple fixes
1989	NASA Satellite Control Project 1 40 KLOC (FORTRAN)	Certification testing failure rate: 4.5 errors/KLOC 50% improvement in quality Productivity 780 LOC/PM 80% improvement in productivity
1990	Martin Marietta: automated documentation system 1.8 KLOC (FOXBASE)	First compilation: no errors found Certification testing failure rate: 0.0 errors/KLOC (no errors found)
1991	IBM System Software First increment 0.6 KLOC (C)	First compilation: no errors found Certification testing failure rate: 0.0 errors/KLOC (no errors found)

Year	Project	Results
1991	IBM AOEXPERT/MVS™ product 107 KLOC (mixed languages)	Testing failure rate: 2.6 errors/KLOC Productivity 486 LOC/PM No operational errors from Beta test sites
1991	IBM Language Product First increment 21.9 KLOC (PL/X)	Testing failure rate: 2.1 errors/KLOC
1991	IBM Image Product Component 3.5 KLOC (c)	First compilation: 5 syntax errors Certification testing failure rate: 0.9 errors/KLOC
1992	IBM Printer Application First increment 6.7 KLOC (c)	Certification testing failure rate: 5.1 errors/KLOC
1992	IBM Knowledge Based System Application 17.8 KLOC (TIRS™)	Testing failure rate: 3.5 errors/KLOC
1992	NASA Satellite Control Projects 2 and 3 170 KLOC (FORTRAN)	Testing failure rate: 4.2 errors/KLOC
1993	University of Tennessee: Cleanroom tool 20 KLOC (c)	Certification testing failure rate: 6.1 errors/KLOC
1993	IBM 3490E Tape Drive 86 KLOC (c)	Certification testing failure rate: 1.2 errors/KLOC

Table 1.1 – *continued*

Year	Project	Quality and productivity
1993	IBM Database Transaction Processor First increment 21.5 KLOC (JOVIAL)	Testing failure rate: 2.4 errors/KLOC No design errors, all simple fixes
1993	IBM LAN Software First increment 4.8 KLOC (C)	Testing failure rate: 0.8 errors/KLOC
1993	IBM Workstation Application Component 3.0 KLOC (JOVIAL)	Testing failure rate: 4.1 errors/KLOC
1993	Ericsson Telecom AB Switching Computer OS32 Operating System 350 KLOC (PLEX, C)	Testing failure rate: 1 error/KLOC 70% improvement in development productivity 100% improvement in testing productivity

Note: All testing failure rates are measured from first-ever execution.
Key: KLOC = thousand lines of code; PM = person month; × = (mathematical) times.

small fraction of the maintenance budget associated with traditionally developed products of similar size and complexity. The product was developed and certified by a team averaging six members, with productivity five times the IBM averages.[16]

IBM 3490E tape drive

The 3490E tape drive is a real-time, embedded software system developed by a five-person team in three increments of C design with a code total of 86 KLOC. It provides high-performance tape cartridge support through a multiple processor bus architecture that processes multiple real-time input and output data streams. The product experienced 1.2 errors/KLOC in all statistical testing. To meet an urgent business need, the third increment was shipped straight from development to the hardware and software integration team with no testing whatsoever. Customer evaluation testing with live data by the integration team resulted in no errors being found.

In a comparison experiment, the project team subjected a selected module to both unit testing and correctness verification. Development of execution scaffolding, definition and execution of test cases, and checking of results required one- and one-half person-weeks of effort and resulted in the detection of seven errors. Correctness verification of the same program by the development team required one and one-half hours, and resulted in the detection of the same seven errors, plus three additional errors.[1]

Ericsson os32 operating system

Ellemtel Telecommunications Systems Laboratories is completing a 350 KLOC operating system for a new family of switching computers for Ericsson Telecom AB. The code is written in PLEX and C. The 73-person, 33-month Cleanroom project experienced productivity improvements of 70 percent and 100 percent in development and testing, respectively, and the product averaged under one error/KLOC in all testing. Project management reported that an average of less than one person–hour was required to detect an error in team reviews, compared to an average of 17.5 person–hours to detect an error in testing. The project allocated two days per week to prepare and conduct team reviews. The product team was honored by Ericsson as the single project that had contributed the most to the company in 1993.[18]

CLEANROOM TECHNOLOGIES

In the Cleanroom process, the objective of the development team is to deliver software to the test team that approaches zero defects; the objective of the test team is to scientifically certify the quality of software, not to attempt to "test in" quality. These objectives are achieved through management and technical practices based on the technologies of incremental development, box structure specification and design, correctness verification, and statistical quality certification.

Incremental development

Management planning and control in Cleanroom is based on development and certification of a *pipeline of increments* that represent operational user function, accumulate top-down into the final product, and execute in the system environment.[22] Following specification of required external system behavior, an incremental development plan is created to define schedules, resources, and functional content of a series of code increments to be developed and certified. The initial increment contains stubs (small placeholder programs) that stand in for later increments and permit early execution of the code. The ultimate functionality of the code that will replace the stubs is fully defined in subspecifications for team verification of each increment prior to testing. As incremental development progresses, stubs are replaced by corresponding code increments, possibly containing stubs of their own, in a stepwise system integration process. When the final increment is integrated, the system is complete and no stubs remain.

As each increment is integrated, the evolving system of increments undergoes a new step in statistical usage testing for quality certification. Statistical measures of quality provide feedback for reinforcement or improvement of the development process as necessary. Early increments can serve as system prototypes, providing an opportunity to elicit feedback from customers to validate requirements and functionality. As inevitable changes occur, incremental development provides a framework for revising schedules, resources, and function, and permits changes to be incorporated in a systematic manner.

Box structure specification and design

Box structures provide a stepwise refinement and verification process based on *black box*, *state box*, and *clear box* forms for defining system behavior and deriving and connecting objects comprising a system architecture.[5,23] Boxes are object-based, and the box structure process provides a systematic means for developing object-based systems.[24] Specifically, the black box form is a specification of required behavior of a system or system part in all circumstances of use, defined in terms of stimuli, responses, and transition rules that map stimulus histories to responses. The state box form is refined from and verified against the black box, and defines encapsulated state data required to satisfy black box behavior. The clear box form is refined from and verified against the state box, and defines procedural design of services on state data to satisfy black box behavior, often introducing new black boxes at the next level of refinement. New black boxes (specifications) are similarly refined into state boxes (state designs) and clear boxes (procedure designs), continuing in this manner until no new black boxes are required. Specification and design steps are interleaved in a seamless, integrated hierarchy affording complete verifiability and traceability.

Box structures isolate and separate the creative definition of behavior, data, and procedures at each level of refinement. They incorporate the essential property of *referential transparency*, such that the information content of an abstraction, for example, a black box, is sufficient to define and verify its refinement into state and clear box forms without reference to other specification parts. Referential transparency is crucial to maintaining intellectual control in complex system developments. Box-structured systems are developed as *usage hierarchies* of boxes, where each box provides services on encapsulated state data, and where its services may be used and reused in many places in the hierarchy as required. Box-structured systems are developed according to the following principles:[25] (1) all data to be defined and retained in a design are encapsulated in boxes, (2) all processing is defined by sequential and concurrent use of boxes, and (3) each use of a box occupies a distinct place in the usage hierarchy of the system. Clear boxes play an important role in the hierarchy by defining and controlling the correct operation of box services at the next level of refinement.

Correctness verification

As noted, in the Cleanroom process, verification of program correctness in team reviews replaces private unit testing and debugging by individuals. Debugging is an inefficient and error-prone process that undermines the mental discipline and concentration that can achieve zero defects. The intellectual control of software development afforded by team verification is a strong incentive for the prohibition against unit testing. "No unit testing" does not, however, mean "no use of the machine." It is essential to use the machine for experimentation, to evaluate algorithms, to benchmark performance, and to understand and document the semantics of interfacing software. These exploratory activities are entirely consistent with the Cleanroom objective of software that is correct by design.

Elimination of unit testing motivates tremendous determination in developers to ensure that the code they deliver for independent testing is error-free on first execution. But there is a deeper reason to adopt correctness verification – it is more efficient and effective than unit testing. Programs of any size can contain an essentially infinite number of possible execution paths and states, but only a minute fraction of those can be exercised in unit testing. Correctness verification, however, reduces the verification of programs to a finite and complete process.

In more detail, all clear box programs are composed of nested and sequenced control structures, such as sequence, IF–THEN–ELSE, WHILE–DO, and their variants. Each such control structure is a rule for a mathematical function,[9] that is, a mapping from a domain or initial state to a range or final state. The function mapping carried out by each control structure can be documented in the design as an *intended function*. For correctness, each control structure must implement the precise mapping defined by its intended function. The Correctness Theorem[4] shows that verification of sequence, IF–THEN–ELSE, and WHILE–DO structures requires checking exactly one, two, and three *correctness conditions*, respectively. While programs can exhibit an essentially infinite number of execution paths and states, they are composed of a finite number of control structures, and their verification can be carried out in a finite number of steps by checking each correctness condition in team reviews. Furthermore, verification is complete, that is, it deals with all possible program behavior at each level of refinement. The verification process defined by the Correctness Theorem accounts for all possible mappings from the domain to the range of each control structure, not just a handful of mappings exercised by particular unit tests. For these reasons, verification far surpasses unit testing in effectiveness.

Statistical quality certification

In the Cleanroom process, statistical usage testing for certification replaces coverage testing for debugging. Testing is carried out by the certification team based on anticipated usage by customers. *Usage probability distributions* are developed to define system inputs for all aspects of usage, including nominal scenarios as well as error and stress situations. The distributions can be organized into probabilistic state transition matrices or formal grammars. Test cases are generated based on random sampling of usage distributions. The correct output for each test input is specified with reference to an oracle, that is, an independent authority on correctness, typically the software specification. System reliability is predicted based on analysis of test results by a *formal reliability model*, and the development process for each increment is evaluated based on the extent to which the reliability results attained objectives. In effect, statistical usage testing is based on a *formal statistical design*, from which statistical inferences of software quality and reliability can be derived.[3,11,26]

Coverage testing can provide no more than anecdotal evidence of reliability. Thus, if many errors are found, does that mean that the code is of poor quality and many errors remain, or that most of the errors have been discovered? Conversely, if few errors are found, does that mean that the code is of good quality, or that the testing process is ineffective? Statistical testing provides scientifically valid measures of reliability, such as mean-time-to-failure (MTTF), as a basis for objective management decision-making regarding software and development process quality.

Empirical studies have demonstrated enormous variation in the failure rates of errors in operational use.[8] Correcting high-failure-rate errors has a substantial effect on MTTF, while correcting low-failure-rate errors hardly influences MTTF at all. Because usage-based testing exercises software the way users intend to use it, high-frequency, virulent errors tend to be found early in testing. For this reason, statistical usage testing is more effective at improving software reliability than is coverage testing. Statistical testing also provides new management flexibility to certify software quality for varying conditions of use and stress, by developing special usage probability distributions for such situations. For example, the reliability of infrequently used functions with severe consequences of failure can be independently measured and certified.

ADOPTING THE CLEANROOM PROCESS

Rigorous and complete Cleanroom implementation permits development of very high quality software with scientific certification of reliability. However, substantial gains in quality and productivity have also occurred in partial Cleanroom implementations.[15,18] Evidence suggests that a phased approach to implementation can produce concrete benefits and afford increased management control. The phased approach, combined with initial Cleanroom use on selected demonstration projects, provides a systematic management process for reducing risk in technology transfer. Three implementation phases can be defined and sequenced in a systematic technology transfer process. The idea is to first introduce fundamental Cleanroom principles and several key technologies in an *introductory implementation*. As team experience and confidence grows, increased precision and rigor can be achieved in a *full implementation* of Cleanroom technology. Finally, an *advanced implementation* can be introduced to optimize the Cleanroom process. Of course, a particular Cleanroom implementation can combine elements from various phases as necessary and appropriate for the project environment.

Introductory implementation

Key aspects of an introductory implementation are summarized in the first part of table 1.2. The fundamental idea is to shift from craft-based to engineering-based processes. The development objective shifts from defect correction in unit testing to defect prevention in specification, design, and verification. As experience grows, developers learn they can write software that is right the first time, and a psychological change occurs, from expecting errors to expecting correctness. At the same time, the testing objective shifts from debugging in coverage testing to reliability certification in usage testing. Because Cleanroom code is of high quality at first execution, testers learn that little debugging is required, and they can concentrate on evaluating quality. A management opportunity exists to leverage these technology shifts to develop systems on schedule with substantial improvement in quality and reduction in life-cycle costs.

All development and testing is accomplished by small teams. Team operations provide opportunities for cross-training and a ready forum for discussion, review, and improvement. All work products undergo a team-based peer review to ensure the highest level of quality. The size and number of teams varies according to resource availability, skill levels, and project size and complexity. Teams are organized during project planning and their membership should remain stable throughout development. Cooperative team behavior that leverages individual expertise is a key factor in successful Cleanroom operations.

In any Cleanroom implementation, zero-defect software is an explicit design goal, and measured performance at a target level is an explicit reliability goal. The Cleanroom practices necessary to achieve these objectives require substantial management commitment. Because compromises in process inevitably lead to compromises in quality, it is crucial for managers to understand Cleanroom fundamentals – the philosophy, process, and milestones – and demonstrate unequivocal support. Management commitment is essential to successful introduction of the Cleanroom process.

A key aspect of customer interaction is to shift from a technology-driven to a customer-driven approach, whereby system functional and usage requirements are subject to extensive analysis and review with customers to clearly understand their needs. Maintaining customer involvement in specification and certification helps avoid developing a system that approaches zero defects but provides the wrong functionality for the user.

Unlike the traditional life cycle of sequential phases, the Cleanroom life cycle is based on incremental development. In an introductory implementation, a project is scheduled and managed as a pipeline of increments for development and testing. Functional content and sequencing of increments is typically based on a natural subdivision of system functions and their expected usage. Successive increments should implement user function, execute in the system environment, and accumulate top-down into the final product. This incremental strategy supports testing throughout development rather than at completion. It also integrates system increments in multiple steps across the life cycle, to avoid risks of single-step integration of all system components late in a project when little time or resources remain to deal with unforeseen problems.

In an introductory implementation, a black box specification is written that precisely defines required system functionality in terms of inputs, outputs, and behavior in all possible circumstances of use, including correct and incorrect use. The specification focuses on required system behavior from the user's viewpoint and does not describe implementation details. At this level, specifications are generally expressed in an outer syntax of specification structures, such as tabular formats or variants of Box Description Language (BDL),[5] and an inner syntax of natural language. Cleanroom specifications are important working documents that drive design and certification activities, and they must be kept current for effective team operations. Definition of system user's guides is initiated in parallel with specifications, for elaboration and refinement throughout the development.

In the design process of an introductory implementation, state and clear box concepts are implemented using sound software engineering practices, including stepwise refinement, structured programming, modular design, information hiding, and data abstraction. Successive increments are specified and designed top-down through stepwise refinement, with frequent team review and discussion of design strategies.[8] Stepwise refinement requires substantial look-ahead and analysis, as successive design versions are developed and revised. In this process, a relentless team drive for *design simplification* can result in substantial reductions in the size and complexity of systems, for more efficient correctness verification and subsequent maintenance.

Design with intended functions is a fundamental practice at the introductory level. High-level intended functions originate in system specifications, and are refined into control structures and new intended functions.

Table 1.2   A phased implementation for Cleanroom practice
Introductory implementation

Management and team operations	Customer interaction	Incremental development	System specification
• Document an introductory Cleanroom process. • Shift from craft-based to engineering-based processes. • Shift from defect correction in unit testing to defect prevention in specification, design, and verification. • Shift from debugging in coverage testing to quality certification in usage testing. • Shift from individual to small team operations with team review of all work products. • Establish Cleanroom projects and provide commitment, education, and recognition to teams. • Develop to schedule with substantial quality improvement and life cycle cost reduction.	• Shift from technology-driven to customer-driven development. • Analyze and clarify functional requirements with customers to develop functional specifications. • Analyze and clarify usage requirements with customers to develop usage specifications. • Review and validate functional and usage specifications with customers. • Revise functional and usage specifications as necessary for changing requirements.	• Shift from a sequential (waterfall) to an incremental process. • Define increments that implement user function, execute in the system environment, and accumulate top down into the final product. • Define and evolve an incremental development plan for schedules, resources, and increment content. • Carry out scheduled incremental development and testing with stepwise integration of increments.	• Shift from informal, throwaway specifications to precise, working specifications kept current through the project life cycle. • Define specifications of system boundaries, interfaces, and required external behavior in all possible circumstances of use, including correct and incorrect use. • Express specifications in systematic forms such as tables that define required behavior in natural language. • Develop and evolve system user's guides in parallel with specifications.

Table 1.2 – *continued*
Introductory implementation

System Design and Implementation	Correctness Verification	Statistical Testing and Reliability Certification	Process Improvement
• Shift from programming by aggregation of statements to design by stepwise refinement of specifications.	• Shift from unit testing by individuals to correctness verification by teams.	• Shift from coverage testing to usage testing.	• Shift from informal review of lessons learned to a systematic, documented improvement process.
• Refine specifications into structured, modular designs using good software engineering practices with substantial look ahead and analysis.	• Shift from path tracing in code inspections to functional analysis in verification reviews.	• Define high-level usage distributions in systematic structures such as hierarchical decision trees.	• Measure team productivity, quality, and cost, and analyze for process improvements.
• Express designs in control structures and case-structured intended functions expressed in natural language.	• Conduct demonstration verification reviews to set expectations and train teams.	• Develop/acquire test cases from a user perspective based on system specifications and usage distributions.	• Document improvements to the introductory implementation based on lessons learned from each increment.
• Conduct frequent team development reviews to communicate, simplify, and improve evolving designs.	• Verify all control structures in team reviews by reading, function abstraction, and comparison to intended functions.	• Evaluate quality of each increment through analysis of measures such as failure rates and severity levels.	• Improve or sustain the development process based on quality results of increment testing.
• Conduct execution experiments to document the system environment and semantics of interfacing software.	• Verify all design changes in team reviews and deliver verified increments to testing for first execution.	• Return low-quality increments to development for additional design and reverification.	• Assess customer satisfaction with Cleanroom-developed systems for process improvements.

Table 1.2 – *continued*
Full implementation

Management and team operations	Customer interaction	Incremental development	System specification
• Document a full Cleanroom process. • Increase development rigor with box structure specification, design, and correctness verification. • Increase testing rigor with scientific measures of reliability. • Establish larger Cleanroom projects as teams of small teams with experienced leaders from previous projects. • Develop to schedule with substantial quality and productivity improvement and life cycle cost reduction.	• Educate customers in Cleanroom to increase value, cooperation, and responsiveness to customer needs. • Review black box functional specifications with customers to support increased rigor in specification. • Review usage specifications with customers to support increased rigor in statistical usage testing. • Provide customers with prototypes and accumulating increments for evaluation and feedback.	• Define increments to incorporate early availability of important functions for customer feedback and use. • Rapidly revise incremental plans for new requirements and actual team performance, and respond to schedule and budget changes.	• Develop prototypes as necessary to validate customer requirements and operating environment characteristics. • Define black box specifications in systematic structures such as transition tables expressed in conditional rules and precise natural language.

System Design and Implementation	Correctness Verification	Statistical Testing and Reliability Certification	Process Improvement
• Refine black boxes (specifications) into state boxes (data designs) and state boxes into clear boxes (procedure designs) and new black boxes. • Define state boxes in data designs and systematic structures such as transition tables expressed in conditional rules and precise natural language. • Define clear boxes in control structures and intended functions expressed in conditional rules and precise natural language. • Encapsulate system data in boxes and define processing by use of box services. • Identify opportunities for reuse of system components.	• Improve introductory practices through increased precision and formality in verification reviews. • Improve verification by introducing mental proofs of correctness based on box structure theory and Correctness Theorem correctness conditions. • Document and reuse proof arguments for recurring design patterns. • Simplify and standardize designs where possible to reduce proof reasoning.	• Establish reliability targets and conduct statistical usage testing for reliability certification. • Define usage probability distributions for all circumstances of use in formal grammars or state transition matrices. • Define alternative distributions for special environments and critical and unusual usage. • Use automated generators to create test cases randomized against usage probability distributions. • Use reliability models to produce statistical reliability measures based on analysis of test results.	• Document improvements to the full implementation based on team decisions in process reviews after each increment • Use baseline measurements from introductory projects to set quality and productivity objectives. • Improve or sustain the development process based on reliability measurements of each increment. • Conduct causal analysis of failures found in testing and use to identify process areas for improvement. • Conduct surveys of customer satisfaction with Cleanroom-developed systems for process improvement.

Table 1.2 – *continued*
Advanced implementation

Management and team operations	Customer interaction	Incremental development	System specification
• Document an advanced Cleanroom process. • Establish a Cleanroom Center of Competency to monitor Cleanroom technology and train and consult with teams. • Establish Cleanroom projects across the organization led by experienced Cleanroom practitioners. • Develop to schedule with substantial quality and productivity improvements and life cycle cost reduction, even in emergency and adverse circumstances.	• Assist customers in leveraging the quality of Cleanroom-developed software for competitive advantage. • Contract with customer for reliability warranties based on certification with agreed usage distributions and reliability models. • Establish cooperative processes with customers for recording operational system usage to calibrate and improve reliability certification.	• Incorporate comprehensive reuse analysis and reliability planning in incremental development plans. • Plan increment content to manage project risk by early development of interface dependencies, critical functions, and performance-sensitive processes.	• Incorporate advances in formal specification methods into local practices. • Develop guidelines for specification formats and conventions based on team experience. • Apply mathematical techniques in black box specifications to define complex behavior with precision. • Express black box specifications where appropriate with specification functions and abstract models. • Develop a specification review protocol for team reviews based on team experience.

System Design and Implementation	Correctness Verification	Statistical Testing and Reliability Certification	Process Improvement
• Incorporate advances in formal design methods into local practices.	• Incorporate advances in formal verification methods into local practices.	• Incorporate advances in scientific software certification methods into local practices.	• Use the full rigor of statistical process control to analyze team performance.
• Use box structures to document the precise semantics of interfacing software.	• Use trace tables as necessary to support mental proofs of correctness.	• Apply experience of prior Cleanroom projects and customers in setting reliability targets.	• Compare team performance with locally-defined process control standards for performance.
• Develop guidelines for design formats and conventions based on team experience.	• Document written proofs of correctness as required for critical system functions.	• Employ usage analysis to validate functional specifications and plan increment content.	• Use error classification schemes to improve specific Cleanroom practices in specification, design, verification, and testing.
• Apply mathematical techniques in state and clear box designs to define complex behavior with precision.	• Develop verification protocols and extended proof rules for application-, language-, and environment-specific semantics.	• Use automated tools to generate self-checking test cases.	
• Develop a design review protocol for team development reviews based on team experience.		• Collect customer usage data to track conformance of usage distributions to actual field use.	
• Establish libraries of reusable, certified designs.		• Apply and evaluate multiple reliability models for best prediction of system reliability in the usage environment.	

Expressed primarily in natural language, intended functions are recorded as comments attached to key control structures in designs. Intended functions precisely define required behavior of their control structure refinements. Behavior is defined in functional, non-procedural descriptions of the derivation of output data from input data. Intended function refinements are expressed in a restricted set of single-entry, single-exit control structures with no side effects, such as sequence, IF–THEN–ELSE, WHILE–DO, and their variants. Each control structure may contain additional intended functions for further refinement. This stepwise specification and design process continues until no further intended functions remain to be elaborated. Intended functions provide a precise road map for designers in refining design structures, and are essential to team verification reviews.

The *last intellectual pass* through a design occurs in team-based correctness verification, another fundamental practice in an introductory implementation. At the design level, verification reviews prove correctness of program control structures, unlike traditional code inspections that trace program flow paths to look for errors. The verification process is based on reading and abstracting the functionality of control structures in designs and comparing the abstractions with specified intended functions to assess correctness. Team members read, discuss, evaluate, and indicate agreement (or not) that designs are correct with respect to their intended behavior. If changes are required, the team must review and verify the modifications before the designs can be considered finished. Verification reviews provide team members with deep understandings of designs and their correctness arguments. Reviews are conducted with the understanding that the entire team is responsible for correctness. Ultimate successes are team successes, and failures are team failures. All specifications and designs are subject to team review, without exception. Following verification, increments are delivered to the test team for first execution.

In an introductory implementation, usage testing based on external system behavior replaces coverage testing based on design internals. Usage information is collected by analyzing functional specifications and surveying prospective users (where users may be people or other programs). Based on this information, a high-level usage profile is developed, including nominal scenarios of use, as well as error and stress situations. A usage profile can be recorded in systematic structures such as hierarchical decision trees that embody possible usage patterns in compact form. Next, test scenarios are defined based on the usage profile. The idea is that the test cases represent realistic scenarios of user interaction, including both correct and incorrect usage. For example, if particular system functions are used frequently in particular patterns with occasional user mistakes, this usage should be reflected in the test suite. At this stage, the usage profile may not be extremely precise or detailed, but it does contain sufficient information for the test team to generate realistic test cases.

The effectiveness of the development process is measured by system performance in testing with respect to predetermined quality standards, such as failure rates and severity levels. (More precise statistical measures, such as MTTF and improvement ratio, are introduced in the full implementation.) If test results show that the development process is not meeting quality objectives, testing ceases and the code is removed from the machine for redevelopment and reverification by the development team.

Process improvement is a fundamental activity in an introductory implementation. The idea is to shift from informal discussions of lessons learned to a systematic, documented improvement process. Baseline measurements of fundamental project characteristics, such as quality, productivity, and cost, provide a basis for assessing progress and making improvements. The quality results of usage testing can guide changes to the development process. In addition, customer satisfaction with Cleanroom-developed systems can highlight process areas requiring improvements.

Full implementation

Introductory Cleanroom implementation establishes a framework for maturing the process to a full implementation. As summarized in the second part of table 1.2, full implementation adds rigor to practices established in the introductory phase through formal methods of box structure specification and design, correctness verification, statistical testing, and reliability certification. For a Cleanroom project of substantial size and complexity, a *team-of-teams* approach can be applied, whereby the hierarchical structure of the system under development forms the basis for organizing, partitioning, and allocating work among a corresponding hierarchy of small teams.

An opportunity exists for more extensive customer interaction in a full Cleanroom implementation. Customers can be provided with education on Cleanroom practices to improve the effectiveness of functional and usage specification analysis and review. In addition, prototypes and accumulating increments can be provided to customers for evaluation and feedback.

Managers and team leaders can leverage Cleanroom experience into additional flexibility in incremental development to accommodate changing requirements, and shortfalls and windfalls in team performance within remaining schedule and budget. Increment planning can emphasize early development of useful system functionality for customer feedback and operational use.

In specification and design, prototyping and experimentation are encouraged to clarify and validate requirements, and to understand and document semantics of interfacing software. The formal syntax and semantics of box structures are used for black, state, and clear box refinements. Black boxes and state boxes are recorded in an outer syntax of formal structures, such as transition tables, with inner syntax expressed in precise *conditional rules*, often given as *conditional concurrent assignments* combined with precise natural language. In clear box design, intended functions are recorded at every level of refinement, expressed in conditional concurrent assignments and precise natural language.

A box-structured system is specified and designed as a hierarchy of boxes, such that appropriate system data are encapsulated in boxes, processing is defined by using box services, and every use of a box service occupies a distinct place in the hierarchy. Box structures promote early identification of common services, that is, reusable objects, that can simplify development and improve productivity. Duplication of effort is avoided when team members have an early awareness of opportunities for use and reuse of common services. Rigorous team verification reviews are conducted for all program structures, using *mental proofs of correctness* based on box structure theory and the correctness conditions of the Correctness Theorem.

Statistical testing involves a more complete and experimentally valid approach than in an introductory implementation. Reliability objectives are established and extensive analysis of anticipated system usage is carried out. Comprehensive specifications of the population of possible system inputs are defined in usage probability distributions recorded in formal grammars or state transition matrices. Automated tools are used to randomly generate test cases from the distributions, and the correct output for each test input is defined based on the system specification. For example, the IBM Cleanroom Certification Assistant (CCA)[27] automates elements of the statistical testing process based on a formal grammar model for usage probability distributions. It contains a Statistical Testcase Generation Facility for compiling distributions (expressed in a Usage Distribution Language) and creating randomized test cases. Reliability models are employed to measure system reliability based on test results, and the development process for each increment is evaluated based on the extent to which reliability results meet objectives. The CCA provides an automated reliability model, the Cleanroom Certification Model, that analyzes test results to compute MTTF, improvement ratio, and other statistical measures. Alternative distributions are often employed to certify the reliability of special aspects of system behavior, for example, infrequently used functions that exhibit high consequences of failure.

Process improvement is established through reviews, following completion of each increment, to incorporate team recommendations into the documented Cleanroom process. Causal analysis of failures and comprehensive customer surveys can provide additional insight into process areas requiring improvement.

Advanced implementation

Key elements of an advanced implementation are summarized in the third part of table 1.2. At this level of experience, the Cleanroom process is optimized for the local environment and continually improved through advances in software engineering technology. A Cleanroom center of competency can be established, staffed by expert practitioners to monitor advances in Cleanroom technology and provide training and consultation to project teams. The Cleanroom process can be scaled up to ever larger projects and applied across an organization. An opportunity exists to achieve Cleanroom quality, productivity, and cost improvements even in emergency and adverse circumstances.

Product warranties may be possible in customer contracts, based on certification with usage distributions and reliability models agreed to by both parties. In the future, a capability for developing software with warranted reliability could become a major differentiating characteristic of software development organizations. Customers can benefit by capturing actual usage from specially instrumented versions of Cleanroom-developed systems, to permit test teams to improve the accuracy of usage distributions employed in certification.

Incremental development can be used to manage project risk through early development of key interfaces with pre-existing software, important user functions, and performance-sensitive components. Increments can also be defined to isolate and reduce dependence on areas of incomplete or volatile requirements, and to focus on early initiation of complex, long-lead-time components. Advanced incremental development also includes systematic reuse and reliability planning,[28] facilitated by such tools as the Cleanroom Reliability Manager.[29] In this approach, libraries of reusable components are searched for functions identified in specification and top-level design. If the reliability of candidate components is not known, statistically valid experiments are conducted to estimate reliability. If reliability of a candidate component has previously been certified, the usage profile used in that certification is compared with the new usage profile to determine if the previous certification is valid for the new use. Once reliability estimates exist for new and reused components, an estimate of total system reliability is generated through calculations based on top-level transition probabilities between subsystems. The results of this analysis are used to set reliability requirements for components, evaluate the viability of component reuse, and factor reliability risks into increment planning.

An advanced use of box structure specification involves formal mathematical and computer science models appropriate to the application. Formal black box and state box outer syntax used in full Cleanroom implementation is combined with formal inner syntax expressed as propositional logic, predicate calculus, algebraic function composition, BNF (Backus Naur form) grammars, or other formal notation that affords a clear and concise representation of function. Clear box designs are expressed in design languages for which target language code generators exist, or in restricted subsets of implementation languages, thereby eliminating opportunities for new errors in translation.

In verification reviews, trace tables are employed where appropriate for analysis of correctness, and written proofs are recorded for critical functions, particularly in life-, mission-, and enterprise-critical systems. Application-, language-, and environment-specific proof rules and standards provide a more complete framework for team verification. Locally defined standards have been shown to be more effective than generic standards in producing consistent practitioner judgment about software quality.[30] In an advanced implementation, the documented process includes environment-specific protocols for specification, design, and verification based on team experience.

In an advanced approach to statistical testing, Markov- or grammar-based automated tools can be used to improve efficiency and effectiveness. For example, the IBM Cleanroom Certification Assistant permits generation of any required number of unique, self-checking test cases. In addition, the rich body of theory, analytical results, and computational algorithms associated with Markov processes have important applications in software development.[31] Both formal grammars and Markov usage models can reveal errors, inconsistencies, ambiguities, and data dependencies in specifications early in development, and serve as test case generators for statistical testing. Initial versions of systems can be instrumented to record their own usage on command, as a baseline for analysis and calibration of usage distributions in certification of subsequent system versions.

An advanced implementation can benefit from a locally validated reliability model for software certification. Just as locally validated standards enable more consistent practitioner judgment about software quality, a locally validated reliability model will enable more accurate prediction of operational reliability from testing results.

In an advanced implementation, the full rigor of statistical process control can be applied to process improvement. Team accomplishments can be compared to locally defined process control standards for performance. Errors can be categorized according to an error classification scheme to target specific Cleanroom practices for improvement.

CHOOSING AN IMPLEMENTATION APPROACH

Cleanroom software engineering represents a shift from a paradigm of traditional, craft-based practices to rigorous, engineering-based practices, specifically as follows:

From:		To:
Individual operations	→	Team operations
Waterfall development	→	Incremental development
Informal specification	→	Black box specification
Informal design	→	Box structure refinement
Defect correction	→	Defect prevention
Individual unit testing	→	Team correctness verification
Path-based inspection	→	Function-based verification
Coverage testing	→	Statistical usage testing
Indeterminate reliability	→	Certified reliability

A phased approach to Cleanroom implementation enables an organization to build confidence and capability through gradual introduction of new practices with corresponding growth in process control. If organizational support and capability is sufficient for full implementation, the highest software quality and reliability afforded by Cleanroom practices can be achieved. Otherwise, a phased implementation is recommended. In general, a software organization that employs informal methods of specification and design, relies on coverage testing and defect correction to achieve quality, and has little experience with team-based operations, can gain the most benefit through an introductory implementation. This first phase introduces a comprehensive set of practices spanning project management, development, and testing, but without the full formality of Cleanroom technology. Once an organization successfully completes a project using the introductory practices, it has prepared itself for a full implementation. Likewise, maturation from full to advanced implementation can occur when the practices of the second stage have been successfully demonstrated.

Note that very few teams in reality will implement the precise set of practices defined within each implementation. Each team embodies unique skills, process, and experiences that must be assessed when choosing an appropriate implementation. It is often the case that a team can best utilize practices from more than one implementation level. For example, a team using an introductory implementation may have had prior experience with inspections and code reviews. Consequently, it may shift to a full or advanced implementation of the system design and verification practices. Perhaps another mature Cleanroom team, using primarily advanced practices, will find the rigor of the second phase of system specification to be sufficient.

The well-known Software Engineering Institute Capability Maturity Model provides a useful assessment technique to help define the best Cleanroom approach.[32,33] In general, higher assessment levels indicate that an organization can successfully adopt a more complete Cleanroom implementation. Organizations assessed at levels 1 and 2 will likely benefit from an introductory implementation, at levels 2 and 3, a full implementation, and at levels 4 and 5, an advanced implementation.

Acknowledgments

The growing worldwide community of Cleanroom practitioners and researchers, as well as Cleanroom-developed software owners and users, owes an enormous debt of gratitude to Harlan Mills, a retired IBM Fellow, for his groundbreaking development of theoretical foundations for the Cleanroom process. Mills' insight that programs are rules for mathematical functions became the foundation for a disciplined engineering process of program development that replaced a sea of *ad hoc* methods. His insight that program reliability can be scientifically certified in formal statistical designs brought the power of statistical quality control to software engineering and management.

Those of us who worked with Mills during the formative years of the Cleanroom process were indeed fortunate to have shared in the exciting intellectual climate he created, and to have contributed to the development of the Cleanroom process.

Acknowledgment is also due to members of the Cleanroom teams whose accomplishments are reported in this chapter. These practitioners are setting whole new standards of professional excellence and achievement in software engineering.

The authors would like to thank Mark Pleszkoch of the IBM Cleanroom Software Technology Center for his suggestions.

References

1   H. D. Mills, M. Dyer, and R. C. Linger, "Cleanroom Software Engineering," *IEEE Software* **4**, No. 5, 19–24 (September 1987).

2   R. C. Linger, "Cleanroom Software Engineering for Zero-Defect Software," *Proceedings of 15th International Conference on Software Engineering*, IEEE Computer Society Press, Los Alamitos, CA (1993), pp. 2–13.

3   P. A. Curritt, M. Dyer, and H. D. Mills, "Certifying the Reliability of Software," *IEEE Transactions on Software Engineering* **SE-12**, No. 1, 3–11 (January 1986).

4   R. C. Linger, H. D. Mills, and B. J. Witt, "Structured Programming: Theory and Practice," Addison-Wesley Publishing Co., Reading, MA (1979).

5   H. D. Mills, R. C. Linger, and A. R. Hevner, "Principles of Information Systems Analysis and Design," Academic Press, Inc., New York (1986).

6   H. D. Mills, "Certifying the Correctness of Software," *Proceedings of 25th Hawaii International Conference on System Sciences*, IEEE Computer Society Press, Los Alamitos, CA (January 1992), pp. 373–381.

7   M. D. Deck and P. A. Hausler, "Cleanroom Software Engineering: Theory and Practice," *Proceedings of Software Engineering and Knowledge Engineering*: Second International Conference, Skokie, IL, June 21–23, 1990. Knowledge Systems Institute, 3420 Main St., Skokie, IL 60076.

8   E. N. Adams, "Optimizing Preventive Service of Software Products," *IBM Journal of Research and Development* **28**, No. 1, 2–14 (1984).

9   H. D. Mills, "Mathematical Foundations for Structured Programming," *Software Productivity*, Little, Brown and Company, Boston, MA (1983), pp. 115–178.

10 P. A. Hausler, "Software Quality Through IBM's Cleanroom Software Engineering," *Creativity!* (ASD-WMA Edition), IBM, Austin, TX, March 1991.

11 H. D. Mills and J. H. Poore, "Bringing Software Under Statistical Quality Control," *Quality Progress* (November 1988), pp. 52–56.

12 R. C. Linger and R. A. Spangler, "The IBM Cleanroom Software Engineering Technology Transfer Program," *Proceedings of SEI Software Engineering Education Conference*, C. Sledge, Editor, Springer-Verlag, Inc., New York (1992).

13 B. W. Boehm, *Software Engineering Economics*, Prentice-Hall, Inc., Englewood Cliffs, NJ (1981).

14 S. E. Green, A. Kouchakdjian, and V. R. Basili, "Evaluation of the Cleanroom Methodology in the Software Engineering Laboratory," *Proceedings of Fourteenth Annual Software Engineering Workshop*, NASA, Goddard Space Flight Center, Greenbelt, MD 20771 (November 1989), pp. 1–22.

15 P. A. Hausler, "A Recent Cleanroom Success Story: The Redwing Project," *Proceedings of Seventeenth Annual Software Engineering Workshop*, NASA, Goddard Space Flight Center, Greenbelt, MD 20771 (December 1992), pp. 256–285.

16 R. C. Linger and H. D. Mills, "A Case Study in Cleanroom Software Engineering:

The IBM COBOL Structuring Facility," *Proceedings of the 12th Annual International Computer Software and Applications Conference (COMPSAC '88)*, IEEE Computer Society Press, Los Alamitos, CA (1988), pp. 10–17.

17   S. E. Green and R. Pajersky, "Cleanroom Process Evolution in the SEL," *Proceedings of 16th Annual Software Engineering Workshop*, NASA, Goddard Space Flight Center, Greenbelt, MD 20771 (December 1991), pp. 47–63.

18   L.-G. Tann, "OS32 and Cleanroom," *Proceedings of 1st Annual European Industrial Symposium on Cleanroom Software Engineering* (Copenhagen, Denmark), Q-Labs AB, IDEON Research Park, S-233 70 Lund, Sweden (1993), Section 5, pp. 1–40.

19   C. J. Trammell, L. H. Binder, and C. E. Snyder, "The Automated Production Control Documentation System: A Case Study in Cleanroom Software Engineering," *ACM Transactions on Software Engineering and Methodology* **1**, No. 1, 81–84 (January 1992).

20   M. Dyer, *The Cleanroom Approach to Quality Software Development*, John Wiley & Sons, Inc., New York (1992).

21   *A Success Story at Pratt and Whitney: On Track for the Future with IBM's VS COBOL II and COBOL Structuring Facility*, GK20-2326, IBM Corporation (1989); no longer available through IBM branch offices.

22   R. C. Linger and A. R. Hevner, "The Incremental Development Process in Cleanroom Software Engineering," *Proceedings of Workshop on Information Technologies and Systems (WITS-93)*, A. R. Hevner, Editor, College of Business and Management, University of Maryland, College Park, MD (December 4–5, 1993), pp. 162–171.

23   H. D. Mills, R. C. Linger, and A. R. Hevner, "Box Structured Information Systems," *IBM Systems Journal* **26**, No. 4, 395–413 (1987).

24   A. R. Hevner and H. D. Mills, "Box-Structured Methods for Systems Development with Objects," *IBM Systems Journal* **32**, No. 2, 232–251 (1993).

25   H. D. Mills, "Stepwise Refinement and Verification in Box Structured Systems," *IEEE Computer* **21**, No. 6, 23–35 (June 1988).

26   R. H. Cobb and H. D. Mills, "Engineering Software Under Statistical Quality Control," *IEEE Software* **7**, No. 6, 44–54 (November 1990).

27   R. C. Linger, "An Overview of Cleanroom Software Engineering," *Proceedings of 1st Annual European Industrial Symposium on Cleanroom Software Engineering* (Copenhagen, Denmark), Q-Labs AB, IDEON Research Park, S-223 70 Lund, Sweden (1993), Section 7, pp. 1–19.

28   J. H. Poore, H. D. Mills, and D. Mutchler, "Planning and Certifying Software System Reliability," *IEEE Software* **10**, No. 1, 88–99 (January 1993).

29   J. H. Poore, H. D. Mills, S. L. Hopkins, and J. A. Whittaker, *Cleanroom Reliability Manager: A Case Study Using Cleanroom with Box Structures ADL*, Software Engineering Technology Report, IBM STARS CDRL 1940 (May 1990). STARS Asset Reuse Repository, 2611 Cranberry Square, Morgantown, West Virginia 26505.

30   C. J. Trammell and J. H. Poore, "A Group Process for Defining Local Software Quality: Field Applications and Validation Experiments," *Software Practice and Experience* **22**, No. 8, 603–636 (August 1992).

31 J. A. Whittaker and J. H. Poore, "Markov Analysis of Software Specifications," ACM *Transactions on Software Engineering and Methodology* **2**, No. 1, 93–106 (January 1993).

32 M. C. Paulk, W. Curtis, M. B. Chrissis, C. V. Weber, *Capability Maturity Model for Software, Version 1.1*, CMU/SEI-93-TR-24, Software Engineering Institute, Carnegie Mellon University, Pittsburg, PA 15213 (February 1993).

33 M. C. Paulk, C. V. Weber, S. M. Garcia, and M. B. Chrissis, *Key Practices of the Capability Maturity Model, Version 1.1*, CMU/SEI-93-TR-25, Software Engineering Institute, Carnegie Mellon University, Pittsburgh, PA 15213 (February 1993).

PART II

Cleanroom Management

Current Practice in Cleanroom Management

Cleanroom Management treats the software enterprise as an engineering practice. The classical engineering principles of controlled iteration, peer review, and measured performance can be seen in the following chapters about Cleanroom incremental development, team operations, and quantified reliability.

- "Cleanroom software engineering" (Mills, Dyer, and Linger, 1987) was the "coming out" of Cleanroom. This paper marked the gathering of Mills' key ideas under a single umbrella, and their movement out of the IBM laboratory and into the marketplace. The rationale for the Cleanroom method is explained and the results of early pilot projects are given.
- In "Cleanroom: an alternative software development process," originally a chapter in *Aerospace Software Engineering* (Anderson and Dorfman, eds, AIAA, 1990), Mills elaborates on the key ideas in the preceding chapter. The section of this chapter that details the motivation for statistical testing is essential reading for any Cleanroom practitioner. Mills' analysis of Adams' data about differential failure rates among errors leads to the conclusion that, on the average, fixing an error found in statistical testing is 30 times more effective in reducing mean-time-to-failure (MTTF) than fixing an error found in coverage testing.
- "The Cleanroom approach to six sigma: combining information" (developed from Poore, 1990) addresses the infeasibility of demonstrating six-sigma quality during development and the difficulty of doing so even over the life of a software system. The basis for counting (software uses) and the basis for inference (the binomial distribution) are shown to lead to the conclusion that six-sigma quality means that a software system exhibits no more than two failures in a billion uses.

- "Planning and certifying software system reliability" (Poore, Mills, and Mutchler, 1993) describes an approach to evaluating components for reuse in terms of their impact on the target level of system reliability. The chapter covers the theoretical basis for the approach and works through an example using a tool developed to support the approach. This was the only paper selected by both the IEEE Software Editorial and Industrial Advisory Boards as one of the best papers in 1993.
- "Cleanroom process model" (Linger, 1994) is a concise description of the generic Cleanroom process by a colleague who was among Mills' closest associates during his tenure at IBM, and who was the project manager for the first major application of Cleanroom at IBM. An organization that intends to tailor the Cleanroom process for its environment might use this excellent description of the central ideas and methods as a basis.

2 Cleanroom Software Engineering

H. D. MILLS, M. DYER, AND R. C. LINGER

INTRODUCTION

Recent experience demonstrates that software can be engineered under statistical quality control and that certified reliability statistics can be provided with delivered software. IBM's Cleanroom process[1] has uncovered a surprising synergy between mathematical verification and statistical testing of software, as well as a major difference between mathematical fallibility and debugging fallibility in people.

With the Cleanroom process, you can engineer software under statistical quality control. As with Cleanroom hardware development, the process's first priority is defect prevention rather than defect removal (of course, any defects not prevented should be removed). This first priority is achieved by using human mathematical verification in place of program debugging to prepare software for system test.

Its next priority is to provide valid, statistical certification of the software's quality through representative-user testing at the system level. The measure of quality is the mean time to failure in appropriate units of time (real or processor time) of the delivered product. The certification takes into account the growth of reliability achieved during system testing before delivery.

To gain the benefits of quality control during development, Cleanroom software engineering requires a development cycle of concurrent fabrication and certification of product increments that accumulate into the system to be delivered. This lets the fabrication process be altered on the basis of early certification results to achieve the quality desired.

© 1987 IEEE. Reprinted, with permission, from *IEEE Software*, vol. 4, no. 5, pp. 19–24, September 1987.

CLEANROOM EXPERIENCE

Typical of our experience with the Cleanroom process were three projects: an IBM language product (40,000 lines of code), an Air Force contract helicopter flight program (35,000 lines), and a NASA contract space-transportation planning system (45,000 lines). A major finding in these cases was that human verification, even though fallible, could replace debugging in software development – even informal human verification can produce software sufficiently robust to go to system test without debugging.

Typical program increments were 5000 to 15,000 lines of code. With experience and confidence, such increments can be expected to increase in size significantly. All three projects showed productivity equal to or better than expected for ordinary software development: Human verification need take *no more time* than debugging (although it takes place earlier in the cycle).

The combination of formal design methods and mathematics-based verification had a positive development effect: More than 90 percent of total product defects were found before first execution. This is in marked contrast to the more customary experience of finding 60 percent of product defects before first execution. This effect is probably directly related to the added care and attention given to design in lieu of rushing into code and relying on testing to achieve product quality.

A second encouraging trend is the drop in total defect count (by as much as half), which highlights the Cleanroom focus on error prevention as opposed to error detection. With industry averages at 50 to 60 errors per 1000 lines of code, halving these numbers is significant.

The IBM language product (COBOL/SF[2]) experience is especially instructive. This advanced technology product, comparable in complexity to a compiler, was formally specified and then designed in a process-design language. Specification text exceeded design text by about four to one. Every control structure in the design text was verified in formal, mathematics-based group inspection, so the product proved very robust. A first phase of development (20,000 lines) had just 53 errors found during testing.

Correctness verification was the cornerstone of the project; many programs were redesigned to permit simpler verification arguments. Productivity averaged more than 400 lines of code per man–month, largely as a result of sharply reduced testing time and effort compared to conventional developments.

A controlled experiment at the University of Maryland, with student teams developing a common project in message processing (1000 to 2000 lines), indicates better productivity and quality with the Cleanroom process than with interactive debugging and integration – even the first time you use it.[3]

MANAGEMENT PERSPECTIVE

At first glance, statistical quality control and software development seem incompatible. Statistical quality control seems to apply to manufacturing, especially manufacturing of multiple copies of a previously specified and designed part or product. Software development seems to be a one-of-a-kind logical process with no statistical properties at all. After all, if the software ever fails under certain conditions, it will always fail under those conditions.

However, by rethinking the process of statistical quality control itself from a management perspective, we can find a way to put software development under statistical quality control with significant management benefits.

But where do the statistics come from, when neither software nor its development have any statistical properties at all? The statistics come from the usage of the software, not from its intrinsic properties. Engineering software under statistical quality control requires that we not only specify the functional behavior of the software but also its statistical usage.

Cleanroom software engineering is a practical process to place software development under statistical quality control. The significance of a process under statistical quality control is well-illustrated by modern manufacturing techniques where the sampling of output is directly fed back into the process to control quality. Once the discipline of statistical quality control is in place, management can see the development process and can control process changes to control product quality.

The Cleanroom process permits a sharper structuring of development work between specification, design, and testing, with clearer accountabilities for each part of the process. This structuring increases management's ability to monitor work in progress. Inexperienced software managers often fail to recognize and expose early software problems (like hardware or specification instability, inexperienced personnel, and incomplete design solutions) and mistakenly think they can resolve and manage these problems over time. The Cleanroom process forces these early problems into the open, giving all levels of management an opportunity to resolve them.

The Cleanroom process requires stable specifications as its basis. Because specifications are often not fully known or verified during initial development, it might appear at first glance that the Cleanroom process does not apply. But, in fact, the discipline of the Cleanroom process is most useful in forcing specification deficiencies into the open and giving management control of the specification process.

As long as development is treated as a trial-and-error process, the incompleteness of specification can be accommodated as just one more source of trial and error. The result is diluted accountability between specifiers and developers. A better way is to develop software to early, stable specifications that remain stable in each iteration. This establishes a clear accountability between specification and development, keeping management in control of specification changes.

STATISTICAL QUALITY CONTROL

Statistical quality control begins with an agreement between a producer and receiver. A critical part of this agreement, explicit or implicit, is how to measure quality, particularly *statistical* quality. For simple products with straightforward physical, electrical, or other measurements, the agreement may be simply stated – for example, 99 percent of certain filaments are to exhibit an electrical resistance within 10 percent of a fixed value. However, software is complex enough to require a new understanding on how statistical quality can be measured.

For even the simplest of products, there is no absolute best statistical measure of quality. For example, a statistical average can be computed many ways – an arithmetic average, a weighted average, a geometric average, and a reciprocal average can each be better than the others in various circumstances.

It finally comes down to a judgment of business and management – in every case. In most cases, the judgment is practically automatic from experience and precedent, but it *is* a judgment. In the case of software, that judgment has no precedent because the concept of producing software under statistical quality control is just at its inception.

A new basis for the certification of software quality, given in Currit, Dyer, and Mills,[1] is based on a new software-engineering process.[4] This basis requires a software specification and a probability distribution on scenarios of the software's use; it then defines a testing procedure and a prescribed computation from test data results to provide a certified statistical quality of delivered software.

This new basis represents scientific and engineering judgment of a fair and reasonable way to measure statistical quality of software. As for simpler products, there is no absolute best and no logical arguments for it beyond business and management judgment. But it can provide a basis for software statistical quality as a contractual item where no such reasonable item existed before.

The certification of software quality is given in terms of its measured reliability over a probability distribution of usage scenarios in statistical testing. Certification is an ordinary process in business – even in the certification of the net worth of a bank. As in software certification, there is a fact-finding process, followed by a prescribed computation.

In the case of a bank, the fact-finding produces assets and liabilities, and the computation subtracts the sum of the liabilities from the sum of the assets. For the bank, there are other measures of importance besides net worth – such as goodwill, growth, and security assets – just as there are other measures for software than reliability – such as maintainability and performance. So a certification of software quality is a business measure, part of the overall consideration in producing and receiving software.

Once a basis for measuring statistical quality of delivered software is available, creating a management process for statistical quality control is relatively straightforward. In principle, the goal is to find ways to repeatedly rehearse the final measurement during software development and to modify the development process, where necessary, to achieve a desired level of statistical quality.

The Cleanroom process has been designed to carry out this principle. It calls for the development of software in increments that permit realistic measurements of statistical quality during development, with provision for improving the measured quality by additional testing, by process changes (such as increased inspections and configuration control), or by both methods.

MATHEMATICAL VERIFICATION

Software engineering without mathematical verification is no more than a buzzword. When Dijkstra introduced the idea of structured programming at an early software-engineering conference,[5] his principal motivation was to reduce the length of mathematical verifications of programs by using a few basic control structures and eliminating gotos.

Many popularizers of structured programming have cut out the rigorous part about mathematical verification in favor of the easy part about no gotos. But by cutting out the rigorous part, they have also cut out much of the real benefit of structured programming. As a result, a lot of people have become three-day wonders in having no gotos without acquiring the fundamental discipline of mathematical verification in engineering software – of even discovering that such a discipline exists.

In contrast, learning the rigor of mathematical verification leads to behavioral modification in both individuals and teams of programmers, whether programs are verified formally or not. Mathematical verification requires precise specifications and formal arguments about the correctness with respect to those specifications.

Two main behavioral effects are readily observable. First, communication among programmers (and managers) becomes much more precise, especially about program specifications. Second, a premium is placed on the simplest programs possible to achieve specified function and performance.

If a program looks hard to verify, it is the program that should be revised, *not* the verification. The result is high productivity in producing software that requires little or no debugging.

Cleanroom software engineering uses mathematical verification to replace program debugging before release to statistical testing. This mathematical verification is done by people, based on standard software-engineering practices[4] such as those taught at the IBM Software Engineering Institute. We find that human verification is surprisingly synergistic with statistical testing – that mathematical fallibility is very different from debugging fallibility and that errors of mathematical fallibility are much easier to discover in statistical testing than are errors of debugging fallibility.

Perhaps one day automatic verification of software will be practical. But there is no need to wait for the engineering value and discipline of mathematical verification until that day.

Experimental data from projects where both Cleanroom verification and more traditional debugging techniques were used offers evidence that the Cleanroom-verified software exhibited higher quality. For the verified software, fewer errors were injected, and these errors were less severe and required less time to find and fix. The verified product also experienced better field quality, all of which was due to the added care and attention paid during design.

Findings from an early Cleanroom project (where verified software accounted for approximately half the product's function) indicate that verified software accounted for only one fourth the error count. Moreover, the verified software was responsible for less than 10 percent of the severe failures. These findings substantiated that verified software contains fewer defects and that those defects that are present are simpler and have less effect on product execution.

The method of human mathematical verification used in Cleanroom development, called functional verification, is quite different than the method of axiomatic verification usually taught in universities. It is based on functional semantics and on the reduction of software verification to ordinary mathematical reasoning about sets and functions as directly as possible.

The motivation for functional verification and for the earliest possible reduction of verification reasoning to sets and functions is the problem of scaling up. A set or function can be described in three lines of ordinary mathematics notation or in 300 lines of English text. There is more human fallibility in 300 lines of English than in three lines of mathematical notation, but the verification paradigm is the same.

By introducing verification in terms of sets and functions, you establish a basis for reasoning that scales up. Large programs have many variables, but only one function. Mills and Linger[6] gave an additional basis for verifying large programs by designing with sets, stacks, and queues rather than with arrays and pointers.

While initially harder to teach than axiomatic verification, functional verification scales up to reasoning for million-line systems in top-level design as well as for hundred-line programs at the bottom level. The evidence that such reasoning is effective is in the small amount of back-tracking required in very large systems designed top-down with functional verification.[7]

CLEANROOM SOFTWARE ENGINEERING

While it may sound revolutionary at first glance, the Cleanroom software engineering process is an *evolutionary* step in software development. It is evolutionary in eliminating debugging because, over the past 20 years, more and more program design has been developed in design languages that must be verified rather than executed. So the relative effort for advanced teams in debugging, compared to verifying, is now quite small, even in non-Cleanroom development.

It is evolutionary in statistical testing because with higher quality programs at the outset, representative-user testing is correspondingly a greater and greater fraction of the total testing effort. And, as already noted, we have found a surprising synergism between human verification and statistical testing: People are fallible with human verification, but the errors they leave behind for system testing are much easier to find and fix than those left behind from debugging.

Results from an early Cleanroom project where verification and debugging were used to develop different parts of the software indicate that corrections to the verified software were accomplished in about one fifth the average time of corrections to the debugged software. In the verified software case, the developers essentially never resorted to debugging (less than 0.1 percent of the cases) to isolate and repair reported defects.

The feasibility of combining human verification with statistical testing makes it possible to define a new software-engineering process under statistical quality control.[1] For that purpose, we define a new development life cycle of successive incremental releases to achieve a structured specification of function and statistical usage. A structured specification is a formal specification (a relation or set of ordered pairs) for a decomposition into a nested set of subspecifications for successive product releases. A structured specification defines not only the final software but also a release plan for its incremental implementation and statistical testing.

A stepwise refinement or decomposition of requirements creates successive levels of software design. At each level of decomposition, mathematics-based correctness arguments ensure the accuracy of the evolving design and the continued integrity of the product requirements. The work strategy is to create specifications and then design to those specifications, as well as to check the correctness of that design before proceeding to the next decomposition.

The Cleanroom design methods use a limited set of design primitives to capture software logic (sequence, selection, and iteration). They use module and procedure primitives to package software designs into products. Decomposition of software data requirements is handled by a companion set of data-structuring primitives (sets, stacks, and queues) that ensure product designs with strongly typed data operations. Specially defined design languages document designs and provide a straightforward translation to standard programming forms.

In the Cleanroom model, structural testing that requires knowledge of the design is replaced by formal verification, but functional testing is retained. In fact, this testing can be performed with the two goals of demonstrating that the product requirements are correctly implemented in the software and of providing a basis for product-reliability prediction. The latter is a unique Cleanroom capability that results from its statistical testing method, which supports statistical inference from the test to operating environments.

The Cleanroom life cycle of incremental product releases supports software testing throughout the product development rather than only when it is completed. This allows the continuous assessment of product quality from an execution perspective and permits any necessary adjustments in the process to improve observed product quality.

As each release becomes available, statistical testing provides statistical estimates of its reliability. Software process analysis and feedback can be used to meet reliability goals (for example, by increased verification inspections and by more intermediate specification formality) for subsequent releases. As errors are found and fixed during system testing, the growth in reliability of the maturing system can also be estimated so a certified reliability estimate of the system-tested software can be provided at final release.

Cho[8] has also proposed the development of software under statistical quality control, using as a measure the ratio of correct outputs to total outputs. He regards software as a factory for producing output, rather than for producing a product itself. The ratio of correct outputs to total outputs is directly related to the mean time between failures, where time is normalized to output production. Such a normalization is one possibility in the Cleanroom process, but other normalizations may be more meaningful in most system applications.

A principal difference between the Cleanroom and Cho's ideas is the use of a certification model to account for the growth in reliability during development. Another major difference is an insistence on human mathematical verification with no program debugging before representative-user testing at the system level. As Mills discussed,[9] human mathematical verification is possible and practical at high production rates. The time spent on verification can be less than the time spent on debugging.

STATISTICAL BASIS

Software people customarily talk about errors in the software, typically measured in errors per thousand lines of code. Current postdelivery levels in ordinary software are one to 10 errors per thousand lines. Good methodology produces postdelivery levels under one error per thousand lines. But such numbers are irrelevant and misleading when you consider software reliability. Users do not see errors in the software, they see failures in execution, so the measurement of times between failures is more relevant.

If each error had the same or similar failure rate, there would be a direct relationship between the number of errors in software and the time between failures in its execution. Half as many errors would mean half the failure rate and twice the mean time between failures. In this case, efforts to reduce errors would automatically increase reliability.

It turns out that every major IBM software product – without exception – has an extremely high error-failure rate variation. In stable released products, these failure rates run from 18 months between failures to more than 5000 years. More than half the errors have failure rates of more than 1500 years between failures. Fixing these errors will reduce the number of errors by more than half, but the decrease in the product failure rate will be imperceptible. More precisely, you could remove more than 60 percent of the errors but only decrease the failure rate by less than 3 percent.

These surprising refutations of conventional wisdom in software reliability are due to data painstakingly developed over many years by Adams.[10]

To be more precise about software errors and failures, assume that a specification and its software exist. Then, when the software is executed, its behavior can be compared with its specification and any discrepancies (failures). Such failures may be catastrophic and prevent further execution (for example, by abnormal termination). Other failures may be so serious that every response from then on is incorrect (for example, if a database is compromised). Less serious failures represent the case in which the software continues to execute with at least partially correct behavior beyond the failure.

These examples illustrate that failures represent different levels of severity, beginning with three major levels:

- terminating failures
- permanent failures (but not terminating), and
- sporadic failures

Even terminating or permanent failures may be followed by a restart of the software, so you can imagine a long history of execution and, in this history, the failures marked at each instant of time. Clearly, this history will depend on the software's initial conditions (and data) and on the subsequent inputs (as commands and data) to it. Such a history can be very arbitrary, but suppose for argument's sake that representative histories (scenarios of use) are conceivable.

The behavior of software is deterministic in that repeating an initial condition and history of use will reproduce the same outputs (with the same failures). But, in fact, if software is used in more than one history by more than one user, the histories of use will usually be different. For that reason, we consider as part of a structured specification a probability distribution of usage histories, typically defined as a stochastic process.

This probability distribution of usage histories will, in turn, induce a probability distribution of failure histories in which statistics about times between failures, failure-free intervals, and the like can be defined and estimated. So, even though software behavior is deterministic, its reliability can be defined relative to its statistical usage. Such a probability distribution of usage histories provides a statistical basis for software quality control.

CERTIFYING STATISTICAL QUALITY

For software already released, it is simple to estimate its reliability in mean times to failure: merely take the average of its times between failure in statistical testing. However, for software under Cleanroom development, the problem is more complicated, for two reasons:

1   In each Cleanroom increment, results of system testing may indicate software changes to correct failures found.
2   With each Cleanroom increment release, untested new software will be added to software already under test.

In fact, each change or set of changes to correct failures in a release creates a new software product very much like its predecessor but with a different reliability (intended to be better, but possibly worse). However, each of these corrected software products, by itself, will be subject to a strictly limited amount of testing before it is superseded by its successor, and statistical estimates of reliability will be correspondingly limited in confidence.

Therefore, to aggregate the testing experience for an increment release, we define a model of reliability change with parameters M and R (as discussed in Currit, Dyer, and Mills[1]) for the mean time to failure after c software changes, of the form $\text{MTTF} = MR^c$ where M is the initial mean time to failure of the release and where R is the observed effectiveness ratio for improving mean time to failure with software changes.

Although various technical rationales are given for this model by Currit, Dyer, and Mills,[1] it should be considered a contractual basis for the eventual certification of the finally released software by the developer to the user. Moreover, because there is no way to know that the model parameters M and R are absolutely correct, we define statistical estimators for them in terms of the test data. The choice of these estimators is based on statistical analysis, but the choice should also be a contractual basis for certification.

The net result of these two contractual bases – a reliability change model and statistical estimators for its parameters – gives producer and receiver (seller and purchaser) a common, objective way to certify the reliability of the delivered software. The certification is a scientific, statistical inference obtained by a prescribed computation on test data arranged to be correct by the developer.

In principle, the estimators for software reliability are no more than a sophisticated way to average the times between failure, taking into account the change activity called for during statistical testing. As test data materializes, the reliability can be estimated, even change by change. And with successful corrections, the reliability estimates will improve with further testing, providing objective, quantitative evidence of the achievement of reliability goals.

This objective evidence is itself a basis for management control of the software development to meet reliability goals. For example, process analysis may reveal both unexpected sources of errors (such as poor understanding of the underlying hardware) and appropriate corrections in the process itself for later increments. Intermediate rehearsals of the final certification provide a basis for management feedback to meet final goals.

The treatment of separate increment releases should also be part of the contractual basis between the developer and user. Perhaps the simplest treatment is to treat separate increments independently. However, more statistical confidence in the final certification will result from aggregate testing experience across increments. A simple aggregation could complement separately treated increments with management judgment.

A more sophisticated treatment of separate releases would be to model the failure contribution of each newly released part of the software and to develop stratified estimators release by release. Earlier releases can be expected to mature while later releases come under test. This maturation rate in reliability improvement can be used to estimate the amount of test time required to reach prescribed reliability levels.

Mean time to failure and the rate of change in mean time to failure can be useful decision tools for project management. For software under test, which has both an estimated mean time to failure and a known rate of change in mean time to failure, decisions on releasability can be based on an evaluation of life-cycle costs rather than on just marketing effect.

When the software is delivered, the average cost for each failure must include both the direct costs of repair and the indirect costs to the users (which may be much larger). These postdelivery costs can be estimated from the number of expected failures and compared with the costs for additional predelivery testing. Judgments could then be made about the profitability of continuing tests to minimize lifetime costs.

References

1   A. Currit, M. Dyer, and H. D. Mills, "Certifying the Reliability of Software," IEEE *Trans. Software Eng.*, Jan. 1986, pp. 3–11.

2   COBOL *Structuring Facility Users Guide*, IBM Corp., Armonk, N.Y., 1986.

3   R. W. Selby, V. R. Basili, and F. T. Baker, "Cleanroom Software Development: An Empirical Evaluation," Tech. Report TR-1415, Computer Science Dept., Univ. of Maryland, College Park, Md., Feb. 1985.

4   R. C. Linger, H. D. Mills, and B. I. Witt, *Structured Programming: Theory and Practice*, Addison-Wesley, Reading, Mass., 1979.

5   E. W. Dijkstra, "Structured Programming," in *Software Engineering Techniques*, J. N. Burton and B. Randell, eds., NATO Science Committee, New York, 1969, pp. 88–93.

6   H. D. Mills and R. C. Linger, "Data Structured Programming," *IEEE Trans. Software Eng.*, Feb. 1986, pp. 192–197.

7   A. J. Jordano, "DSM Software Architecture and Development," *IBM Technical Directions*, No. 3, 1984, pp. 17–28.

8   C. K. Cho, *Quality Programming: Developing and Testing Software with Statistical Quality Control*, John Wiley & Sons, New York, 1987.

9   H. D. Mills, "Structured Programming: Retrospect and Prospect," *IEEE Software*, Nov. 1986, pp. 58–66.

10 E. N. Adams, "Optimizing Preventive Service of Software Products," *IBM J. Research and Development*, Jan. 1984.

3 Cleanroom: an Alternative Software Development Process

H. D. MILLS

WHAT IS CLEANROOM SOFTWARE ENGINEERING?

The Cleanroom software engineering process develops software of certified reliability under statistical quality control in a pipeline of increments,
with no program debugging before independent statistical usage testing of
the increments. It requires rigorous methods of software specification,
design, and testing, with which disciplined software engineering teams are
capable of producing low- or zero-defect software of arbitrary size and
complexity. Such engineering discipline is not only capable of producing
highly reliable software, but also the certification of the reliability of the
software as specified.

The term "Cleanroom" is taken from the hardware industry to mean an
emphasis on preventing errors to begin with, rather than removing them
later (of course any errors introduced should be removed). Cleanroom
software engineering involves rigorous methods that enable greater control over both product and process. The Cleanroom process not only produces software of high reliability and high performance, but does so while
yielding high productivity and schedule reliability. The intellectual control
provided by the rigorous Cleanroom process allows both technical and
management control.

As stated, Cleanroom software engineering is a process for software development under statistical quality control.[1-2] It recognizes software development as an engineering process with mathematical foundations rather than as a trial-and-error programming process.[3-5] But it also defines a new basis for statistical quality control in a design process, rather than the well-known idea of statistical quality control in manufacturing to accepted product designs.

In this first human generation of software development, such mathematical and statistical foundations have been little understood and used, particularly in large projects in which the very management of all of the people required seemed of foremost difficulty. One generation is a very short time for human society to master a subject as complex and novel as software development. For example, after a single generation of civil engineering, the right angle was yet to be discovered. Although many more people are working in software engineering in its first generation, fundamentals and disciplines still take time for discovery, confirmation, and general use.[6]

In Cleanroom software engineering a major discovery is the ability of well-educated and motivated people to create nearly defect-free software before any execution or debugging, less than five defects per thousand lines of code. Such code is ready for usage testing and certification with no unit debugging by the designers. In this first human generation of software development it has been counter intuitive to expect software with so few defects at the outset. Typical heuristic programming creates 50 defects per thousand lines of code, then reduces that number to five or less by debugging. But program debugging often leaves deeper errors behind while doing so. A second major discovery is that defects due to mathematical fallibility in the Cleanroom process are much easier to find and fix than defects due to debugging fallibility, with the time and effort required literally reduced by a factor of five.[1]

The mathematical foundations for Cleanroom software engineering come from the deterministic nature of computers themselves. A computer program is no more and no less than a rule for a mathematical function.[3-5] Such a function need not be numerical, of course, and most programs do not define numerical functions. But for every legal input, a program directs the computer to produce a unique output, whether correct as specified or not. And the set of all such input/output pairs is a mathematical function. A more usual way to view a program in this first generation is as a set of instructions for specific executions with specific input data. Although correct, this view misses a point of reusing well known and tested mathematical ideas, regarding computer programming as new and private art rather than more mature and public engineering.

With these mathematical foundations, software development becomes a process of constructing rules for functions that meet required specifications, which need not be a trial-and-error programming process. The functional semantics of a structured programming language can be expressed in an algebra of functions with function operations corresponding to program sequence, alternation, and iteration.[7] The systematic top-down development of programs is mirrored in describing function rules in terms of algebraic operations among simpler functions, and their rules in terms of still simpler functions until the rules of the programming language are reached. It is a new mental base for most practitioners to consider the complete functions needed, top-down, rather than computer executions for specific data.

The statistical foundations for Cleanroom software engineering come from adding usage statistics to software specifications, along with function and performance requirements.[1,8] Such usage statistics provide a basis for measuring the reliability of the software during its development and thereby measuring the quality of the design in meeting functional and performance requirements. A more usual way to view development in this first generation is as a difficult to predict art form. Software with no known errors at delivery frequently experiences many failures in actual usage.

CLEANROOM EXPERIENCES

The IBM COBOL Structuring Facility (SF), a complex product of some 80K lines of source code, was developed in the Cleanroom discipline, with no debugging before usage testing and certification of its reliability. A version of the HH60 (helicopter) flight control program of over 30 KLOC was also developed using Cleanroom. Smaller student Cleanroom projects have been successful at the Universities of Maryland, Tennessee, and Florida. Just as people learned to type more accurately and faster without looking at the keys, people can also learn to develop software more accurately and faster without looking at its execution.

The IBM COBOL SF is part of a line of products dealing with various levels of COBOL.[9] It converts an unstructured COBOL program into a structured one of identical function. It uses considerable artificial intelligence to transform a flat structured program into one with a deeper hierarchy that is much easier to understand and modify. The product line was prototyped with Cleanroom discipline at the outset, then individual products were generated in Cleanroom extensions. In this development several challenging schedules were defined for competitive reasons, but every schedule was met.

The COBOL/SF products have high function per line of code. The prototype was estimated at 100 KLOC by an experienced language processing group, but the Cleanroom developed prototype was 20 KLOC. The software was designed not only in structured programming, but also in structured data access. No arrays or pointers were used in the design; instead, sets, queues, and stacks were used as primitive data structures.[10] Such data-structured programs are more reliably verified and inspected and also more readily optimized with respect to size or performance, as required.

The HH60 flight control program was developed on schedule. Programmers' morale went from quite low at the outset ("Why us?") to very high on discovering their unexpected capability in accurate software design without debugging. The 12 programmers involved had all passed the pass/fail course work in mathematical (functional) verification of the IBM Software Engineering Institute, but were provided a week's review as a team for the project. The testers had much more to learn about certification by objective statistics.[8]

In the 80K COBOL/SF product the defect rate of the original, unexecuted, undebugged software was 3.4/KLOC. Such defects were discovered during the statistical certification process and duly fixed. In the 30K HH60 flight control product the defect rate was 2.5/KLOC. As already noted, defects from mathematical fallibility are much easier to find and fix, quantified in the latter case by a factor of five to one in decreased time required.[1]

V. R. Basili and F. T. Baker introduced Cleanroom ideas in an undergraduate software engineering course at the University of Maryland, assisted by R. W. Selby. As a result, a controlled experiment in a small software project was carried out over two academic years, using 15 teams with both traditional and Cleanroom methods. The result, even on first exposure to Cleanroom, was positive in the production of reliable software, compared with traditional results.[11]

Cleanroom projects have been carried out at the University of Tennessee, under the leadership of J. H. Poore,[2] and at the University of Florida under H. D. Mills. At Florida, seven teams of undergraduates produced uniformly successful systems for a common structured specification of three increments. It is a surprise for undergraduates to consider software development as a serious engineering activity using mathematical verification instead of debugging, because it is introduced primarily as a trial-and-error activity with no real technical standards.

TWO SACRED COWS OF THE FIRST HUMAN GENERATION IN SOFTWARE

Software engineering and computer science are new subjects, only a human generation old. In this first generation, two major sacred cows have emerged from the heuristic, error-prone software development of this entirely new human activity, namely, program debugging and coverage testing. As noted earlier, program debugging before independent usage testing is unnecessary and creates deeper errors in software than are found and fixed. It is also a surprise to discover that coverage testing is very inefficient for getting reliable software and provides no capability for scientific certification of reliability in use.

As a first-generation effort, it has seemed only natural to debug programs as they are written and even to establish technical and management standards for such debugging. For example, in the first generation in typing, it seemed only natural to look at the keys. Touch typing without looking at the keys must have looked very strange to the first generation of hunt-and-peck typists. Similarly, software development without debugging before independent certification testing of user function looks very strange to the first generation of trial-and-error programmers. It is quite usual for human performance to be surprising in new areas, and software development will prove to be no exception.

Just as debugging programs has seemed natural, coverage testing has also seemed to be a natural and powerful process. Although 100% coverage testing is known to still possibly leave errors behind, coverage testing seems to provide a systematic process for developing tests and recording results in well managed development. Thus, it comes as a major surprise to discover that statistical usage testing is more than an order of magnitude more effective than coverage testing in increasing the time between failures in use. Coverage testing may, indeed, discover more errors in error prone software than usage testing. But it discovers errors of all failure rates, whereas usage testing discovers the high failure rate errors more critical to users.

CLEANROOM STATISTICAL QUALITY CONTROL

Cleanroom software engineering achieves statistical quality control over software development by strictly separating the design process from the testing process in a pipeline of incremental software development. There are three major engineering activities in the process:[1,9]

(1) structured architecture and precise specification of a pipeline of software increments that accumulate into the final software product, which includes the statistics of its use as well as its function and performance requirements;
(2) box-structured design and functional verification of each increment, delivery for certification without debugging beforehand, and subse-

quent correction of any failures that may be uncovered during certification; and

(3)   statistical testing and certification of the software reliability for the usage specification, notification to designers of any failures discovered during certification, and subsequent recertification as failures are corrected.

These three activities are defined and discussed in the next three sections.

As noted, there is an explicit feedback process between certification and design on any failures found in statistical usage testing. This feedback process provides an objective measure of the reliability of the software as it matures in the development pipeline. It does, indeed, provide a statistical quality control process for software development that has not been available in this first human generation of trial-and-error programming.

Humans are fallible, even in using sound mathematical processes in functional verification; thus, software failures are possible during the certification process. But there is a surprising power and synergism between functional verification and statistical usage testing.[1] First, as already noted, functional verification can be scaled up for high productivity and still leave no more errors than heuristic programming often leaves after unit and system testing combined. Second, it turns out that the mathematical errors left are much easier to find and fix during testing than errors left behind in debugging, measured at a factor of five in practice.[1] Mathematical errors usually turn out to be simple blunders in the software, whereas errors left behind or introduced in debugging are usually deeper in logic or wider in system scope than those fixed. As a result, statistical usage testing not only provides a formal, objective basis for the certification of reliability under use, but also uncovers the errors of mathematical fallibility with remarkable efficiency.

STRUCTURED ARCHITECTURE

In this first human generation of software development, most of the progress and discipline has been discovered in the later parts of the life cycle, first in coding machine programs in higher-level languages, then in areas such as structured programming and object-oriented design. Problems in requirements analyses and specifications are more difficult. Defining precisely what is needed and what should be provided by software is more general and difficult than simply producing working software with the hope that it will be satisfactory on trial by users. Even when specifications are required, they are frequently provided in informal, natural languages with considerable room for misunderstandings between designers and users and with gaps in exact details in which programming mis-interpretations are possible and likely.

Precision specifications require formal languages, just as programming does. In the case of programming the need is very obvious because computer machine languages are formal. But as systems become more complex and are used by more people with more critical impacts on business, industrial, and governmental institutions, the need for formal languages for specifications becomes clearer. New programming languages have improved primarily in their ability to provide explicit structure in data and procedure. For example, Ada has no more capability in defining machine operations than FORTRAN or COBOL. But it has more explicit design structures for people to use, for example, in packages for data abstractions or objects. Specification languages also need explicit structures for the same reason, to allow people to express requirements as directly as possible.

Regardless of the language, formal or informal, a functional specification defines not only legal system inputs, but legal input histories, and for each legal input history, a set of one or more legal outputs. Such legal input histories may be defined in real-time in systems in which real-time is a critical factor, and the outputs given real-time requirements as well. Illegal inputs and histories may be treated in various ways, from ignoring them to attempts to decipher or correct them. Any definite treatments of illegal inputs or histories become part of the specification as well. The abstraction of any such functional specification, in any language, is a mathematical relation, a set of ordered pairs whose first members are input histories and second members are outputs. Then, there is a very direct and simple mathematical definition for a program meeting a specification. The definition is that the function defined by the program determines a value for every argument in the domain of the specification relation and that this value be associated with that argument in the relation.[5,6]

In Cleanroom software engineering precision specifications are extended in two separate ways to create a structured architecture. First, the functional specifications are designed as a set of nested subspecifications, each a strict subset of the preceding subspecification. Then, beginning with the smallest subspecification, a pipeline of software increments is defined with each step going to the next larger subspecification.[1] Second, the usage of the functional specifications is defined as a statistical distribution over all possible input histories.[8] The structured architecture makes statistical quality control possible in subsequent incremental software development to the functional specifications. The usage statistics provide a statistical basis for testing and certification of the reliability of the software in meeting its specifications.

The creation of a structured architecture defines not only what a software system is to be when finished, but also a construction plan to design and test the software in a pipeline of subsystems, step by step. The pipeline must define step sizes that the design group can complete without debugging prior to delivery to the certification group. Well-educated and disciplined design groups may handle step sizes up to 200,000 lines of high-level code. But the structured architecture must also determine a satisfactory set of user-executable increments for the development pipeline of overlapping design and test operations.

BOX-STRUCTURED DESIGN

Box-structured design is defined by the top-down design of a Parnas usage hierarchy of modules.[12] Such modules, also known as data abstractions or objects,[17] are described by a set of operations that may define and access internally stored data. Stacks, queues, and sequential files provide simple examples of such modules. Part of their discipline is that internally stored data cannot be accessed or altered in any way except through the explicit operations of the module. It is critical in box-structured design to recognize that modules exist at every level from complete systems to individual program variables. It is also critical to recognize that a verifiable design must deal with a usage hierarchy rather than a parts hierarchy in its structure. A program that stores no data between invocations can be described in terms of a parts hierarchy of its smaller and smaller parts, because any use depends only on data supplied to it on its call with no dependence on previous calls. But an invocation of a module, say, a queue, may depend not only on the present call and data supplied to it, but also on previous calls and data supplied then.

The parts hierarchy of a structured program identifies every sequence, selection, and iteration (say, every begin–end, if–then–else, while–do) at every level. It turns out that the usage hierarchy of a system of modules (say, an object-oriented design with all objects identified) also identifies every call (use) of every operation of every module. The semantics of the structured program is defined by a mathematical function for each sequence, selection, and iteration in the parts hierarchy. That does not quite work for the operations of modules because of usage history dependencies, but there is a simple extension for modules that does work. The solution is to model the behavior of a module as a state machine, with the calls of its several operations as inputs to the common state machine. Then the semantics of such a module is defined by the transition function of its state machine (with an initial state). When the operations are defined by structured programs, the semantics of modules becomes a simple extension of the semantics of structured programs.

Although theoretically straightforward, the practical design of systems of Parnas modules (object-oriented systems) in usage hierarchies can become quite complex. It seems much simpler to outline such designs in parts hierarchies and structures, for example in data flow diagrams, without distinguishing between separate usages of the same module. Although that may seem simpler at the moment, such design outlines are incomplete and often lead to faulty completions at the detailed programming levels.

In order to create and control such designs based on usage hierarchies in more practical ways, their box structures provide standard, finer-grained subdescriptions for any module of three forms, namely, as black boxes, state boxes, and clear boxes, defined as follows:[13–15]

(1)   black box – an external view of a Parnas module, describing its behavior as a mathematical function from historical sequences of stimuli to its next response;

(2)   state box – an intermediate view of a Parnas module, describing its behavior by use of an internal state and internal black box with a mathematical function from historical sequences of stimuli and states to its next response and state, and an initial internal state; and

(3)   clear box – an internal view of a Parnas module, describing the internal black box of its state box in a usage control structure of other Parnas modules (such a control structure may define sequential or concurrent use of the other modules).

Box structures enforce completeness and precision in design of software systems as usage hierarchies of Parnas modules. Such completeness and precision lead to pleasant surprises in human capabilities in software engineering and development. The surprises are in capabilities to move from system specifications to design in programs without the need for unit/module testing and debugging before delivery to system usage testing. In this first generation of software development, it has been widely assumed that trial-and-error programming, testing, and debugging were necessary. But well-educated, well-motivated software professionals are, indeed, capable of developing software systems of arbitrary size and complexity without program debugging before system usage testing.[9]

STATISTICAL CERTIFICATION

Cleanroom statistical certification of software involves, first, the specification of usage statistics in addition to function and performance specifications. Such usage statistics provide a basis for assessing the reliability of the software being tested under expected use. An efficient estimation process has been developed for projecting mean time to failures (MTTF) of software under test while also under correction for previously discovered failures.[8]

As each specified increment is completed by the designers, it is delivered to the certifiers, combined with preceding increments, for testing based on usage statistics. As noted, the Cleanroom architecture must define a sequence of nested increments that are to be executed exclusively by user commands as they accumulate into the entire system required. Each subsequence represents a subsystem complete in itself, even though not all of the user function may be provided in it. For each subsystem a certified reliability is defined from the usage testing and failures discovered, if any.

It is characteristic that each increment goes through a maturation during the testing, becoming more reliable from corrections required for failures found, serving thereby as a stable base as later increments are delivered and added to the developing system. For example, the HH60 flight control program had three increments[8] of over 10 KLOC each. Increment 1 required 27 corrections for failures discovered in its first appearance in increment 1 testing, but then only one correction during increment 1/2 testing, and two corrections during increment 1/2/3 testing. Increment 2 required 20 corrections during its first appearance in increment 1/2 testing, and only five corrections during increment 1/2/3 testing. Increment 3 required 21 corrections on its first appearance in increment 1/2/3 testing. In this case 76 corrections were required in a system of over 30 KLOC, under 2.5 corrections per KLOC for verified and inspected code, with no previous execution.

The COBOL SF consisted of 80 KLOC, 28 KLOC reused from previous products, 52 KLOC new or changed, designed, and tested in a pipeline of five increments,[9] the largest over 19 KLOC. A total of 179 corrections were required during certification, under 3.5 corrections per KLOC for code with no previous execution. The productivity of the development was 740 LOC per person month, including all specification, design, implementation, and management, in meeting a very short deadline.

In the certification process it is not only important to observe failures in execution, but also the times between such failures in execution of usage representative statistically generated inputs. Such test data must be developed to represent the sequential usage of the software by users, which, of course, will account for previous outputs seen by the users and what needs the users will have in various circumstances. The state of mind of a user and the current need can be represented by a stochastic process determined by a state machine whose present state is defined by previous inputs/outputs and a statistical model that provides the next input based on that present state.[1]

THE POWER OF USAGE TESTING OVER
COVERAGE TESTING

The insights and data of Adams[16] in the analysis of software testing, and the differences between software errors and failures, give entirely new understandings in software testing. Since Adams has discovered an amazingly wide spectrum in failure rates for software errors, it is no longer sensible to treat errors as homogeneous objects to find and fix. Finding and fixing errors with high failure rates produces much more reliable software than finding and fixing just any errors, which may have average or low failure rates.

The major surprise in Adams' data is the relative power of finding and fixing errors in usage testing over coverage testing, a factor of 30 in increasing MTTF. That factor of 30 seems incredible until the facts are worked out from Adams' data. But it explains many anecdotes about experiences in testing. In one such experience, an operating systems development group used coverage testing systematically in a major revision and for weeks found mean time to abends in seconds. It reluctantly allowed user tapes in one weekend, but on fixing those errors, found that the mean time to abends jumped literally from seconds to minutes.

The Adams data are given in Table 3.1 taken from ref. 16. The data describe distributions of failure rates for errors in nine major IBM products, including the major operating systems, language compilers, and data base systems. The uniformity of the failure rate distributions among these very different products is truly amazing. But even more amazing is a spread in

Table 3.1 Distributions of errors (in %) among mean time to failure (MTTF) classes

Product	MTTF in K months							
	60	19	6	1.9	0.6	0.19	0.06	0.019
1	34.2	28.8	17.8	10.3	5.0	2.1	1.2	0.7
2	34.2	28.0	18.2	9.7	4.5	3.2	1.5	0.7
3	33.7	28.5	18.0	8.7	6.5	2.8	1.4	0.4
4	34.2	28.5	18.7	11.9	4.4	2.0	0.3	0.1
5	34.2	28.5	18.4	9.4	4.4	2.9	1.4	0.7
6	32.0	28.2	20.1	11.5	5.0	2.1	0.8	0.3
7	34.0	28.5	18.5	9.9	4.5	2.7	1.4	0.6
8	31.9	27.1	18.4	11.1	6.5	2.7	1.4	1.1
9	31.2	27.6	20.4	12.8	5.6	1.9	0.5	0.0

failure rates over four orders of magnitude, from 19 months to 5000 years (60 K months) calendar time in MTTF, with about a third of the errors having an MTTF of 5000 years, and 1% having an MTTF of 19 months.

With such a range in failure rates, it is easy to see that coverage testing will find the very low failure rate errors a third of the time with practically no effect on the MTTF by the fix, whereas usage testing will find many more of the high failure rate errors with much greater effect. Table 3.2 develops the data, using Table 3.1, that show the relative effectiveness of fixes in usage testing and coverage testing, in terms of increased MTTF. Table 3.2 develops the change in failure rates for each MTTF class of Table 3.1, because it is the failure rates of the MTTF classes that add up to the failure rate of the product.

First, in Table 3.2, line 1, denoted M (MTTF), is repeated directly from Table 3.1, namely, the mean time between failures of the MTTF class. Next, line 2, denoted ED (error density), is the average of the error densities of the nine products of Table 3.1, column by column, which represents a typical software product. Line 3, denoted ED/M, is the contribution of each class, on the average, in reducing the failure rate by fixing the next error found by coverage testing (1/M is the failure rate of the class, ED the probability a member of this class will be found next in coverage testing; hence, their product, ED/M, is the expected reduction in the total failure rate from that class). Now ED/M is also proportional to the usage failure rate in each class, since failures of that rate will be distributed by just that amount. Therefore, this line 3 is normalized to add to 100% in line 4, denoted FD (failure density). It is interesting to note that ED and FD are almost reverse distributions, ED about a third at the high end of MTTFs and FD about a third at the low end of MTTFs. Finally, line 5, denoted FD/M, is the contribution of each class, on the average, in reducing the failure rate by fixing the next error found by usage testing.

The sums of the two lines ED/M and FD/M turn out to be proportional to the decrease in failure rate from the respective fixes of errors found by coverage testing and usage testing, respectively. Their sums are 77.3 and

Table 3.2 Error densities and failure densities in the MTTF classes of Table 3.1

Property								
M	60	19	6	1.9	0.6	0.19	0.06	0.019
ED	33.2	28.2	18.7	10.6	5.2	2.5	1.1	0.5
ED/M	0.6	1.5	3.1	5.6	8.7	13.2	18.3	26.3
FD	0.8	2.0	3.9	7.3	11.1	17.1	23.6	34.2
FD/M	0	0	1	4	18	90	393	1800

2306, with a ratio of about 30 between them. That is the basis for the statement of their relative worth in increasing MTTF. It seems incredible at first glance, but that is the number!

To see that in more detail, consider, first, the relative decreases in failure rate R in the two cases:

Fix next error from coverage testing
$$R \rightarrow R - (\text{sum of ED/M values})/(\text{errors remaining})$$
$$= R - 77.3/E$$

Fix next error from usage testing
$$R \rightarrow R - (\text{sum of FD/M values})/(\text{errors remaining})$$
$$= R - 2306/E$$

Next, the increase in MTTF in each case will be

$$1/(R - 77.3/E) - 1/R = 77.3/(R*(E*R - 77.3))$$

and

$$1/(R - 2306/E) - 1/R = 2306/(R*(E*R - 2306))$$

In these expressions the numerator values 77.3 and 2306 dominate, and the denominators are nearly equal when $E*R$ is much larger than 77.3 or 2306 (either $77.3/(E*R)$ or $2306/(E*R)$ is the fraction of R reduced by the next fix and is supposed to be small in this analysis). As noted, the ratio of these numerators is about 30 to 1, in favor of the fix with usage testing.

SUMMARY

In summary, the Cleanroom software engineering process develops software of certified reliability under statistical quality control in a pipeline of increments that accumulate into the specified software. In the Cleanroom process there is no program debugging before independent statistical usage testing of the increments as they accumulate into the final product. The Cleanroom process requires rigorous methods of software specification, design, and testing, through which disciplined software engineering teams are capable of producing low- or zero-defect software of arbitrary size and complexity. Such engineering discipline is not only capable of producing highly reliable software, but also the certification of the reliability of the software as specified.

In a major application the IBM COBOL Structuring Facility, a complex product of some 80K lines of source code was developed in the Cleanroom discipline, with no debugging before usage testing and certification of its reliability. The product was completed with high productivity (740 SLOC/pm) and under 3.5 defects/KLOC in its initial design. A version of the HH60 (helicopter) flight control program of over 30 KLOC was also developed Cleanroom with under 2.5 defects/KLOC in its initial design.

In Cleanroom software engineering a major discovery is the ability of well-educated and motivated people to create nearly defect-free software before any execution or debugging, less than 5 defects/KLOC. In this first human generation of software development it has been counter intuitive to expect software with so few defects at the outset. Typical heuristic programming creates 50 defects/KLOC, then reduces that number to 5 or less by debugging. But such program debugging often leaves deeper errors behind while doing so.

Software engineering and computer science are new subjects, only a human generation old. In this first generation two major sacred cows have emerged from the heuristic, error-prone software development of this entirely new human activity, namely, program debugging and coverage testing. As noted earlier, program debugging before independent usage testing is unnecessary and creates deeper errors in software than are found and fixed. It is also a surprise to discover that coverage testing is very inefficient for getting reliable software in comparison with statistical usage testing (a factor of 30 in increasing MTTF). In addition, coverage testing provides no capability for scientific certification of reliability in use.

Of course, humans are fallible, even in using sound mathematical processes in functional verification; hence, software failures are possible during the certification process in the Cleanroom process. But there is a surprising power and synergism between functional verification and statistical usage testing.[1] First, as already noted, functional verification can be scaled up for high productivity and still leave no more errors than heuristic programming often leaves after unit and system testing combined. And second, it turns out that the mathematical errors left are much easier to find and fix during certification testing than errors left behind in debugging, measured at a factor of five in practice.[1]

Acknowledgments

The author is indebted to many people, many referenced, in the discovery and development of the idea of Cleanroom software engineering. For this paper the author notes special thanks to M. Dorfman, R. C. Linger, J. H. Poore, and C. Trammell for comments and suggestions.

References

1   Mills, H. D., Dyer, M., and Linger, R. C., "Cleanroom Software Engineering," *IEEE Software*, Sept. 1987, pp. 19–24.

2   Mills, H. D., and Poore, J. H., "Bringing Software Under Statistical Quality Control," *Quality Progress*, Nov. 1988. pp. 52–55.

3   Linger, R. C., Mills, H. D., and Witt, B. I., *Structured Programming: Theory and Practice*, Addison-Wesley, Reading, MA, 1979.

4   Mills, H. D., "The New Math of Computer Programming," *Communications of the ACM*, Vol. 18, No. 1, 1975.

5   Mills, H. D., Basili, V. R., Gannon, J. D., and Hamlet, R. G., *Principles of Computer Programming: A Mathematical Approach*, Brown, 1987.

6   Mills, H. D., "Structured Programming: Retrospect and Prospect," *IEEE Software*, Nov. 1986, pp. 58–66.

7   Mills, H. D., *Software Productivity*, Little, Brown, Boston, MA, 1983.

8   Currit, P. A., Dyer, M., and Mills, H. D., "Certifying the Reliability of Software," *IEEE Transactions on Software Engineering*, Vol. SE-12, No. 1, Jan. 1986, pp. 3–11.

9   Linger, R. C., and Mills, H. D., "A Case Study in Cleanroom Software Engineering: The IBM COBOL Structuring Facility," *Proceedings of COMPSAC '88*, IEEE, New York, 1988.

10 Mills, H. D., and Linger, R. C., "Data-Structured Programming: Program Design Without Arrays and Pointers," *IEEE Transactions on Software Engineering*, Vol. SE-12, No. 2, Feb. 1986, pp. 192–197.

11 Selby, R. W., Basili, V. R., and Baker, F. T., "Cleanroom Software Development: An Empirical Evaluation," *IEEE Transactions on Software Engineering*, Vol. SE-13, No. 9, Sept. 1987.

12 Parnas, D. L., "Designing Software for Ease of Extension and Contraction," *IEEE Transactions on Software Engineering*, Vol. SE-5, No. 3, March 1979, pp. 128–138.

13 Mills, H. D., "Stepwise Refinement and Verification in Box-Structured Systems," *IEEE Computer*, June 1988, pp. 23–36.

14 Mills, H. D., Linger, R. C., and Hevner, A. R., *Principles of Information Systems Analysis and Design*, Academic, New York, 1986.

15 Mills, H. D., Linger, R. C., and Hevner, A. R., "Box-Structured Information Systems," *IBM Systems Journal*, Vol. 26, No. 4, 1987, pp. 395–413.

16 Adams, E. N., "Optimizing Preventive Service of Software Products," *IBM Journal of Research and Development*, Jan. 1984.

17 Booch, G., *Software Components with Ada*, Benjamin/Cummings, Menlo Park, CA, 1987.

4 The Cleanroom Approach to Six Sigma: Combining Information

J. H. POORE

INTRODUCTION

A new release of a software product reaches the field and triggers a flood of "customer problem reports". Each of these reports is given a number and is logged into a data base with all pertinent information. If the "problem" is declared "critical" special teams spring into action. Short-term fixes are devised for the site, and these fixes take on an identity and become part of the data base. As the new release amasses thousands or millions of hours of field use across the entire customer base, problems are identified and fixed and the flood recedes. Attention drifts from the critical fixes toward judgment calls as to whether certain customer problems were actually just discrepancies between the documentation and the field performance. Some problems prove to be urgently needed enhancements going well beyond the specifications of the release as marketed. The cycle is so predictable that companies have created bureaucracies to record the data, react to the severe problems, control the marketing damage and glean new marketing opportunities from the troubles. Customers, through user organizations, become an integral part of the socialization of expected software failures.

Most software releases follow the familiar scenario of alpha testing by the development organization, then beta testing at selected customer sites, followed by general release to the field. As figure 4.1 suggests, in general we do not know what occurs in alpha and beta testing as each company will have its own methods, but we do know what occurs when the software reaches the field-usage testing! The customers or users are not sinister.

This contribution was first presented at a Technical Vitality Seminar, and was revised for this publication.

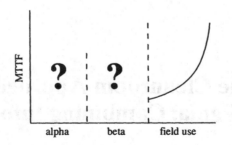

Figure 4.1   Traditional MTTF profile of software.

They do not contrive ways to crash the new software release. Customers just continue to do what they had been doing long before the new release, plus try new capability delivered with the release. The customers are the true usage population. For this reason, they experience the usage-critical errors first; they see and report failures in proportion to the likelihood of those failures being experienced. Experience shows that high frequency errors are fixed and the mean time to failure rises exponentially after the software is introduced to the field.

There may be errors in the software that are never exposed by field use. Finding and fixing these errors would have little or no impact on customers' mean time to failure.

Beta testing is generally the release of software to a few selected sites. Site selection is often based on such criteria as technical strength of the customer, leadership image of the site among customers, interplay with other products, marketing reasons and many other criteria. The selection process tends to guarantee that the beta site is atypical of the user community as a whole. Consequently, the beta site is not representative of the usage base in a statistical sense. Therefore, the failures seen at beta sites and the errors corrected in beta testing are not typical of the customer base. It should come as no surprise that failures will be seen in field usage immediately following beta testing. Careful selection of the beta sites to be representative of the general customer base would allow one of the question marks of figure 4.1 to be replaced with an exponential segment of known parameters as suggested in figure 4.2.

Alpha testing is typically done by software developers themselves and, like beta testing, will vary greatly among them. Alpha testing will usually involve some form of coverage testing, unit testing, bottom-up integration testing and regression testing. Testing that is independent of the developers,

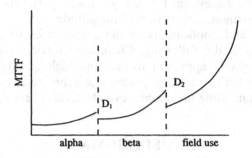

Figure 4.2 MTTF profile with statistical testing.

even "tiger teams," might be used. Many errors are found in alpha testing and surely the product passed on to beta is better because of alpha testing. The question is how much better, and how does this first stage of testing relate to the future performance of the product in the field (if the product ever gets to the field).

This traditional process is under siege. Customers are demanding contracts which provide for cash refunds based on the number of failures experienced in new releases of software. Some would-be products (or new features) never reach the field or are withdrawn. They may be canceled as a consequence of alpha testing or beta testing, or even worse, after being released. Customer user groups are pooling data and tracking failure rates. The enhancement of mature products requires unacceptably long cycle times from inception of a new feature or a response to competition through the development process, the testing process and release to the field.

If statistical usage testing were to replace traditional methods in alpha testing and if beta sites were selected with a statistical basis, then the record would follow the form of figure 4.2. The parameters of the exponential segments in alpha and beta would become measures of the accuracy of the model of the user base. Delta-1 and delta-2 would be measures of the disparity between adjacent phases. A finer grain product testing program could introduce additional test modes over which to spread each phase. This is the certification testing profile of software developed under the Cleanroom process.

Quality cannot be "tested into software"; it must be designed in. There is an awakening to the fact that software is menaced by problems that would be unacceptable and practices that would be unthinkable in engineering projects in other fields. This has led to the "six sigma" concept of delivering software that performs to new standards of excellence as measured by two defects per billion events. For many software products this would represent an improvement of six orders of magnitude.

The meaning and implications of the ambition of six sigma software will be explored in the following. Cleanroom software development[1] is suggested as a viable approach to creating high quality software, and Cleanroom's statistical testing process can be extended in a viable strategy for documenting the quality, even to levels of six sigma.

SIX SIGMA

"Six sigma" derives from the use of the Greek letter sigma to denote the statistic called standard deviation and 6σ represents the area under the curve of the normal distribution in the interval of six standard deviations about the mean. This turns out to be approximately 99.9999998% of the total area under the curve. Those are the good events. The bad events are to the left and right of the 6σ points. Only two parts per billion are found beyond the 6σ points: see figure 4.3.

Six sigma is an allusion to a statistical concept to measure the quality or reliability of a product or process.[2] Where do the statistics come from in software? The statistics come from the use of the software. Software performs a service and the concept of use should relate to the service performed. Six sigma software will operate correctly 99.9999998% of the time and fail only on two uses per billion. Notice that this is very different from saying that of a billion lines of code only two will be incorrect – the traditional expression of errors per KLOC (thousand lines of code) is not operable here. A 2,000 line program must have the same opportunity to be of six sigma quality as a 12 million line system. Suppose a program contains many faults as a consequence of errors in specifications, design and programming, but that the users never exercise the features where the faults lie and so the software exhibits failure free performance throughout its life across all users. Suppose a huge program contains only one fault, only one line of code is wrong, but users exercise that line of code on average once each thousand uses. Six sigma performance is not related to the size of a program or the number of faults in it; it is simply related to the performance in customer usage.

Since the statistics are in the use of software, the basic measure of use is critical. Use might be measured in calendar-clock time, number of transactions, or in other independently occurring units. For example, if the software is a word processor, to consider each keystroke a use or test of the software would lack credibility; however, it would not be necessary to write a book as a single use or test case. Each software product will have its own definition of a single use, and mean time to failure for the software will be expressed in terms of its units of use.

Figure 4.3 and some closely associated information are summarized in table 4.1.

If six sigma software is to be fielded, how is one to know in advance that it is of such quality? In order to conduct an experiment to demonstrate empirically that one has six sigma quality and to have, say, 90% confidence in the demonstration, one would have to run 10^9 independent, randomly selected uses from the user population without failure. At the level of 99% confidence in the experiment, the number of test cases must be approximately double the target

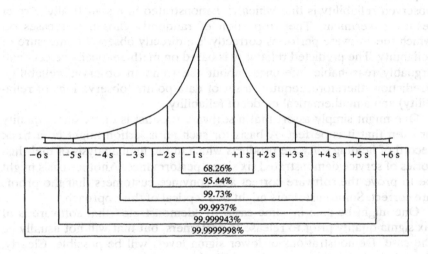

Figure 4.3   Standard deviation marks on normal curve.

Table 4.1   Failure rates by sigma levels

Percent of correct uses	Mean time to failure	Failures per billion uses
$1\sigma = 68.26\%$	4	317,400,000
$2\sigma = 95.44\%$	22	45,600,000
$3\sigma = 99.73\%$	371	2,700,000
$4\sigma = 99.9937\%$	15,873	63,000
$5\sigma = 99.999943\%$	1,754,386	570
$6\sigma = 99.9999998\%$	500,000,000	2

MTTF,[3] and the number grows as the required level of confidence in the demonstration grows. For 3σ quality, generating and applying the requisite number of test cases appears to be a reasonable task, given a model of the user distribution. Even so, 742 suitable test uses is not insignificant and is very likely far more rigorous and meaningful than most current testing regimes.

Three aspects of the reliability of a software product must be distinguished: the actual reliability, the observed reliability, and the predicted reliability. The actual reliability of a software product may never become known because such knowledge would require the application of all possible input histories to the software. Exhaustive testing is a practical impossibility, of course, for all but the most trivial of software. The observed reliability is that which is demonstrated in a statistically correct testing experiment. The proportion of randomly chosen test cases on which the software performs correctly is a directly observable measure of reliability. The predicted reliability is based on mathematically correct and arguably reasonable inferences about the trend in observed reliability. Prediction, therefore, requires a set of data points (observations of reliability) and a mathematical model of reliability.

One might simply assert that a software product is of six sigma quality or even that it is perfect. A basis for such an assertion might be a track record of fielding software products which in the final analysis of their histories of service demonstrated six sigma performance. Another basis might be to prove the software correct and convince customers that the proofs are correct. Some customers might be skeptical of this approach.

One might be able in some cases to "demonstrate" that software is of six sigma quality prior to release to customers, but that will not usually be the case. Demonstrations of lower sigma levels will be possible. Clearly, the relationship of real calendar or clock time to the basic measure of use is important. One can envision settings in which a single usage requires the passage of hours.

One might "predict" six sigma quality based upon a model of growth in quality coupled with supporting empirical evidence that the growth is on track. This is the approach that is used in the example in the "Certification Model" section of this chapter.

STATISTICAL TESTING

In Cleanroom, statistical testing controls the entire testing budget. The prohibition against developer debugging before statistical testing is motivated by the need to take seriously the importance of rigor in writing specifications, designing systems, writing code and verifying code. Formal methods strive for zero-defect work. Six sigma ambitions underscore the futility of debugging and the necessity of spending the entire testing budget, whatever the amount, in a way that contributes to the certification process. It is clearly impossible to debug your way to six sigma. Six sigma requires a paradigm shift.

Imagine a large software product of several million lines of code that has a customer base of 2,000. Let us suppose that the product operates 24 hours per day as might the software in a reservation system. Suppose that all customer sites put the new release into operation at the same time. On the first day of field use, the product will record 48,000 hours of usage testing. By the end of the first week "customer problem reports" will be reflecting a base of usage testing of 336,000 hours. Problems will be addressed based on some criteria of criticality, frequency and first-come-first-served. If the mean time to failure for the product over all usage grows exponentially as the failures are resolved then the release will succeed however bitter the initial experience. If the mean time to failure does not exhibit exponential growth, in all likelihood the release will be withdrawn.

The goal of six sigma is to deliver software that has very high mean time to failure in customer usage upon release. Therefore beta testing should be conducted in the way that will bring the software to this point. If the beta sites are statistically representative of the user base, then errors corrected during beta testing will be the errors with high failure rates in the field, rather than errors with low failure rates. The failure rates of errors vary greatly.

The power of usage testing was shown by Adams,[5] provided the motivation for the Cleanroom Certification Model[6] and is fully explicated by Mills in reference 1. Adams' data describes distributions of failure rates for errors in nine major software products, including operating systems, language compilers, and data base systems. The spread in failure rates is from 19 system–months to 60,000 system–months, about one-third of the errors having a MTTF of 60,000 months and 1% having a MTTF of 19 months. If one assumes that in coverage testing all errors are equally likely to be found, then one-third of the errors found will have little or no improvement on the MTTF.

In the hypothetical case sketched above, suppose four beta sites are used for three months. During beta testing 8,760 hours of usage testing will occur. If an hour of failure free operation equates to a use, then by referring to the table above, it may be seen that this has the potential to demonstrate 3σ quality but not 4σ. Later, we will consider the predictive contribution of such a data point. In order to demonstrate 4σ, the beta testing would have to generate some 32,000 hours of testing either by increasing the number of sites or extending the test period.

It is easier to see the applicability of statistical usage testing in beta than in alpha. Beta testing occurs after the software is ready to deliver, so far as programmers are concerned. Alpha testing directly involves the programmers and the software in an acknowledged "pre-release" state. Two questions are involved in assessing statistical testing in alpha and should be considered separately. First, which is more effective in finding errors with high failure rates, traditional testing methods or statistical testing? Second, what does the testing methodology contribute toward the certification statement? These constitute the management questions as to the best way to spend the testing budget.

Prima facie evidence shows that current methods are not effective in finding high failure rate errors. No one doubts that many errors are found and fixed in developer and alpha testing. If these are truly high failure-rate errors then the acceptable level of workmanship for professionals is called into question. If they are not high failure-rate errors then the budget is being spent inefficiently.

The second question is easier; anecdotal testing cannot be used in classical (also known as "frequentist") statistical models for predicting software performance. Independent statistical testing in the alpha stage will not amass many usage instances, but every usage test contributes to the certification. The major costs of statistical testing lie in modeling the usage distribution and creating the test generator and oracle. Once this is done, the stage is set for more extensive testing on a marginally small budget increase. More importantly, one has a quantitative basis on which to move the product into customer sites at the beta stage. Even demonstrations at 1σ and 2σ are more impressive than no statistical certification at all, but their real significance lies in the fact that a systematic record of certification is being established with each test case, and this record is the basis for both demonstrated reliability and meaningful prediction of exponentially greater levels.

Cleanroom advocates a way of training and working that has the potential to produce a work product of sufficiently high quality that developer testing is not economical. Certain tests may still be in order as matters of safety, risk reduction, policy or law, but these are separately justified on a moral or economic basis.

CERTIFICATION MODEL[6]

While it is well known that most software companies release software only after certain measures are reached, the nature of those measures is disconcerting. For example, the software might be released after a percentage of known errors are corrected. Or, if a certain number of errors are found in unit testing, then the software will be released only after a related number are found in system testing. A perverse thing happens. Errors take on a positive quality, finding errors takes on a heroic quality, and the number found and removed becomes a basis for confidence in the product! It is difficult to find a similar phenomenon in any human activity. Software errors are the result of poor management and poor workmanship; correcting an error is rework. Making and correcting errors must be replaced as a basis for confidence in software by an empirical, auditable, scientific demonstration of the absence of errors when software is used as intended. (If software must function in adverse circumstances, then the adversity should be part of the specification and part of the intended use.)

Six sigma software will necessarily require certification of correctness based upon empirical demonstration and mathematically sound prediction. Certification and prediction are an integral part of Cleanroom. Whether or not one requires a six sigma certification is simply an issue of time and money and does not require a change in philosophy or the mathematical models.

Cleanroom strives for zero defect software, based upon functional verification[7] of the design to the specifications and the code to the design. Cleanroom statistical testing is performed independently of the developers for the purpose of certification, i.e., for the purpose of providing empirical evidence of the high quality of the code, not for the purpose of finding errors. Humans are fallible even when well trained, skilled and motivated to excellent work. If a failure is found in the course of certification testing, the developers review the design and code and make an engineering change to correct the error. This is more than a matter of semantics. Very few such failures are expected, each is treated as a serious shortcoming, root causes are analyzed, and the changes are carefully reasoned.

The Certification Model is based on the concept of an exponential growth in the MTTF of the software with each engineering change. Experience with this model has shown that if the software is of high quality, that is, if the errors are few and the interfail times are increasing exponentially, then the model becomes a bold predictor of high MTTF with subsequent engineering changes. However, if the errors are frequent and early engineering changes do not result in exponential growth, then the model will require extensive empirical evidence before MTTF predictions will be large. Six sigma software must be good from the very first version and must get dramatically better with each engineering change as the data below illustrate.

Consider the following hypothetical situation. Suppose that a software product goes directly from the developers to independent statistical testing. Suppose that exactly four randomly selected test cases run before a failure occurs; this is the estimate of the MTTF of the initial version of the software and because the testing represents a statistically correct experiment, the software has been demonstrated to be of 1σ quality. The developers then review the design and code and make the appropriate engineering change. The new version of the software is sent to independent statistical testing and runs 22 cases before failure. Suppose that this scenario continues with exactly one failure found in each phase and such that the failures exactly correspond with having run the minimum number of cases to demonstrate the corresponding sigma level of quality through 4σ. The first version exhibits 1σ, the second version exhibits 2σ, etc. as illustrated in table 4.2.

After the third data point, the model will predict for the fourth version a MTTF of only 1,038. In the hypothetical situation we assume that the fourth version is much better, 4σ in fact. After four data points, i.e. after the software has demonstrated 4σ performance, the model still predicts that the next version will perform far below 5σ. Suppose that after demonstrating 4σ we do exactly what the model predicts; in other words, we do not disappoint the model. Finally, the model predicts 6σ quality after the eighth engineering change level.

Of course, other models exist, there are other methods of estimating parameters, and there are innumerable performance histories. The purpose of this illustration was to convey some intuitive feel for the enormity of the task of predicting 6σ quality even with an uncharacteristically strong performance record. This in turn underscores the importance of having every dollar of the testing budget focused on certification.

The above scenario suggests a reasonable plan for fielding 6σ software. Levels 1, 2 and 3 are demonstrated in an alpha test phase, level 4 in a beta phase, level 5 in a controlled release. After general release one strives to maintain the improvement factor in the 13–14 range and hit three more

Table 4.2 Certification model

Version number	Observed MTTF	Predicted reliability	Predicted MTTF	Improvement factor
0	4	—	—	—
1	22	—	—	—
2	371	0.99903	1,038	6.13
3	15,873	0.999989	97,319	13.45
4	97,319	0.99999928	1,400,000	13.39
5	1,400,000	0.999999952	21,000,000	13.51
6	21,000,000	0.9999999968	320,000,000	13.70
7	320,000,000	0.99999999980	5,000,000,000	13.90

benchmarks after which one has a strong performance history for a prediction that the software will exhibit 6σ quality during its product life. Six sigma requires the statistical combining of information across the life cycle of testing and usage.

COMBINING INFORMATION[8]

Modern Cleanroom methods use a Markov chain model of software specification and use to conduct statistical certification testing. The applicability of Markov theory for modeling software specifications,[9] use,[10] and design[3] has been established. However, the Markov model can play a higher level role as the unifying formalism in a new model for combining information from all testing and use of a software system and its variants across the entire life cycle. Such a new model would support six sigma ambitions far better than the classical model.

As an illustration, assume a software item is taken from operational field use, enhanced by two increments of development, ported to two new environments, made available for reuse, and is heavily used. Table 4.3 illustrates how the testing and use information at each stage might contribute to a composite view used to make assessments at each stage. Each column represents a given version of the software, with percentages allocated to the relevant sources of information for decisions about its use. (Accordingly, columns sum to 100%.)

Table 4.3   Combining testing and usage information across the life cycle

Version 1	Version 2	Version 3	Version 4	Version 5	Version 6	Version 7	Version 8	Version 9
Inc 1 100%	Inc 1 40%	Inc 1 10%						
	Inc 2 60%	Inc 2 20%	Inc 2 10%					
		Alpha 70%	Alpha 60%	Alpha 50%	Alpha 40%	Alpha 20%		
			Beta 1 30%	Beta 1 25%	Beta 1 20%	Beta 1 20%		
				Beta 2 25%	Beta 2 20%	Beta 2 20%		
					User A 20%	User A 20%	User A 20%	User A 10%
						User B 20%	User B 30%	User B 30%
							User C 50%	User C 30%
								User D 30%

As time goes by, the more current analytical and experimental (testing) information "pushes out" less relevant, older testing information. The "pushing out" should happen mathematically, i.e., as a consequence of the statistical models, so that it really doesn't matter whether the data is kept in the analysis or is literally discarded; impact assessment and decision support information will be the same either way. Combining information across usage environments entails a certain amount of risk or statistical uncertainty. It is essential to be able to quantify the risk and to appropriately weight various components of information. Data and judgement must come together in the statistical models.

Zero-defects is a Cleanroom development goal. Failure-free performance is a Cleanroom operational goal. Six sigma quality in software pertains only to the performance of the product in customer use. The formal methods of Cleanroom have the potential to produce such high quality code that it is economical to use the testing budget for the purpose of simulating the intended usage environment and conducting demonstrations of reliability. These demonstrations coupled with well reasoned predictions can form the basis for asserting that a software product will exhibit six sigma quality in its lifetime.

References

1 Mills, Harlan D., "Cleanroom: An Alternative Software Development Approach" in *Aerospace Engineering Software*, Ed. C. Anderson, AIAA, 1990.
2 Harry, Mikel J., *The Nature of Six Sigma Quality*, Motorola, Inc., 1988.
3 Poore, J. H., Harlan D. Mills, and David Mutchler, "Planning and Certifying Software System Reliability", *IEEE Software*, January 1993, pp. 88–99.
4 Mills, Harlan D., and J. H. Poore, "Bringing Software Under Statistical Quality Control", *Quality Progress*, November, 1988.
5 Adams, E. N., "Optimizing Preventive Services of Software Products", *IBM Journal of Research and Development*, January, 1984.
6 Currit, A., M. Dyer, and Harlan D. Mills, "Certifying the Reliability of Software", *IEEE Transactions on Software Engineering*, Vol. SE-12, No. 1, pp. 3–11, January, 1989.
7 Linger, R. C., Harlan D. Mills, and B. I. Witt, *Structured Programming: Theory and Practice*, Addison-Wesley, 1979.
8 "Combining Information: Statistical Issues and Opportunities for Research", National Research Council, Washington D.C., 1992.
9 Whittaker, J. A. and J. H. Poore, "Markov Analysis of Software Specifications", *ACM Transactions on Software Engineering and Methodology*, January 1993.
10 Walton, G. H., J. H. Poore, and C. J. Trammell, "Statistical Testing Based on a Software Usage Model", *Software Practice and Experience*, January 1995.

5   Planning and Certifying Software System Reliability

J. H. POORE, H. D. MILLS, AND D. MUTCHLER

INTRODUCTION

Hardware-reliability engineers have long been able to design a hardware system to a target reliability by determining the reliability of system components or allocating reliability budgets to component developers. Software engineers can also design for reliability, but they seldom do because they view the process as too complex or not applicable to software. With the growing emphasis on reuse, however, and the need to demonstrate that the software to be reused is indeed reliable, they can no longer afford to shy away from reliability planning.

To make reliability planning and certification more accessible, we developed an approach based on the use of three mathematical models – the sampling,[1,2] component,[1,3,4] and certification[5] models – although other models may be equally suitable. This approach, which helps reduce reliability analysis to a problem that can be evaluated and manipulated through a series of spreadsheets, addresses the three reasons we believe most developers avoid these activities:

- They do not differentiate between planning and certifying and the tasks associated with each.
- They find it difficult to choose from among the many available reliability models.

© 1993 IEEE. Reprinted, with permission, from *IEEE Software*, vol. 10 no. 1, pp. 88–99, January 1993.

- They find the mathematical models difficult to manipulate for what-if analyses.

The first reason is the result of trying to apply concepts that are relatively new to software engineering, the second stems from a lack of consensus about reliability itself, and the third may be caused by a lack of tools for manipulating model results. As part of our experiment, we developed a system to handle all the calculations in a spreadsheet format.

Our approach has three aspects which address these reasons for avoidance. First, we believe that developers need to thoroughly understand the tasks involved in planning and certification. Second, armed with that insight, they can choose a reliability model similar to the ones we describe here. Finally, they can develop a spreadsheet system similar to our own to manipulate model results in enlightening what-if analyses.

This approach was motivated by our interest in applying the Cleanroom software-engineering method in environments that require extensive code reuse. Two models for certification, including the one we used in our experiment, are part of accepted Cleanroom practice.[5–8]

WHAT IS RELIABILITY?

Like hardware reliability, software reliability is based on modes[1] of failure. Hardware modes of failure – wear, design flaws, and unintentional environmental phenomena – are more tangible because hardware is a physical entity. In fact, it is this very physical quality that prompts hardware designers to assume that hardware cannot be perfect. Ironically, the same designers often assign perfect reliability to a software component because it can't "wear out," for example.

But software does have a model of failure, which is based on the assumption that design and development are not perfect processes. The mistakes made during these processes manifest as faults in the code, which are revealed as inputs are processed. That is, a failure occurs when the software does not perform according to specification for an input history.

Thus, like hardware, software is deemed reliable in relation to its use and intended performance. Use, the basic unit of reliability measurement, can be a keystroke, work session, transaction, completed telephone call, or any other unit of performance appropriate to the service the software is expected to perform.

To quantify reliability in a meaningful way, software use must be modeled as a random process in which a use is selected according to some probability distribution, or *use distribution*. Reliability then becomes the probability that the software will perform according to specification for a randomly selected use. When the software fails to meet specification during use, a failure occurs.

Reliability can be a useful metric. You can use it to help guide software development. You can use it to assess a program's fitness for use by conducting experiments to establish empirical evidence of quality.

These dual uses of reliability have slightly different definitions. Reliability as a function of time, perhaps the more traditional definition, addresses the design of software that will operate according to specification for a period of time. But you can also use a simpler definition – reliability is the probability that a randomly chosen use (test case) will be processed correctly.

In most instances, we use this simpler definition because it is well suited to the idea of conducting experiments to establish empirical evidence of quality. It also proves to be a very conservative notion of reliability, well suited to dealing with the reuse of software for which little may be known about the process of its development but much may be known about its operational history.

In the time-based definition of reliability, the choice of time as the random variable is based on the idea that randomly selected uses (according to a use distribution) will cause paths through the program to execute randomly; consequently, as operating time increases, the probability of encountering a fault in the code increases. Time can be execution time, calendar time, number of instructions executed, number of input cases, or number of uses, to name the most common interpretations. These conditions represent a constant failure rate.

Using the definition that reliability is the probability that the software will give the correct result for a single, randomly chosen (according to the use distribution) use, then the mean time to failure is the average number of uses between failures. MTTF and reliability can be related mathematically in the models.

Some models deal with system reliability (in all uses of "system," we are referring to a software system) as a function of the modules or units that comprise the system. Other models estimate or predict system reliability without regard to what the system comprises.

PLANNING VERSUS CERTIFICATION

An understanding of reliability planning and certification is based on the progression of four basic ideas:

- Systems are composed of components.
- Component reliability can be measured.

- System reliability can be calculated from component information.
- System certification may be based on a different model from that used in reliability planning.

Systems are composed of components

We define a system as a collection of programs and system files such that the system files are accessed and altered only by the programs in the collection. This definition is not intended to rule out systems, but is given to establish the boundary of responsibility. Clearly, if files are altered by agents outside the system, we cannot vouch for the consequences. These programs and system files are what we mean by components. Components may be systems, modules, packages, programs, or files.

An additional constraint on the system, to satisfy a technical assumption of one of the mathematical models, is that it must be proper. A proper system must have a single entry and a single exit, and for each executable component there must be a path from the entrance through the component to the exit.

If a system is being planned that will comprise new and reused components, in the final analysis you will either use or not use a specific component. You can make this binary decision on the basis of somewhat crude information. In particular, you must know or conjecture how the component will interplay with the rest of the system and what its reliability will be during this interplay, so that you can assess the effect on the reliability of the system as a whole. The quality of component information must be good enough to support a determination that it is the best among alternatives, including a newly developed component.

In reliability planning, you must model the interaction of all system components – an inexact activity. While the error in this process is bearable for reaching the binary decision to use or not use a given component, it need not be accepted in calculating final system reliability. For this reason, we recommend that you independently certify the completed system on the basis of statistical use testing.

In this type of testing, the testing process constitutes a statistical experiment. It consists of processing a random sample of test cases selected according to intended system use to present empirical evidence that the system performs correctly. The statistical qualities of the testing process let you make scientific statements about the predicted reliability of the system, in essence certifying it.

Calculating the Metrics

The mathematics of the sampling, component, and certification models are based on the relationship of reliability and the mean time to failure. MTTF is the average number of uses between failures. Time is measured as the number of uses (or test cases). Reliability is related to MTTF by

$$MTTF = \frac{1}{1 - reliability}$$

If time is interpreted in any other way, the relationship is

$$MTTF = \frac{L}{1 - reliability}$$

where L is the average number of time units per use. By defining L, you can choose an arbitrary time unit or convert various time units to a common one and move easily between MTTF and reliability.

Sampling model

If $100c$ is the percentage of confidence you want in the experiment, the number of test cases that must run without a failure to report a reliability of r is

$$Number\ of\ test\ cases = \left\lceil \frac{\log(1 - c)}{\log(r)} \right\rceil$$

The $100c$-percent confidence means that if you adopt this testing method and test software frequently, it is almost certain that the claims would be true at least $100c$ percent of the time. This is not the same as saying that the claim itself is right with probability c, there is no probability involved in the claim itself because a claim is either right or wrong. As table A shows, you can obtain additional confidence without greatly increasing the number of tests; additional reliability, however, does require large increases in the number of tests.

Table A   Zero failures

	Confidence level (percent)			
Reliability	90	95	99	99.9
0.9	22	29	44	66
0.95	45	59	90	135
0.99	230	299	459	688
0.999	2302	2995	4603	6905

This formula uses a zero-failures certification method. The software is tested on m random test cases (chosen according to the use distribution) and is certified if no failures occur. The number of tests is m, the minimal number to ensure that unreliable software is not certified too frequently.

Another approach is to test m_k random test cases, where k is any non-negative integer, and certify if at most k failures are found. m_k is chosen just as m was; it is the minimal number of tests that ensures that unreliable software is not certified too frequently. For example, to allow up to two failures, and certify with 90-percent confidence that r is at least 0.99, you must run 531 test cases.

You can compute m_k numerically for any k and for the other parameters as follows: m_k must satisfy

Pr(k or fewer failures in m_k trials | actual reliability $< r$) $\leq 1 - c$

where Pr is probability. The smallest m that satisfies this requirement is the smallest m such that

$$\sum_{j=m-k}^{m} \binom{m}{j} r^j (1-r)^{m-j} \leq (1-c).$$

You can then solve for m numerically.

The major disadvantage of this k-failures method over the zero-failures method is that it requires more tests. A second disadvantage is that it certifies software with known errors; if the errors are corrected, the certification is no longer valid because the test was conducted on the software before the changes. The statement must apply to the software on which the experiment was conducted.

The advantage of the k-failures method over the zero-failures method is that the k-failures method will deny certification less often. If the software has an MTTF of 500 with a goal MTTF of 100, the zero-failures method will deny certification more than a third of the time, the k-failures (two-failures) method will deny certification less than 10 percent of the time.

Thus, the sampling model can produce certification errors in two ways: First, it can certify software that is, in fact, unreliable. Second, it can deny certification to software that is, in fact, reliable. The zero-failures method lets you control the likelihood of errors of the first kind by setting the confidence level as desired. You can use the k-failures method to control the likelihood of errors of the second kind as well by setting k large enough. However, you pay the price for this extra control in more tests.

Component model

Calculations in the planning spreadsheets of the CRM are based on a Markov model. Here we present only the formulas used in the calculations.

Consider a system that consists of n components, 1 to n, with component 1 being the single entry point to the system. Let r_i denote the probability that when component i is being executed, the system continues to another component without an error. Thus, $(1 - r_i)$ is the probability of a failure (fatal error) during component i's execution. For $i = 1, \ldots, n$ and for $j = 1, \ldots, n, T$, where component T is interpreted as the successful termination of the system, define p_{ij} by

$r_i p_{ij}$ = probability that component j will be executed next if component i is currently being executed

When i is fixed, p_{ij}'s sum to r_i. The model makes the Markovian assumption that transfer of control (to another component, to successful termination, or to unsuccessful termination) is conditionally independent of execution history.

Calculating system reliabilities and component sensitivities requires the following: For i and j from 1 to n, define n by n matrices $\mathbf{G}$ and $\mathbf{H}$ by $G_{ij} = p_{ij}$ and $H_{ij} = r_i p_{ij}$. Perform two matrix inversions to obtain $\mathbf{S} = (\mathbf{I} - \mathbf{G})^{-1}$ and $\mathbf{T} = (\mathbf{I} - \mathbf{H})^{-1}$. For i from 1 to n, define column vectors f and R by $f_i = r_i p_{iT}$ and $R = Tf$.

Because component 1 is the sole entry point to the system, system reliability R is R_1. The sensitivity of system reliability to the reliability of component i is (by definition)

$$\frac{\partial R_1}{\partial r_i}$$

and is given by

$$\frac{\partial R_1}{\partial r_i} = R_i \frac{T_{1i}}{r_i}$$

Suppose you set a target system reliability R_{tgt}. To meet it, the r_i needed for component i, assuming all other components are reliable, is

$$r_i = \left[\frac{c_i(1 - R_{tgt})}{R_{tgt} - a_i} + 1 \right]^{-1}$$

where

$$c_i = \frac{1}{S_{ii}} \quad \text{and} \quad a_i = 1 - \left(\frac{S_{1i}}{S_{ii}} \right)$$

You can use this formula to allocate reliabilities to the components. However, because allocated reliabilities yield a system reliability less than the target reliability, you must increase each allocated reliability somewhat to meet the target.

Certification model
In the certification model, MTTF_k denotes the MTTF of version k of the system. Suppose that for all k, $\text{MTTF}_k = (B)(\text{MTTF}_{k-1})$ where B is some constant. Then $\text{MTTF}_k = AB^k$ where $A = \text{MTTF}_0$.

The certification model has three independent aspects:

1   The parametric form of AB^k, which is used to estimate the MTTF of version k.
2   The corrected-log least-squares technique, which is used to compute A and B from the data points.
3   The technique for obtaining the data points.

You can estimate A and B directly from statistical data using either maximum-likelihood or least-squares techniques. However, the corrected-log least-squares technique is not only a better estimator but also a simpler computation.

This technique starts with the original equation $\text{MTTF}_k = AB^k$. You then take the logarithms of both sides to get

$$\log(\text{MTTF}_k) = \log A + k(\log B).$$

By letting a equal $\log A$ and b equal $\log B$, you can then rewrite the equation as

$$\log(\text{MTTF}_k) = a + kb.$$

You can compute the estimates for a and b using standard linear regression. This minimizes the sum of the squares of the differences between the logarithms of $\text{MTTF}_0, \ldots, \text{MTTF}_{n-1}$ and the estimate for $a + 0b, \ldots, a + (n-1)b$. To do this linear regression, take partial derivatives with respect to a and b, set them to zero, and solve the two linear equations that result.

From the previous step, you have estimates α for $\log A$ and β for $\log B$. Tentative estimates for A and B are e^{α} and e^{β}. The estimate of the MTTF for version d is $e^{\alpha}(e^{\beta})^d$. However, this estimate is biased; its mean is not equal to the true value of AB^d. Using the model's assumption that the MTTF (measured by sampling) for version k is an independent random variable exponentially distributed with mean AB^k, you can compute an unbiased estimate.

To get confidence intervals for various aspects of the curve from a least-squares linear regression, assume that the residuals are independent and normally distributed with a mean of zero and common variance of σ^2. You can estimate this variance and then compute a confidence interval for the log-transformed data.

The power of a model is the ratio of the released product's predicted MTTF to the number of tests. To estimate the power of the certification model, assume that the estimates of A and B are exact and that all the data points lie exactly on the curve. Suppose that version n is released after versions 0 through $n - 1$ have been tested. The estimated MTTF of version n is then AB^n; the number of tests conducted is

$$\sum_{k=0}^{n-1} AB^k = \frac{A(B^n - 1)}{(B - 1)}$$

so the power of the certification model is the ratio of the released product's predicted MTTF to the number of tests:

$$AB^n : \frac{A(B^n - 1)}{(B - 1)}$$

which is equal to

$$\left[\frac{(B - 1)(B^n)}{(B^n - 1)} \right] \approx (B - 1)$$

for B not near 1. As we described earlier, the power of the sampling model is about $1 : 2$ at 90 percent confidence levels and less at higher confidence levels. Thus, if you do N tests under the certification model, you expect to do roughly $2N(B - 1)$ tests to achieve the same level of MTTF certification under the sampling model.

Component reliability

The quality of information about the component must be good enough to support your decision to use or not use it. There are many sources of component information, and even a crude form of any of these may be enough to make that binary decision:

- *Developer's records.* If the component developer has by reputation or contract asserted the component's reliability, you may be able to use this assertion.

- *Development method.* If a certain development method was used and that method includes a reliability standard, you may be able to know the reliability by knowing the method.
- *Proof of correctness.* If the component has been verified by a mathematical proof of correctness, you may be able to attribute a high degree of reliability to it.[9]
- *Field performance.* If records of field use and failures are available, you can estimate reliability from the field data.
- *Statistical experiment.* You can always conduct a specific statistical testing experiment using the sampling model as described in the box on pp. 87–91.

System reliability

To calculate system reliability using the component model as shown in the box on pp. 87–91, you will need both estimates of component reliabilities and the structure of component interactions. The structure and relative frequency of these interactions is determined by transition probabilities – the probability of transition from one component to another. You must estimate transition probabilities on the basis of design and intended use.

Given the system structure, component reliabilities, and transition probabilities, you can perform calculations in an enlightening what-if analysis. What if a certain component were more or less reliable? How would that affect system reliability? What if a certain component were perfect, with a reliability of 1.0?

You can also estimate the sensitivity of the total system to each component through what-if analysis. You can calculate system reliability from component information, or you can stipulate a system reliability and calculate an allocated reliability to the components. The what-if analysis gives insight to the decision to use or not to use a component. Coupled with the sampling model, it can show the scale and scope of effort needed to demonstrate the required levels of component reliabilities. Finally, it can shed light on the reasonableness of building a system to desired levels of reliability on the basis of reusing a specific collection of components.

System certification

Certification of a completed system is based on a different model from that used in planning, and the model criteria are substantially different. Developers must take responsibility for the completed system as an operational entity, without regard for the parts and why or how they are used. A good certification model must focus on the performance of the system in statistical use testing and in field use. Exponential growth in MTTF is the goal in certification.

System certification should be based on generating or selecting inputs and input histories according to the system's intended use. To the extent that files are a part of the system, you must achieve representative steady states in these files through input histories. You can conduct a statistical experiment to collect data points on performance and use a reliability model to analyze them and predict system reliability.

RELIABILITY MODELS

To illustrate our approach, we used the sampling, component, and certification models, which have been useful in practice.[10] Each model has certain mathematical properties, described in the box on pp. 87–91. You can apply the models to your development process to the extent that your process is characterized by these properties. Because many aspects of planning and certifying system reliability do not require an exact analysis, the models can be meaningful to your process even if they only partially characterize it.

Sampling model

This model is useful for estimating the reliability of an existing component as an entity without regard to its composition.

In a simple sampling experiment, you must draw a number of test cases from the use distribution – which mirrors actual software use – run these test cases and record the number processed correctly. You can then report that the software has the estimated reliability at a set confidence level. The appeal of the sampling model is that you can make a quantitative claim about software quality subject to only two sources of error: sampling error, which you can control through a set confidence level, and error in the use distribution.

The sampling model has drawbacks as well. It may be difficult to model use distribution. Testing may be expensive. If you need a 90 percent or better confidence level, the number of tests required to demonstrate a certain MTTF is more than twice that MTTF. Certification will often be denied because of bad luck if the true MTTF is close to the certified MTTF. For example, if the certified MTTF is 100 and the true MTTF is 200, then certification at 90 percent confidence will be denied merely because of chance more than two-thirds of the time! Even if the true MTTF is 1,000, certification will still be denied more than 20 percent of the time.

Because the sampling model is conservative in its estimates, certification of unreliable software is rare. But this very conservatism coupled with the economic pressure to limit the number of tests might deny certification to much software that is in fact quite reliable. Fortunately, there are mathematical ways to control the likelihood that reliable software is denied certification, but for the most part you are better off certifying the system through statistical testing.

Component model

The component model is useful for estimating how the reliability of components – both new and used – can affect system reliability. You can calculate system reliability from information about the components, or you can stipulate a system reliability and calculate an allocated reliability to the components.

The component model can use existing component data to estimate system reliability with no additional testing. Also, the planner can use the component model for what-if analyses. The model's simplicity is both a strength and a weakness. It makes the model easy to use, but reliability estimates may be inaccurate. For the qualitative decisions involved in planning system reliability, this inaccuracy is acceptable. For certifying the complete system, however, a more accurate model is required.

Certification model

Certification is essentially a statistical experiment to collect data points, which are the times between failures on successive system versions or engineering-change levels. A curve is fitted to this data, which is useful in monitoring progress during development and predicting the MTTF of the released product. The model assumes that MTTF grows exponentially over successive versions of a system.

The certification model is more powerful than the sampling model, in that far fewer test cases are required to certify the system at a set reliability. It is also usually more accurate than the component model, but will yield poor estimates if the curve being fitted does not, in fact, exhibit exponential growth. A promising alternative to the certification model is the Markov Testing Model.[7,8]

APPLYING THE MODELS

Figure 5.1 shows a system represented by a network of components. Each directed arc indicates that control passes from one component to another

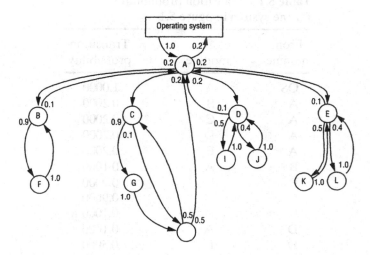

Figure 5.1 A software system as a network of components. Each directed arc, labeled with its transition probability, indicates that control passes from one component to another in the direction of the arrow.

in the direction of the arrow. There is a single point of entry into the system from the operating system and single point of return to the operating system and, for each node, there is a path from entry to exit that passes through that node – the definition of a proper system.

As we described earlier, you must estimate component-transition probabilities. In a well-designed system, communication among components is limited. Table 5.1 shows the transition probabilities for the network in figure 5.1, listing the probability associated with each arc. This information may also be represented as a matrix with a zero probability assigned to impossible transitions.

Using just the transition probabilities, you can learn some interesting information about how a component can affect system reliability. Managers can use this information to rethink the system's architecture and to plan resource allocation, for example.

To assist in manipulating the necessary calculations for planning and certification, we designed the Cleanroom Reliability Manager.[10] Table 5.2 shows the information the CRM will display given only transition probabilities as input. The CRM uses certain defaults. For each component, the default reliability is 1.0, and the default confidence level is 90 percent. The defaults are displayed until the planner enters new information.

Table 5.1   Transition probabilities
for the system in figure 5.1

From module	To module	Transition probability
OS	A	1.0000
A	B	0.2000
A	C	0.2000
A	D	0.2000
A	E	0.2000
B	A	0.1000
B	F	0.9000
C	G	0.9000
C	H	0.1000
D	A	0.1000
D	I	0.5000
D	J	0.4000
E	A	0.1000
E	K	0.5000
E	L	0.4000
F	B	1.0000
G	H	1.0000
H	A	0.5000
H	C	0.5000
I	D	1.0000
J	D	1.0000
K	E	1.0000
L	E	1.0000
A	OS	0.2000

At the top of the table are system reliability, system MTTF, target reliability, and the test-scale factor. The CRM calculates system reliability from transition probabilities and component reliabilities. Since each component has a default reliability of 1.0, the entire system has a 1.0 reliability.

If the reliability is perfect, the MTTF is undefined (because there are no failures). Target reliability is undefined until the reliability planner enters it into the CRM. Test-scale factor lets you equate one study to another when that is possible simply by scaling all data by a constant factor; it will remain 1.0 throughout this example.

The columns reliability, confidence, test cases, and MTTF are related mathematically, and you should interpret them collectively. For example,

Table 5.2 CRM display given only transition probabilities.

System reliability: 1.0000
System MTTF: undefined

Target reliability: undefined
Test-scale factor, 1.000

Module name	Reliability	Confidence	Test cases	MTTF	Sensitivity	Allocated reliability
Enter_system	1.0000	0.900	Infinite	Undefined	1.00	Undefined
A	1.0000	0.900	Infinite	Undefined	5.00	Undefined
B	1.0000	0.900	Infinite	Undefined	10.00	Undefined
C	1.0000	0.900	Infinite	Undefined	2.00	Undefined
D	1.0000	0.900	Infinite	Undefined	10.00	Undefined
E	1.0000	0.900	Infinite	Undefined	10.00	Undefined
F	1.0000	0.900	Infinite	Undefined	9.00	Undefined
G	1.0000	0.900	Infinite	Undefined	1.80	Undefined
H	1.0000	0.900	Infinite	Undefined	2.00	Undefined
I	1.0000	0.900	Infinite	Undefined	5.00	Undefined
J	1.0000	0.900	Infinite	Undefined	4.00	Undefined
K	1.0000	0.900	Infinite	Undefined	5.00	Undefined
L	1.0000	0.900	Infinite	Undefined	4.00	Undefined

you would need an infinite number of test cases to demonstrate a reliability of 1.0, and you would have no failures on which to base an MTTF. Test cases tell you how many test cases you must run without a failure to demonstrate the given reliability at the given level of confidence. You can enter either reliability or MTTF, whichever is more directly available, and the CRM will calculate the other.

Likewise, you can enter the number of possible or affordable test cases, and the CRM will show the reliability that such an experiment would demonstrate at the chosen confidence level. If you change the confidence level, the CRM will recalculate the number of test cases. If you enter a change for any of the four items, it calculates and displays an appropriate change to one of the other three.

The CRM calculates sensitivity (sixth column) from the transition matrix. In our example, components B, D, and E have the greatest effect on the total system. Thus, system reliability is twice as sensitive to these components as it is to A, I, and K. The component's sensitivity shows its relative importance to system reliability, rather than any absolute information.

Allocated reliability (last column) is the reliability allocated or budgeted to each component and is calculated whenever the target reliability is changed. The allocated reliability for each component is based on the target reliability for the entire system and the sensitivity of the system to the component. If some components have higher reliabilities than are budgeted to them, the demand on other components is lower.

Thus, the CRM provides a good deal of flexibility in what-if analysis. If you change the target reliability, you will cause a reliability budget to be allocated to each component. You can also change any one of reliability, confidence, test cases, or MTTF for an individual component. By changing individual component information, you will cause a change in the calculated system reliability and system MTTF. Finally, if you change the transition probabilities assigned to network arcs, you will change the sensitivities – the relative contributions of each component to the system's reliability.

As an example, suppose you are certifying a system at 0.999 reliability, which in the long run means we can expect one failure in 1,000 uses. Using the CRM, you set the target reliability to the goal of 0.999 to produce the display in table 5.3. To abbreviate reliability figures and to draw attention to the number of nines, the CRM displays 0.999 as (3)00, 0.99980 as (3)80, 0.99999 as (5)00, and so on.

Using the target reliability of (3)00 (0.999) and the known sensitivities, the CRM allocates a reliability budget to each component. If component reliabilities are set at the allocated levels, the system reliability will be slightly less than the target reliability because of the nature of the model.

Table 5.3 CRM display given a target reliability of 0.999

System reliability: 1.0000

System MTTF: undefined

Target reliability: (3)00

Test-scale factor: 1.000

Module name	Reliability	Confidence	Test cases	MTTF	Sensitivity	Allocated reliability
Enter_system	1.0000	0.900	Infinite	Undefined	1.00	(3)00
A	1.0000	0.900	Infinite	Undefined	5.00	(3)80
B	1.0000	0.900	Infinite	Undefined	10.00	(4)00
C	1.0000	0.900	Infinite	Undefined	2.00	(3)50
D	1.0000	0.900	Infinite	Undefined	10.00	(4)00
E	1.0000	0.900	Infinite	Undefined	10.00	(4)00
F	1.0000	0.900	Infinite	Undefined	9.00	(3)88
G	1.0000	0.900	Infinite	Undefined	1.80	(3)44
H	1.0000	0.900	Infinite	Undefined	2.00	(3)50
I	1.0000	0.900	Infinite	Undefined	5.00	(3)80
J	1.0000	0.900	Infinite	Undefined	4.00	(3)75
K	1.0000	0.900	Infinite	Undefined	5.00	(3)80
L	1.0000	0.900	Infinite	Undefined	4.00	(3)75

Adjusting component reliabilities

To illustrate the relationships just described, assume that you have the following information on components A through L:

- *Components A, B, C, D and E.* New, to be programmed and certified at 0.999 reliability.
- *Components, F, G and I.* Existing in a library with 0.99999 field-use reliability. Performance records are sufficiently well-established to justify this reliability claim.
- *Component H.* New, to be programmed and certified at 0.99999 reliability.
- *Components J and L.* Numerical-function library packages with such an extensive field-use record that we are justified in asserting a reliability of 1.0. (Asserting a reliability of 1.0 does not mean you can demonstrate or even believe that, however. The assertion is merely a way of taking a component with exceptionally high reliability out of play.)
- *Component K.* Existing in a library with such an extensive field-use record that we are justified in asserting a reliability of 1.0.

If you enter this component information into the model, you get the display in table 5.4. The table shows that the reliability entries for components A through I have changed, which caused the entries for the associated test cases and MTTF entries to change. Now, to demonstrate a reliability of 0.999 ((3)00) and to have 90 percent confidence in the demonstration, you must run 2,301 test cases without a failure. Moreover, you might also require a similar demonstration for each new component (A through E). (Cleanroom takes a different and more efficient approach, as we will show later.) This table shows that, under our definitions, a reliability of 0.999 corresponds to an MTTF of 1,000 uses.

Entries for components F, G, and I – which have well-established field-use records justifying a reliability of 0.99999 ((5)00) – show the value of carefully documented field performance. To demonstrate a 90 percent confidence level in this reliability, you would have to run 230,257 randomly selected test cases without a failure!

The table shows a system reliability of 0.964 ((1)64), the same as an MTTF of 28.09 uses, which the CRM calculated from the network relationships and component information. Because the allocated-reliability column shows that some components with high sensitivities (B, D, and E) have lower reliabilities than allocated, it should not be surprising that system reliability is less than target reliability.

New components B, D, and E (components A and C, although new, have lower sensitivities) are actually more critical to system reliability than

Table 5.4 CRM display given component reliabilities

System reliability: (1)64
System MTTF: 28.09

Target reliability: (3)00
Test-scale factor target: 1.000

Module name	Reliability	Confidence	Test cases	MTTF	Sensitivity	Allocated reliability
Enter_system	1.0000	0.900	Infinite	Undefined	0.96	(3)00
A	(3)00	0.900	2301	1000.00	4.66	(3)80
B	(3)00	0.900	2301	1000.00	9.13	(4)00
C	(3)00	0.900	2301	1000.00	1.86	(3)50
D	(3)00	0.900	2301	1000.00	9.13	(4)00
E	(3)00	0.900	2301	1000.00	9.14	(4)00
F	(5)00	0.900	230257	100000.00	8.20	(3)88
G	(5)00	0.900	230257	100000.00	1.67	(3)44
H	(5)00	0.900	230257	100000.00	1.85	(3)50
I	(5)00	0.900	230257	100000.00	4.56	(3)80
J	1.0000	0.900	Infinite	Undefined	3.65	(3)75
K	1.0000	0.900	Infinite	Undefined	4.56	(3)80
L	1.0000	0.900	Infinite	Undefined	3.65	(3)75

Table 5.5 CRM display given increased component reliabilities

System reliability: (1)89
System MTTF: 99.25

Target reliability: (3)00
Test-scale factor: 1.000

Module name	Reliability	Confidence	Test cases	MTTF	Sensitivity	Allocated reliability
Enter_system	1.0000					
A	(3)00	0.900	Infinite	Undefined	0.99	(3)00
B	(4)00	0.900	2301	1000.00	4.91	(3)80
C	(3)00	0.900	23025	10000.00	9.78	(4)00
D	(4)00	0.900	2301	1000.00	1.96	(3)50
E	(4)00	0.900	23025	10000.00	9.78	(4)00
F	(5)00	0.900	23025	10000.00	9.78	(4)00
G	(5)00	0.900	230257	100000.00	8.80	(3)88
H	(5)00	0.900	230257	100000.00	1.76	(3)44
I	(5)00	0.900	230257	100000.00	1.95	(3)50
J	1.0000	0.900	230257	100000.00	4.89	(3)80
K	1.0000	0.900	Infinite	Undefined	3.91	(3)75
L	1.0000	0.900	Infinite	Undefined	4.89	(3)80
		0.900	Infinite	Undefined	3.91	(3)75

the reused components with well-established records of highly reliable performance. In table 5.5, the reliabilities for components B, D and E have been increased, and, as you would expect, system reliability has also increased.

Adjusting system structure

The most fundamental change a planner can make is to revise the network that describes component interaction. The most radical change is to remove or add a node and associated arcs, which corresponds to a major architectural change. A less radical change is to remove or add arcs –

Table 5.6 Revised transition probabilities for the system in figure 5.1

From module	To module	Transition probability
OS	A	1.0000
A	B	0.0500
A	C	0.4000
A	D	0.4000
A	E	0.1000
B	A	0.1000
B	F	0.9000
C	G	0.9000
C	H	0.1000
D	A	0.1000
D	I	0.5000
D	J	0.4000
E	A	0.1000
E	K	0.5000
E	L	0.4000
F	B	1.0000
G	H	1.0000
H	A	0.5000
H	C	0.5000
I	D	1.0000
J	D	1.0000
K	E	1.0000
L	E	1.0000
A	OS	0.0500

Table 5.7 CRM display given revised transition probabilities

System reliability: (1)54
System MTTF: 21.92

Target reliability: (3)00
Test-scale factor: 1.000

Module name	Reliability	Confidence	Test cases	MTTF	Sensitivity	Allocated reliability
Enter_system	1.0000		Infinite	Undefined	0.95	(3)00
A	(3)00	0.900	2301	1000.00	18.25	(4)50
B	(4)00	0.900	23025	10000.00	9.09	(4)00
C	(3)00	0.900	2301	1000.00	14.54	(4)37
D	(4)00	0.900	23025	10000.00	72.73	(4)87
E	(4)00	0.900	23025	10000.00	18.18	(4)50
F	(5)00	0.900	230257	100000.00	8.18	(3)88
G	(5)00	0.900	230257	100000.00	13.08	(4)30
H	(5)00	0.900	230257	100000.00	14.53	(4)37
I	(5)00	0.900	230257	100000.00	36.36	(4)75
J	1.0000	0.900	Infinite	Undefined	29.09	(4)68
K	1.0000	0.900	Infinite	Undefined	9.09	(4)00
L	1.0000	0.900	Infinite	Undefined	7.27	(3)87

Table 5.8 CRM display given very high component reliabilities

System reliability: (2)68
System MTTF: 318.18
Target reliability: (3)00
Test-scale factor: 1.000

Module name	Reliability	Confidence	Test cases	MTTF	Sensitivity	Allocated
Enter_system	1.0000		Infinite	Undefined	1.00	(3)00
A	(5)00	0.900	230257	100000.00	19.87	(4)50
B	(4)00	0.900	23025	10000.00	9.92	(4)00
C	(5)00	0.900	230257	100000.00	15.90	(4)37
D	(5)00	0.900	230257	100000.00	79.48	(4)87
E	(5)00	0.900	230257	100000.00	19.87	(4)50
F	(5)00	0.900	230257	100000.00	8.92	(3)88
G	(5)00	0.900	230257	100000.00	14.31	(4)30
H	(5)00	0.900	230257	100000.00	15.90	(4)37
I	(5)00	0.900	230257	100000.00	39.74	(4)75
J	1.0000	0.900	Infinite	Undefined	31.79	(4)68
K	1.0000	0.900	Infinite	Undefined	9.94	(4)00
L	1.0000	0.900	Infinite	Undefined	7.95	(3)87

change the transition probabilities without changing the components themselves – after carefully studying and analyzing the system's intended use. Table 5.6 shows transition probabilities revised from those in table 5.1. The reliability information for table 5.6 is shown in table 5.7 (which contrasts with table 5.5).

A change like this will definitely affect system reliability and component sensitivities, as a comparison of tables 5.5 and 5.7 shows. Particularly important is that the relative values within each table are different, which may cause the planner to reallocate development resources. In table 5.5, components B, D, and E affect system reliability the most; in table 5.7, components D, I, and J have the greatest effect.

Also important is that the components in table 5.7 have much higher sensitivities than those in table 5.5. This difference implies that changes in component reliabilities will affect system reliability more under the revised transition probabilities (as in table 5.7) than under the original ones (as in table 5.5). Table 5.8 shows what happens when component reliabilities are pushed very high.

Cleanroom certification

Continuing with the assumed component information, if you are going to enter the new components individually into a repository or library, you must certify each one individually. In this illustration of Cleanroom certification, we assume that new components do not have an existence or applicability outside the new system. The task is to certify the completed system, not its components, although you should know a great deal by now about how each component affects system reliability.

Cleanroom certification is based on the Cleanroom approach to management and development, which means that system development will be segmented into increments, and each increment will be certified to the target level. Since the increments are cumulative, component interactions are fully certified in the final increment.

The data in table 5.9 is based on an actual project that resulted in approximately 24,000 lines of Ada, of which half was newly developed code and half was reused from a library.[10] The formulas used in the CRM to calculate the data in table 5.9 are given in the box on pp. 87–91. The increments, with components given in the order they were implemented, are as follows:

- *Increment 1.* Components A, B, and F.
- *Increment 2.* Components A, B, F, C, G, H.
- *Increment 3.* Components A, B, F, C, G, H, D, I, J.
- *Increment 4.* Components A, B, F, C, G, H, D, I, J, E, K, L.

Table 5.9 Certification of increments

Version number	Observed MTTF	Predicted reliability	Predicted MTTF	$MTTF_0$	Improvement factor
Increment 1					
0	1.00	—	—	—	—
1	6.00	—	—	—	—
2	1.00	(0)23	0.81	2.09	0.59
3	16.00	(0)77	4.38	1.09	1.36
4	560.00	(2)57	232.62	0.37	3.60
Increment 2					
0	1.00	—	—	—	—
1	1.00	—	—	—	—
2	1.75	(0)37	1.60	1.02	0.99
3	11.00	(0)81	5.38	0.79	1.55
4	37.00	(1)63	27.64	0.55	2.20
5	49.00	(1)88	86.47	0.58	2.31
6	200.00	(2)68	316.52	0.51	2.53
Increment 3					
0	1.00	—	—	—	—
1	1.00	—	—	—	—
2	15.00	(1)23	13.04	0.64	2.31
3	116.00	(2)34	153.84	0.42	4.29
Increment 4					
0	2.00	—	—	—	—
1	1.50	—	—	—	—
2	38.50	(1)78	46.90	0.57	3.97
3	28.00	(2)18	122.40	0.81	3.55
4	12.00	(1)87	80.95	1.55	2.26
5	29.00	(2)05	106.30	1.98	1.99
6	87.00	(2)53	216.24	2.10	1.98
7	200.00	(2)78	472.58	2.13	2.00

Version number (first column in the table) indicates the engineering-change level. Generally, an immediate-repair policy was followed with respect to failures in testing and changes to the code. Whenever it was clear that successive failures were independent, testing continued without code changes and recompilation. When code changes were made, each recompilation resulted in a new version of the system and each new version fixed one or more faults from the previous version. Because there is no failure in the last version, it would be overly conservative to enter just the number of tests run. Thus, the certification model's criterion for stopping testing is based on the last entry for each increment being double the actual number of test cases that ran without failure.

$MTTF_0$ (fifth column) is the estimated MTTF of the software's initial version. Improvement factor (last column) is the estimated factor by which each successive version is an improvement over its predecessor.

The number of test cases required for certification with this model depends not only on the number of failures but also on when they are observed.

To certify increment 1, for example, we had to run 300 randomly generated test cases to reach a predicted reliability of 0.9957 ((2)57). We detected six failures and corrected the faults during certification.

In certifying increment 2, we brought the cumulative number of test cases to 556 and the cumulative error count to 19. We stopped testing when the certification model predicted a 0.9968 ((2)68) reliability.

In certifying increment 3, we required 656 (cumulative) test cases and brought the cumulative error count to 25. We stopped testing when the certification model predicted a 0.9934 ((2)34) reliability.

Finally, in certifying increment 4, the total number of test cases was 989, with 36 total failures (increment 4 is, of course, the total system). We stopped testing when the certification model predicted a 0.9978 ((2)78) reliability.

A few more metrics from this project may be of interest. Of the 36 operational failures, seven were in or related to the reused library software, three were Ada compiler errors, and six were a consequence of the Cleanroom team's lack of Ada knowledge. Twenty failures were caused by logic errors and file-related errors. Of course, all errors are significant in certification because it is from a user perspective, and the customer isn't going to care who made the errors or why.

At this point, we would be justified in putting this system into a library and noting that it has a predicted reliability of 0.99 under the certification model. However, to estimate reliability to this level under the sampling model and to have a certain level of confidence in the demonstration, we might require additional tests. Ideally, the system would first be released to a statistically selected group of users, for whom it might amass a half million failure-free uses, which would justify a claim of five 9s with high confidence. Next the system would be made generally available and followed to see if, after billions of uses, it has earned the status "six sigma."

CONCLUSIONS

Software-reliability models can be applied to software development in typical industrial settings, including the development of entirely new systems and those based on reuse. The models are independent of language and development method, but, for the models to be meaningful, the software must be of high quality. Therefore, these efforts are most significant when they are used in the context of a high-quality development methodology such as Cleanroom software engineering.

Techniques for estimating the reliability of individual software units and an entire system as it is being constructed and prepared for release are within the reach of most organizations. Mathematical complexities notwithstanding, reliability planning and certification lend themselves to straightforward spreadsheet manipulations.

Acknowledgments

We thank R. C. Linger and M. Pleszkoch of the IBM Cleanroom Software Technology Center and C. Trammell of the University of Maryland for their assistance with earlier versions of this article. We also acknowledge suggestions made by anonymous *IEEE Software* referees.

References

1   J. Poore, D. Mutchler, and H. Mills, "STARS-Cleanroom Reliability: Cleanroom Ideas in the STARS Environment," Tech. Report IBM STARS CDRL 1710, Software Engineering Technology (available from Asset, Morgantown, W.V.), 1989.
2   D. Parnas, A. van Schouwen, and S. Kwan, "Evaluation of Safety-Critical Software," *Comm. ACM* June 1990, pp. 636–648.
3   R. Cheung, "A User-Oriented Software Reliability Model," *IEEE Trans. Software Engineering*, Mar. 1980, pp. 118–125.
4   K. Siegrist, "Reliability of Systems with Markov Transfer of Control," *IEEE Trans. Software Engineering*, July 1988, pp. 1049–1053.
5   A. Currit, M. Dyer, and H. Mills, "Certifying the Reliability of Software," *IEEE Trans. Software Engineering*, Jan. 1986, pp. 3–11.
6   H. Mills, M. Dyer, and R. Linger, "Cleanroom Software Engineering," *IEEE Software*, Sept. 1987, pp. 19–24.
7   J. Whittaker, "Markov Chain Techniques for Software Testing and Reliability Analysis," PhD dissertation, CS Dept., Univ. of Tennessee, Knoxville, May 1992.
8   J. Whittaker and J. Poore, "Markov Analysis of Software Specifications," *ACM Trans. Software Engineering and Methodology*, vol. 2, no. 1, Jan. 1993, pp. 93–106.

9   R. Linger, H. Mills, and B. Witt, *Structural Programming: Theory and Practice*, Addison-Wesley, Reading, Mass, 1979.

10   J. Poore et al., "Cleanroom Reliability Manager: A Case Study Using Cleanroom with Box Structures ADL," Tech. Report IBM STARS CDRL 1940, Software Engineering Technology, (available from Asset, Morgantown, W.V.), 1990.

6   Cleanroom Process Model

R. C. LINGER

INTRODUCTION

Today's competitive pressures and society's increasing dependence on software have led to a new focus on development processes. The Cleanroom process, which has evolved over the last decade, has demonstrated that it can improve both the productivity of developers who use it and the quality of the software they produce.

Cleanroom software engineering is a team-oriented process that makes development more manageable and predictable because it is done under statistical quality control.

Cleanroom is a modern approach to software development. In traditional, craft-based development, defects are regarded as inevitable and elaborate defect-removal techniques are a part of the development process. In such a process, software proceeds from development to unit testing and debugging, then to function and system testing for more debugging. In the absence of workable alternatives, managers encourage programmers to get code into execution quickly, so debugging can begin. Today, developers recognize that defect removal is an error-prone, inefficient activity that consumes resources better allocated to getting the code right the first time.

Cleanroom teams at IBM and other organizations are achieving remarkable quality results in both new-system development and modifications and extensions to legacy systems. The quality of software produced by Cleanroom development teams is sufficient (often near zero defects) for the software to enter system testing directly for first-ever execution by test teams.

© 1994 IEEE. Reprinted, with permission, from *IEEE Software*, vol. 11, no. 3, pp. 50–58, March 1994.

The theoretical foundations of Cleanroom – formal specification and design, correctness verification, and statistical testing – have been reduced to practice and demonstrated in nearly a million lines of code. Some Cleanroom projects are profiled in the box on p. 124–126.

QUALITY COMPARISON

Quality comparisons between traditional methods and the Cleanroom process are meaningful when measured from first execution. Most traditional development methods begin to measure errors at function testing (or later), omitting errors found in private unit testing. A traditional project experiencing, say, five errors per thousand lines of code (KLOC) in function testing may have encountered 25 or more errors per KLOC when measured from first execution in unit testing.

At entry to unit testing, traditional software typically exhibits 25 to 35 or more errors per KLOC.[1] In contrast, the weighted average of errors found in 17 Cleanroom projects, involving nearly a million lines of code, is 2.3 errors per KLOC. This number represents all errors found in all testing, measured from first-ever execution through test completion – it is the average number of residual errors present after the development team has performed correctness verification.

In addition to this remarkable difference in the number of errors, experience has shown a qualitative difference in the complexity of errors found in Cleanroom versus traditional software. Errors left behind by Cleanroom correctness verification tend not to be complex design or interface errors, but simple mistakes easily found and fixed by statistical testing.

In this chapter, I describe the Cleanroom development process, from specification and design through correctness verification and statistical usage testing for quality certification.

INCREMENTAL DEVELOPMENT

The Cleanroom process is based on developing and certifying a pipeline of software increments that accumulate into the final system. The increments are developed and certified by small, independent teams, with teams of teams for large projects.

System integration is continual, and functionality grows with the addition of successive increments. In this approach, the harmonious operation of future increments at the next level of refinement is predefined by increments already in execution, thereby minimizing interface and design errors and helping developers maintain intellectual control.

The Cleanroom development process is intended to be "quick and clean," not "quick and dirty." The idea is to quickly develop the right product with high quality for the user, then go on to the next version to incor-porate new requirements arising from user experience.

In the Cleanroom process, correctness is built in by the development team through formal specification, design, and verification. Team correct-ness verification takes the place of unit testing and debugging, and soft-ware enters system testing directly, with no execution by the development team. All errors are accounted for from first execution on, with no private debugging permitted.

Figure 6.1 illustrates the Cleanroom process of incremental develop-ment and quality certification. The Cleanroom team first analyzes and clarifies customer requirements, with substantial user interaction and feed-back. If requirements are in doubt, the team can develop Cleanroom prototypes to elicit feedback iteratively.

As the figure shows, Cleanroom development involves two cooperating teams and five major activities:

- *Specification.* Cleanroom development begins with specification. Together the development team and the certification team produce two specifications: functional and usage. Large projects may have a separate specification team.

  The functional specification defines the required external system behavior in all circumstances of use; the usage specification defines usage scenarios and their probabilities for all possible system usage, both correct and incorrect. The functional specification is the basis for incremental software development. The usage specification is the basis for generating test cases for incremental statistical testing and quality certification. Usage specifications are explained in the section on certi-fication.

- *Increment planning.* On the basis of these specifications, the develop-ment and certification teams together define an initial plan for develop-ing increments that will accumulate into the final system. For example, a 100 KLOC system might be developed in five increments averaging 20 KLOC each. The time it takes to design and verify increments varies with their size and complexity. Increments that require long lead times may call for parallel development.

- *Design and verification.* The development team then carries out a design and correctness verification cycle for each increment. The certi-fication team proceeds in parallel, using the usage specification to gen-

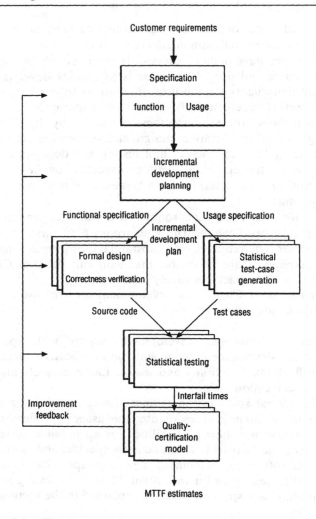

Figure 6.1 Cleanroom process model. The stacked boxes indicate successive increments.

erate test cases that reflect the expected use of the accumulating increments.

- *Quality certification.* Periodically, the development team integrates a completed increment with prior increments and delivers them to the test team for execution of statistical test cases. The test cases are run against the accumulated increments and the results checked for correctness against the functional specification. Interfail times, that is, the elapsed times between failures, are passed to a quality-certification model[2] that computes objective statistical measures of quality, such as mean time to failure. The quality-certification model employs a reliability growth estimator to derive the statistical measures.

Certification is done continuously, over the life of the project. Higher level increments enter the certification pipeline first. This means major architectural and design decisions are validated in execution before the development team elaborates on them. And because certification is done for all increments as they accumulate, higher level increments are subjected to more testing than lower level increments, which implement localized functions.

- *Feedback.* Errors are returned to the development team for correction. If the quality is low, managers and team members initiate process improvement. As with any process, a good deal of iteration and feedback is always present to accommodate problems and solutions.

In the next sections, I describe the specification, design and verification, and quality-certification procedures. A detailed description of increment planning and feedback mechanisms is outside the scope of this chapter.

FUNCTIONAL SPECIFICATION

The object-based technology of box structures has proved to be an effective technique for functional specification.[3] Through stepwise refinement, objects are defined and refined as different box structures, resulting in a usage hierarchy of objects in which the services of an object may be used and reused in many places and at many levels. Box structures, then, define required system behavior and derive and connect objects comprising a system architecture.[4,5]

In the past, without a rigorous specification technology, there was little incentive to devote much effort to the specification process. Specifications were frequently written in natural language, with inevitable ambiguities and omissions, and often regarded as throwaway stepping stones to code.

Box structures provide an economic incentive for precision. Initial box-structure specifications often reveal gaps and misunderstandings in customer requirements that would ordinarily be discovered later in development at high cost and risk to the project.

They also address the two engineering problems associated with system specification: defining the right function for users and defining the right structure for the specification itself. Box structures address the first problem by precisely defining the current understanding of required functions at each stage of development, so that the functions can be reviewed and modified if necessary. The second problem is critical, especially for large-system development. How can we organize the myriad details of behavior and processing into coherent abstractions humans can understand?

Box structures incorporate the crucial mathematical property of referential transparency – the information content of each box specification is sufficient to define its refinement, without depending on the implementation of any other box. This property lets us organize large-system specifications hierarchically, without sacrificing precision at high levels or detail at low levels.

Box structures

Three principles govern the use of box structures.[4]

- All data defined in a design is encapsulated in boxes.
- All processing is defined by using boxes sequentially or concurrently.
- Each box occupies a distinct place in a system's usage hierarchy.

Each box has three forms – black, state, and clear – which have identical external behavior but whose internals are increasingly detailed.

Black box

An object's black box is a precise specification of external, user-visible behavior in all possible circumstances of its use. The object may be an entire system or any part of a system. Its user may be a person or another object.

A black box accepts a stimulus (S) from a user and produces a response (R). Each response of a black box is determined by its current stimulus history (SH), with a black-box transition function

$$(S, SH) \rightarrow (R)$$

A given stimulus will produce different responses that are based on history of use, not just on the current stimulus. Imagine a calculator with two stimulus histories

```
Clear 7 1 3
```

and

```
Clear 7 1 3 +
```

If the next stimulus is 6, the first history produces a response of 7136; the second, 6.

The objective of a black-box specification is to define the responses produced for every possible stimulus and stimulus history, including erroneous and unexpected stimuli. By defining behavior solely in terms of stimulus histories, black-box specifications neither depend on nor prematurely define design internals.

Black-box specifications are often recorded as tables. In each row, the stimulus and the condition on stimulus history are sufficient to define the required response. To record large specifications, classes of behavior are grouped in nested tables and compact specification functions are used to encapsulate conditions on stimulus histories.[6]

State box
An object's state box is derived from its black box by identifying the elements of stimulus history that must be retained as state data between transitions to achieve the required black-box behavior.

The transition function of a state box is

$$(S, OS) \rightarrow (R, NS),$$

where OS and NS represent old state and new state. Although the external behavior of a state box is identical to its corresponding black box, the stimulus histories are replaced with references to an old state and the generation of a new state, as its transitions require.

As in the traditional view of objects, state boxes encapsulate state data and services (methods) on that data. In this view, stimuli and responses are inputs and outputs, respectively, of specific state-box service invocations that operate on state data.

Clear box
An object's clear box is derived from its state box by defining a procedure to carry out the state-box transition function. The transition function of a clear box is

$$(S, OS) \rightarrow (R, NS) \text{ by procedure}$$

So a clear box is simply a program that implements the corresponding state box. A clear box may invoke black boxes at the next level, so the refinement process is recursive, with each clear box possibly introducing opportunities for defining new objects or extensions to existing ones.

Clear boxes play a crucial role in the usage hierarchy by ensuring the harmonious cooperation of objects at the next level of refinement. Objects and their clear-box connections are derived from immediate processing needs at each stage of refinement, not invented *a priori*, with uncertain connections left to be defined later. The design and verification of clear-box procedures is the focus of the next section.

Because state boxes can be verified with respect to their black boxes and clear boxes with respect to their state boxes, box structures bring correctness verification to object architectures.[4]

DESIGN AND VERIFICATION

The procedural control structures of structured programming used in clear-box design – sequence, alternation (if–then–else), and iteration (while–do) – are single-entry, single-exit structures that cannot produce side effects in control flow. (Control structures for concurrent execution are dealt with in box structures, but are outside the scope of this chapter.)

When it executes, a given control structure simply transforms data from an input state to an output state. This transformation, known as its *program function*, corresponds to a mathematical function: it defines a mapping from a domain to a range by a particular rule.

For integers w, x, y, and z, for example, the program function of the sequence,

```
DO
  z := abs(y)
  w := max(x, z)
END
```

is, in concurrent assignment form,

```
w, z := max(x, abs(y)), abs(y)
```

For integer $x \geq 0$, the program function of the iteration

```
WHILE
  x > 1
DO
  x := x - 2
END
```

is, in English,

```
set odd x to 1, even x to 0
```

Design refinement

In designing clear-box procedures, you define an *intended function*, then refine it into a control structure and new intended functions, as figure 6.2 illustrates. Intended functions, enclosed in braces, are recorded in the design and attached to their control-structure refinements. In essence, clear boxes are composed of a finite number of control structures, each of which can be checked for correctness.

Design simplification is an important objective in the stepwise refinement of clear boxes. The goal is to generate compact, straightforward, verifiable designs.

Correctness verification

To verify the correctness of each control structure, you derive its program function – the function it actually computes – and compare it to its intended function, as recorded in the design. A correctness theorem[7] defines how to do this comparison in terms of language- and application-independent *correctness conditions*, which you apply to each control structure.

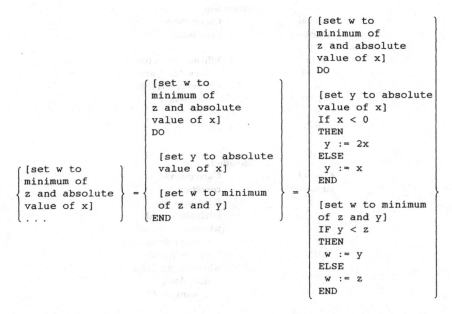

Figure 6.2 Stepwise refinement of a clear-box design fragment that can be verified. Each fragment has identical functional behavior, even though the level of detail increases.

Figure 6.3 shows the correctness conditions for the sequence, alternation, and iteration control structures. Verifying a sequence involves function composition and requires checking exactly one condition. Verifying an alternation involves case analysis and requires checking exactly two conditions. Verifying an iteration involves function composition and case analysis in a recursive equation and requires checking exactly three conditions.

Sequence

Control structure:	Correctness condition (for all arguments)
[f]	
DO	
g;	Does g followed
h	by h do f?
END	

Alternation

Control structure:	Correctness condition:
[f]	
IF p	Whenever p is true
THEN	does g do f, and
g	whenever p is false
ELSE	does h do f?
h	
END	

Iteration

Control structure:	Correctness condition:
[f]	Is termination
WHILE p	guaranteed, and
DO	whenever p is true
g	does g followed
END	by f do f, and
	whenever p is false
	does doing
	nothing do f?

Figure 6.3 Correctness conditions in question form for verifying each type of clear-box control structure.

Correctness verification has several advantages:

* *It reduces verification to a finite process.* As figure 6.4 illustrates, the nested, sequenced way that control structures are organized in a clear box naturally defines a hierarchy that reveals the correctness conditions that must be verified. An axiom of replacement[7] lets us substitute intended functions for their control structure refinements in the hierarchy of subproofs. For example, the subproof for the intended function f1 in figure 6.4 requires proving that the composition of operations g1 and g2 with intended subfunction f2 has the same effect on data as f1. Note that f2 substitutes for all the details of its refinement in this proof. This substitution localizes the proof argument to the control structure at hand. In fact, it lets you carry out proofs in any order.

It is impossible to overstate the positive effect that reducing verification to a finite process has on quality. Even though all but the most trivial programs exhibit an essentially infinite number of execution

Program:	Subproofs:

`[f1]`
`DO`
`  g1`
`  g2`
	`f1 = [DO g1;g2;[f2] END] ?`

`  [f2]`
`  WHILE`
`   p1`
`  DO [f3]`
	`f2 = [WHILE p1 DO [f3] END] ?`

`   g3`
`   [f4]`
`   IF`
	`f3 = [DO g3;[f4];g8 END] ?`

`    p2`
`   THEN [f5]`
`    g4`
`    g5`
	`f4 = [IF p2 THEN [f5] ELSE [f6] END] ?`

`   ELSE [f6]`
`    g6`
`    g7`
	`f5 = [DO g4;g5 END] ?`

`   END`
`   g8`
`  END`
`END`
	`f6 = [DO g6;g7 END] ?`

Figure 6.4 A clear-box procedure and its constituent subproofs. In the figure, each `pi` is a predicate, each `gi` is an operation, and each `fi` is an intended function.

paths, they can be verified in a finite number of steps. For example, the clear box in figure 6.5 has exactly 15 correctness conditions that must be verified.

```
[ Q := odd_numbers(Q) || even_numbers(Q) ]
    PROC Odd_Before_Even (ALT Q)

        DATA
           odds  : queue of integer [initializes to empty]
           evens : queue of integer [initializes to empty]
           x     : integer
        END

        [ Q     := empty,
          odds  := odds  ||odd_numbers(Q),
          evens := evens ||even_numbers(Q) ]
        WHILE Q < > empty
        DO

            x     := end(Q)
                                                          seq
seq         [x is odd → odds  := odds || x                 1
wdo
1           [true     → evens := evens || x ]
3
            If odd(x)
            THEN                                              ite
               end(odds) := x                                 2
             ELSE
               end(evens) := x
            END

        END

        [ Q    := Q || odds,
          odds := empty ]
        WHILE odds < > empty
        DO [end(Q) := end(odds) ]               wdo
                                        seq     3
            x     := end(odds)           1
            end(Q) := x

    END
```

Figure 6.5   A clear-box procedure with 15 correctness conditions to be verified. The procedural control structures and the number of correctness conditions that must be checked are shown in bold. Seq indicates a sequence, ite indicates an alternation (if-then-else), and wdo indicates an iteration (while-do).

- *It lets Cleanroom teams verify every line of design and code.* Teams can carry out the verification through group analysis and discussion on the basis of the correctness theorem, and they can produce written proofs when extra confidence in a life- or mission-critical system is required.
- *It results in a near-zero defect level.* During a team review, every correctness condition of every control structure is verified in turn. Every team member must agree that each condition is correct, so an error is possible only if every team member incorrectly verifies a condition. The requirement for unanimous agreement based on individual verifications results in software that has few or no defects before first execution.
- *It scales up.* Every software system, no matter how large, has top-level, clear-box procedures composed of sequence, alternation, and iteration structures. Each of these typically invokes a large subsystem with thousands of lines of code – and each of those subsystems has its own top-level intended functions and procedures. So the correctness conditions for these high-level control structures are verified in the same way as are those of low-level structures. Verification at high levels may take, and well be worth, more time, but it does not take more theory.
- *It produces better code than unit testing.* Unit testing checks only the effects of executing selected test paths out of many possible paths. By basing verification on function theory, the Cleanroom approach can verify every possible effect on all data, because while a program may have many execution paths, it has only one function. Verification is also more efficient than unit testing. Most verification conditions can be checked in a few minutes, but unit tests take substantial time to prepare, execute, and check.

QUALITY CERTIFICATION

Statistical quality control is used when you have too many items to test all of them exhaustively. Instead, you statistically sample and analyze some items to obtain a scientific assessment of the quality of all items. This technique is widely used in manufacturing, in which items on a production line are sampled, their quality is measured against a presumably perfect design, the sample quality is extrapolated to the entire production line, and flaws in production are corrected if the quality is too low.

In hardware products, the statistics used to establish quality are derived from slight variations in the products' physical properties. But software copies are identical, bit for bit. What statistics can be sample to extrapolate quality?

Cleanroom Quality Results

Cleanroom projects report a *testing error rate per thousand lines of code*, which represents residual errors in the software after correctness verification. The projects briefly described here are among 17 Cleanroom projects, involving nearly a million lines of code, that have reported a *weighted average of 2.3 errors per* KLOC *found in all testing, measured from first-ever execution of the code* – a remarkable quality achievement.[1]

IBM COBOL Structuring Facility (COBOL/SF)

This was IBM's first commercial Cleanroom product, developed by a six-person team. This 85 KLOC PL/I program automatically transforms unstructured COBOL programs into functionally equivalent structured form for improved understandability and maintenance. It had a testing error rate of 3.4 errors per KLOC; several major components completed certification with no errors found. In months of intensive beta testing at a major aerospace corporation, all COBOL programs executed identically before and after structuring.

Productivity, including all specification, design, verification, certification, user publications, and management, averaged 740 LOC per person–month. So far, a small fraction of a person–year per year has been required for all maintenance and customer support. Although the product exhibits a complexity level on the order of a COBOL compiler, just seven minor errors were reported in the first three years of field use, all resulting in simple fixes. – R. C. Linger and H. D. Mills, "A Case Study in Cleanroom Software Engineering: The IBM COBOL Structuring Facility," *Proc. Compsac*, IEEE CS Press, Los Alamitos, Calif., 1988, pp. 10–17.

NASA satellite-control project

The Coarse/Fine Attitude Determination System (CFADS) of the NASA Attitude Ground Support System (AGSS) was the first Cleanroom project carried out by the Software Engineering Laboratory of the NASA Goddard Space Flight Center. The system, comprising 40 KLOC of Fortran, exhibited a testing error rate of 4.5 errors per KLOC. Productivity was 780 LOC per person–month, an 80 percent improvement over previous SEL averages. Some 60 percent of the programs compiled correctly on the first attempt. – A. Kouchakdjian, S. Green, and V. R. Basili, "Evaluation of the Cleanroom Methodology in the Software Engineeering Laboratory," *Proc. 14th Software Eng. Workshop*, NASA Goddard Space Flight Center, Greenbelt, Md., 1989.

Martin Marietta Automated Documentation System
A four-person Cleanroom team developed the prototype for this system, a 1,820-line relational database application written in FOXBASE. It had a testing error rate of 0.0 errors per KLOC – no compilation errors were found and no failures were encountered in statistical testing and quality certification. The software was certified at target levels of reliability and confidence. Team members attributed error-free compilation and failure-free testing to the rigor of the Cleanroom method. – C. J. Trammell, L. H. Binder, and C. E. Snyder, "The Automated Production Control System: A Case Study in Cleanroom Software Engineering," ACM *Trans. Software Eng. and Methodology*, Jan. 1992, pp. 81–94.

IBM AOEXPERT/MVS
A 50-person team developed this complex decision-support facility that uses artificial intelligence to predict and prevent operating problems in an MVS environment. The system, written in PL/I, C, Rexx, and TIRS, totaled 107 KLOC, developed in three increments. It had a testing error rate of 2.6 errors per KLOC. Causal analysis of the first 16-KLOC increment revealed that five of its eight components experienced no errors in testing.

The project reported development team productivity of 486 LOC per person–month. No operational errors have been reported to date from beta test and early user sites. – P. A. Hausler, "A Recent Cleanroom Success Story: The Redwing Project," *Proc. 17th Software Eng. Workshop*, NASA Goddard Space Flight Center, Greenbelt, Md., 1992.

NASA satellite-control projects
Two satellite projects, a 20-KLOC attitude-determination subsystem and a 150-KLOC flight-dynamics system, were the second and third Cleanroom projects undertaken at NASA's Software Engineering Laboratory. These systems had a combined testing error rate of 4.2 errors per KLOC. – S. E. Green and Rose Pajerski, "Cleanroom Process Evolution in the SEL," *Proc. 16th Software Eng. Workshop*, NASA Goddard Space Flight Center, Greenbelt, Md., 1991.

IBM 3090E tape drive
A five-person team developed the device-controller design and microcode in 86 KLOC of C, including 64 KLOC of function definitions. This embedded software processes multiple real-time I/O data streams to support tape-cartridge operations in a multibus architecture. The box-structure specification for the chip-set semantics revealed several hard-

ware errors. The project had a testing error rate of 1.2 errors per KLOC.

A one-module experiment compared the effectiveness of unit testing and correctness verification. In unit testing, the team took 10 person–days to develop scaffolding code, invent and execute test cases, and check results. They found seven errors. Correctness verification, which required an hour-and-a-half in a team review, found the same seven errors plus three more.

To meet a business need, the third code increment went straight from development, with no testing whatsoever, into customer-evaluation demonstrations using live data. There were no errors of any kind. A total of 490 statistical tests were executed against the final version of the system, with no errors found.

Ericsson Telecom os32 operating system

This 70-person, 18-month project specified, developed, and certified a 350-KLOC operating system for a new family of switching computers. The project had a testing error rate of 1.0 errors per KLOC.

Productivity was reported to have increased by 70 percent for development; 100 percent for testing. The team significantly reduced development time, and the project was honored by Ericsson for its contribution to the company. – L.-G. Tann, "os32 and Cleanroom," *Proc. 1st European Industrial Symp. Cleanroom Software Eng.*, Q-labs, Lund, Sweden, 1993.

Reference

1   P. A. Hausler, R. C. Linger, and C. J. Trammell, "Adopting Cleanroom Software Engineering with a Phased Approach," IBM *Systems J.*, vol. 33, no. 1, Mar. 1994, 89–109.

Usage testing

It turns out that software has a statistical property of great interest to developers and users – its execution behaviour. How long, on average, will a software product execute before it fails?

From this notion has evolved the process of *statistical usage testing*,[8] in which you:

* sample the (essentially infinite) population of all possible executions (correct and incorrect) by users (people or other programs) according to how frequently you expect the executions to happen

- measure their quality by determining if the executions are correct
- extrapolate the quality of the sample to the population of possible executions, and
- identify and correct flaws in the development process if the quality is inadequate.

Statistical usage testing amounts to testing software the way users intend to use it. The entire focus is on external system behavior, not the internals of design and implementation. Cleanroom certification teams have deep knowledge of expected usage, but require no knowledge of design internals. Their role is not to debug-in quality, an impossible task, but to scientifically certify software's quality through statistical testing.

In practice, Cleanroom quality certification proceeds in parallel with development, in three steps.

1 *Specify usage-probability distributions.* Usage-probability distributions define all possible usage patterns and scenarios, including erroneous and unexpected usage, together with their probabilities of occurrence. They are defined on the basis of the functional specification and other sources of information, including interviews with prospective users and the pattern of use in prior versions.

Program stimuli	Usage-probability distribution	Distribution interval
U (update)	32%	0–31
D (delete)	14%	32–45
Q (query)	46%	46–91
P (print)	8%	92–99
[A]		

Test number	Random numbers:	Test cases:
1	29 11 47 52 26 94	U U Q Q U P
2	62 98 39 78 82 65	Q P D Q Q Q
3	83 32 58 41 36 17	Q D Q D D U
4	36 49 96 82 20 77	D Q P Q U Q
[B]		

Figure 6.6 (A) Simplified usage probability distribution for a program with four user stimuli and (B) a sample of associated test cases.

Figure 6.6(A) shows a usage specification for a program with four user stimuli: update (U), delete (D), query (Q), and print (P). A simplified distribution that omits scenarios of use and other details shows projected use probabilities of 32, 14, 46, and 8 percent, respectively. These probabilities are mapped onto an interval of 0 to 99, dividing it into four partitions proportional to the probabilities. Usage-probability distributions for large-scale systems are often recorded in formal grammars or Markov chains for analysis and automatic processing.

In incremental development, you can stratify a usage-probability distribution into subsets that exercise increasing functional content as increments are added, with the full distribution in effect once the final increment is in place. In addition, you can define alternate distributions to certify infrequently used system functions whose failure has important consequences, such as the code for a nuclear-reactor shutdown system.

2   Derive test cases that are randomly generated from usage-probability distributions. Test cases are derived from the distributions, such that every test represents actual use and will effectively rehearse user experience with the product. Because test cases are completely prescribed by the distributions, producing them is a mechanical, automatable process.

Figure 6.6(B) shows test cases for the probability distribution in figure 6.6(A). If you assume a test case contains six stimuli, then you generate each test by obtaining six two-digit random numbers. These numbers represent the partition in which the corresponding stimuli (U, D, Q, or P) resides. In this way, each test case is faithful to the distribution and represents a possible user execution. For testing large-scale systems, usage grammars or Markov chains can be processed to generate test cases automatically.

3   Execute test cases, assess results, and compute quality measures. At this point, the development team has released verified code to the certification team for first-ever execution. The certification team executes each test case and checks the results against system specifications. The team records execution time up to the point of any failure in appropriate units, for example, CPU time, wall-clock time, or number of transactions.

These *interfail times* represent the quality of the sample of possible user executions. They are passed to a quality certification model that computes the system's quality, including its mean time to failure. The quality-certification model produces graphs like the one in figure 6.7.

Because the Cleanroom development process rests on a formal, statistical design, these MTTF measures provide a scientific basis for management action, unlike the anecdotal evidence from coverage testing (If few errors are found, is that good or bad? If many errors are found, is that good or bad?). In theory, there is no way to ever know that a software system has

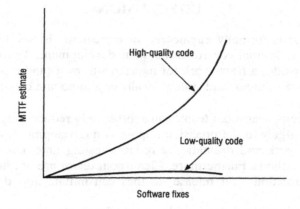

Figure 6.7   Two sample graphs. The curve for high-quality software shows exponential improvement, such that the MTTF quickly exceeds the total test time. The curve for low-quality software shows little MTTF growth.

zero defects. However, as failure-free executions accumulate, it becomes possible to conclude that the software is at or near zero defects with high probability.

Extending MTTF

But there is more to the story of statistical usage testing. Extensive analysis of errors in large-scale software systems reveals a spread in the failure rates of errors of some four orders of magnitude.[9] Virulent, high-rate errors can literally occur every few hours for some users, but low-rate errors may show up only after accumulated decades of use by many users.

High-rate errors are responsible for nearly two-thirds of software failures reported,[10] even though they comprise less than three percent of total errors. Because statistical usage testing amounts to testing software the way users will use it, high-rate errors tend to be found first. Any errors left behind after testing tend to be infrequently encountered by users.

Traditional coverage testing finds errors in random order. Yet finding and fixing low-rate errors has little effect on MTTF and user perception of quality, while finding and fixing errors in failure-rate order has a dramatic effect. Statistical usage testing is far more effective than coverage testing at extending MTTF.[10]

CONCLUSIONS

Software that is formally engineered in increments is well-documented and under intellectual control throughout development. The Cleanroom approach provides a framework for managers to plan (and replan) schedules, allocate resources, and systematically accommodate changes in functional content.

Experienced Cleanroom teams can substantially reduce time to market. This is due largely to the precision imposed on development, which helps eliminate rework and dramatically reduces testing time, compared with traditional methods. Furthermore, Cleanroom teams are not held hostage by error correction after release, so they can initiate new development immediately.

The cost of quality is remarkably low in Cleanroom operations, because it minimizes expensive debugging rework and retesting.

Cleanroom technology builds on existing skills and software-engineering practices. It is readily applied to both new system development and reengineering and extending legacy systems. As the need for higher quality and productivity in software development increases, we believe that use of the Cleanroom process will continue to grow.

Acknowledgments

I thank Kim Hathaway for her assistance in developing this article. Suggestions by Michael Deck, Philip Hausler, Harlan Mills, Mark Pleszkoch, and Alan Spangler are appreciated. I also thank the members of the Cleanroom teams, whose quality results are reported in this chapter, and who continue to achieve new levels of quality and productivity.

References

1 M. Dyer, *The Cleanroom Approach to Software Quality*, John Wiley & Sons, New York, 1992.
2 P. A. Curritt, M. Dyer, and H. D. Mills, "Certifying the Reliability of Software," IEEE *Trans. on Software Eng.*, Jan. 1986, pp. 3–11.
3 H. D. Mills, R. C. Linger, and A. R. Hevner, *Principles of Information Systems Analysis and Design*, Academic Press, San Diego, 1986.
4 H. D. Mills, "Stepwise Refinement and Verification in Box-Structured Systems," *Computer*, June 1988, pp. 23–35.
5 A. R. Hevner and H. D. Mills, "Box Structure Methods for System Development with Objects," IBM *Systems J.*, No. 2, 1993, pp. 232–251.
6 M. G. Pleszkoch et al., "Function-Theoretic Principles of Program

Understanding," *Proc. 23rd Hawaii Int'l Conf. System Sciences*, IEEE CS Press, Los Alamitos, Calif., 1990, pp. 74–81.

7   R. C. Linger, H. D. Mills, and B. I. Witt, *Structured Programming: Theory and Practice*, Addison-Wesley, Reading, Mass., 1979.

8   J. H. Poore and H. D. Mills, "Bringing Software Under Statistical Quality Control," *Quality Progress*, Nov. 1988, pp. 52–55.

9   E. N. Adams, "Optimizing Preventive Service of Software Products," *IBM J. Research and Development*, Jan. 1984, pp. 2–14.

10   R. H. Cobb and H. D. Mills, "Engineering Software Under Statistical Quality Control," *IEEE Software*, Nov. 1990, pp. 44–54.

Evolving Practice in Cleanroom Management

THE CAPABILITY MATURITY MODEL

The Software Engineering Institute's Capability Maturity Model (CMM) is in widespread use as a frame of reference for process maturity. As CMM assessments have become a prerequisite for bidding on federal contracts, organizations have increasingly begun to consider new technologies in light of their impact on a CMM assessment.

The CMM is fundamentally about management, and Cleanroom is fundamentally about methodology. There is considerable overlap between the scope of the two, and there are areas of each that are unaddressed by the other.

The CMM, for example, has Key Process Areas (KPAS) at Level 2 (Repeatable) that are outside the scope of Cleanroom. Configuration Management and Subcontractor Management, for example, are important management issues not addressed by Cleanroom ideas. Cleanroom, on the other hand, enforces the mathematical basis of software development and the statistical basis of software testing, while the CMM is silent on the merits of various methods.

In general, the Cleanroom process addresses a few KPAS at Level 2 (Repeatable), most KPAS at Level 3 (Managed), and all KPAS at Levels 4 (Controlled) and 5 (Optimizing).

AUTOMATED SUPPORT

Pilot efforts in automated support for Cleanroom process management have been sponsored by the US Department of Defense Software Technology for Adaptable, Reliable Systems (STARS) program. The prototype tool described in "Planning and certifying software system reliability" was developed as part of the STARS research by Software Engineering Technology, Inc. A prototype process management tool, the Cleanroom Engineering Process Assistant (CEPA), was field tested at the US Army's Picatinny Arsenal Life Cycle Software Support Center.

The IBM Westlake Laboratory supported research and development of a prototype tool set called the Cleanroom Environment (CRE) for OS/2. The CRE, designed with a Management Assistant, Development Assistant, and Certification Assistant, was the vehicle for several research projects at the University of Tennessee. Several parts of the CRE were used in Cleanroom projects, but support did not continue to the completion of the entire tool set. Experience gained in this project has contributed to the general understanding of tool needs.

Most tool development effort has been in support of certification. A description of current Cleanroom tools and tool development activity is given in Appendix B.

PART III

Cleanroom Development

Current Practice in Cleanroom Development

Cleanroom Development treats software specification, design, and verification as an activity that is fully characterized within mathematical function theory. Hailong Mao explicated the formal syntax and semantics of Box Structure theory and illuminated many technical details (see "Evolving practice in Cleanroom development"). While many adaptations and extensions of Mills' ideas have been proposed, the current state of Cleanroom development practice is substantially as given in his original presentations of the Box Structure Method.

- "Box-structured information systems" (Mills, Linger, and Hevner, 1987) is a synopsis of a book on the Box Structure Method by the same authors. *Principles of Information Systems Analysis and Design* (Academic Press, 1986) was the first full presentation of the Box Structure Method. An earlier book, *Structured Programming: Theory and Practice* (Linger, Mills, and Witt, Addison Wesley, 1979) was an elegant mathematical presentation of the function-theoretical basis for the Box Structure Method.
- "Stepwise refinement and verification in box-structured systems" (Mills, 1988) is a recapitulation of the Box Structure Method in algorithmic form. This treatment also addresses technical issues concerning state boxes. A complete example of the application of Box Structures to real-time software is presented in the classic buoy problem.
- "Correctness verification: alternative to structural software testing" (Dyer and Kouchakdjian, 1990) reports the results of a study in which quality and productivity indices were compared for two defect removal strategies: correctness verification and structural testing. Quality was measured in terms of the percentage of total defects found. Productivity was measured by comparing the number of correctness

verification steps required for a design segment with the number of structural tests that would be required for the segment (making the liberal assumption that the periods of time required for a verification step and a structural test are about the same). Correctness verification proved to be superior to structural testing on measures of both quality and productivity.

- "Reuse and Cleanroom" (Karlsson, 1993) presents an adaptation of the Cleanroom process to maximize reuse. Object-oriented analysis is used in the initial specification phase to capture the reuse opportunities. The modifications in the classical Cleanroom process are intended to accommodate variability in requirements (problems) while leveraging generality in designs (solutions).

- "Six-sigma software using Cleanroom software engineering techniques" (Head, 1994) describes a successful project at Hewlett-Packard. This report is most interesting because of its focus on verification. Whereas many who contemplate Cleanroom want to hold back on functional verification because it is "too mathematical," the HP project reports on both the practicality and rewards of a strong verification effort.

7 Box-structured Information Systems

H. D. MILLS, R. C. LINGER, AND
A. R. HEVNER

INTRODUCTION

Since their inception, information systems have been used in government and business, but research and development in information systems have increased dramatically since the advent of the computer some thirty years ago. As a result, a recognizable discipline of Information Systems is emerging in business and in university curricula. However, Information Systems is still a young field in terms of intellectual growth and development. Even with all the current excitement and progress, there is still a lot to discover. The search for fundamental ideas and deep simplicities takes time.

Structures and data flows

The revolution that changed trial-and-error computer programming into software engineering was triggered by Dijkstra's idea of structured programming.[1] Structured programming cleared a control flow jungle that had grown unchecked for twenty years in dealing with more and more complex software problems. It replaced that control flow jungle with the astonishing assertion that software of any complexity whatsoever could be designed with just three basic control structures – sequence (begin–end), alternation (if–then–else), and iteration (while–do) – which could be nested over and over in a hierarchical structure (the structure of structured programming). The benefits of structured programming to the manage-

© 1987 International Business Machines Corporation. Reprinted, with permission, from *IBM Systems Journal*, vol. 26, no. 4, 1987, pp. 395–413.

ment of large projects are immediate. The work can be structured and progress measured in a top-down development in a direct way.

Even so, information systems development is much more than software development. The operations of a business involve all kinds of data that are transmitted, stored, and processed in all kinds of ways. The total data processing of a business is defined by the activities of all of its people and computers, as they interact with one another and with customer, vendor, and government personnel and computers outside the business. In a large company, it is a massively parallel operation with many thousands of interactions going on simultaneously. Information systems are called on to automate more and more of the information processing in business – in many cases these systems are required for survival in a competitive environment. And for these systems, a complete description of their data operations and uses leads to a data flow jungle that is even more tangled and arcane than the control flow jungle of software.

We will replace that data flow jungle with just three system structures that can be nested over and over in a hierarchical structure (the structure of box structures). Any information system – automatic, manual, or hybrid – can be described or designed in a hierarchy of these system structures step by step in a provable way. The benefits of box structures to the management of large projects are also immediate. The work can be structured and progress measured in top-down system development in a direct way.

State machines and data abstractions

The origins of these system structures are in the hierarchical state machine methodology of software engineering found in references 2, 3, and 4 and taught at the IBM Software Engineering Institute.[5,6] As discussed in the book by Mills, Linger, and Hevner,[7] this methodology was used in the New York Times Information Bank, as reported by Baker,[8,9] with remarkable results in reliability.[9] A very large-scale use of this methodology in the modernization of US Air Force satellite tracking and control systems has been reported by Jordano.[10]

The software counterparts of state machines have also been called data abstractions,[11,12] and more recently, software objects.[13] Their common feature is the presence of a state, represented in stored data, and accessed and altered by procedures that collectively define the state machine transition function. Since these data are accessed and altered by reusing the data abstraction or object, the hierarchy is a usage hierarchy, in the sense found in Parnas,[14] rather than a parts hierarchy. That is, data abstractions appear in the hierarchy at each occasion of use in the design, rather than as a part in the design.

This usage hierarchy of data abstractions cuts a Gordian knot for the effective dual decomposition of data flows and processes in information systems. Data flows are convenient heuristic starting points in information systems analysis, as developed in references 15 through 18, but require a mental discontinuity to move to information systems design. The problem is that data flows describe all that can possibly happen, whereas processes must deal with one data instance at a time and prescribe precisely what will happen at each such instance. Each use of a data abstraction is an instance of data flow through a process, which provides for storage in its state as well. And the collective effects of the usage of the data abstraction throughout a hierarchy are summarized by a data flow through the process. Data abstractions have proved useful in software engineering in several specific languages and systems, as in CLU,[19] VDM,[20,21] HDM,[22] Larch,[23] and object-oriented design.[13]

Box structures and data abstractions

The box structure methodology develops the usage hierarchy of data abstractions in a way especially suited for information systems development, in which the emphasis is jointly on mathematical rigor and management simplicity.[7] For this purpose, we not only need strong system development principles, but must also make these principles obvious in the methodology. We define three distinct forms for any data abstraction, namely, its *black box*, its *state machine*, and its *clear box*. A black box defines a data abstraction entirely in terms of external behavior, in transitions from stimuli to responses. A state machine defines a data abstraction in terms of transitions from a stimulus and internal state to a response and new internal state. A clear box defines a data abstraction in terms of a procedure that accesses the internal state and possibly calls on other black boxes. This recursion of black boxes with clear boxes that call on other black boxes defines a usage hierarchy that supports important principles for system development.

In the next section of this chapter we summarize the principal concepts of the box structure methodology and explain their mathematical foundations. In the subsequent section, box structure hierarchies are defined, and the system development principles of referential transparency, state migration, transaction closure, and common services are described. Finally, we discuss the benefits of these structures in managing a spiral system development process.

BOX STRUCTURES

The behavior of any information system (or subsystem) can be rigorously described in three distinct box structure forms previously mentioned – the black box, state machine, and clear box of the system. We first define each of these structures and then show relationships among them.

Black box behavior

The *black box* gives an external view of a system or subsystem that accepts stimuli, and for each stimulus, S, produces a response, R (which may be null), before accepting the next stimulus. A diagram of a black box is shown in figure 7.1. The system of the diagram could be a hand calculator, a personal computer, an accounts receivable system, or even a manual work procedure that accepts stimuli from the environment and produces responses one by one. As the name implies, a black box description of a system omits all details of internal structure and operations and deals solely with the behavior that is visible to its user in terms of stimuli and responses. Any black box response is uniquely determined by its stimulus history.

For example, an interactive workstation is a computer system that accepts keystrokes, one by one, and returns a new screen with each keystroke. Most keystrokes change the screen in small ways, say, by adding or deleting a character, but some keystrokes bring up entirely new screens, say, by an enter key or a menu choice. Each such keystroke is a stimulus for the black box. The user need have no idea of the internal structure – that some screens are created locally, some indirectly by remote computers, etc. The workstation behaves as a black box for the user.

The idea of describing a system as a black box is useful for analyzing the system from the user's point of view. Only system externals are visible; no system state or procedure is described. The mathematical semantics of black box behavior is a function from system stimulus histories to system responses. A black box is specified by its traces.[24,25] In fact, Parnas uses the term *black box* to motivate the study of traces.[24]

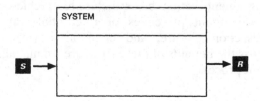

Figure 7.1   A black box diagram.

State machine behavior

The *state machine* gives an intermediate system view that defines an internal system state, namely an abstraction of the data stored from stimulus to stimulus. It can be established mathematically that every system described by a black box has a state machine description. (Consider each stimulus history to be a state.) A state machine diagram is shown in figure 7.2. The state machine part called Machine is a black box that accepts as its stimulus both the external stimulus and the internal state and produces as a response both the external response and a new internal state which replaces the old state. The role of the state machine is to open up the black box description of a system one step by making its state visible. State machine behavior can be described in the transition formula

(stimulus, old state) → (response, new state)

Much of the work in formal specification methods for software applies directly to specification of the state machine system view. These methods, such as those presented in the literature, [11,12,26,27] specify the required properties of programs and abstract data types in axiomatic and algebraic models. The models represent behavior without presenting implementation details.

For information systems, however, we believe that direct descriptions are often sufficient – that indirect axiomatic and algebraic methods of describing data abstractions tend to obscure the essential simplicity of

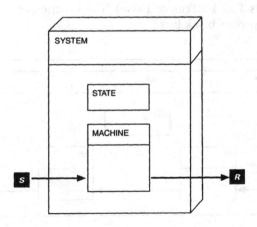

Figure 7.2   A state machine diagram.

state machines. Also, the conceptual work required to derive axioms or algebras for a complete system state can require deep research itself. (For an example of problems associated with the axiomatization of even a simple data abstraction, see Ferrentino and Mills.[2])

Clear box behavior

The *clear box*, as the name suggests, opens up the state machine description of a system one more step in an internal view that describes the system processing of the stimulus and state. The processing is described in terms of three possible sequential structures, namely sequence, alternation, and iteration, and a concurrent structure. Figure 7.3 shows a clear box sequence structure with two internal subsystems represented as black boxes: each accepts both a stimulus and a state and produces both a response and a new state. In the sequence structure, the clear box stimulus is the stimulus to black box M1, whose response becomes the stimulus to M2, whose response is the response of the clear box. At this point, a hierarchical, top-down description can be repeated for each of the embedded black boxes at the next lower level of description. Each black box is described by a state machine, then by a clear box containing even smaller black boxes, and so on.

Figures 7.4, 7.5, and 7.6 show, respectively, the alternation, iteration, and concurrent clear box structures. The internal machines, Mi, can be expanded at lower levels of description in a box structure hierarchy. In alternation and iteration clear boxes, the condition C (denoted by a diamond) is a special black box that accesses the stimulus and old state to return responses T or F (True or False). The function of C is to direct the stimulus to the proper black box.

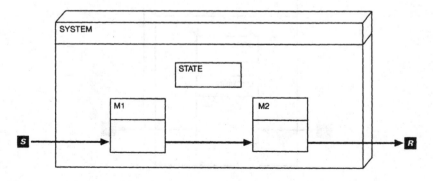

Figure 7.3 The clear box sequence structure.

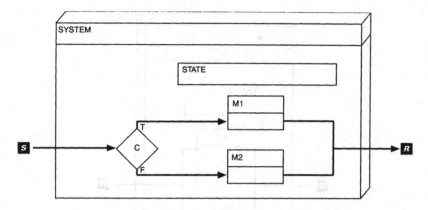

Figure 7.4   The clear box alternation structure.

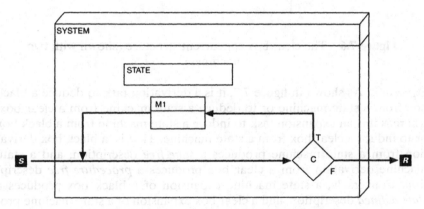

Figure 7.5   The clear box iteration structure.

The clear box is an essential step of system description that is lacking in many information systems development methods. It specifies the procedurality that connects the usage of subsystems to be described at the next lower level in the box structure hierarchy. This explicit connection supports the principle of referential transparency, to be discussed in the next section.

Box structure derivation and expansion

The relationships among the black box, state machine, and clear box views of a system or subsystem precisely define the tasks of *derivation* and

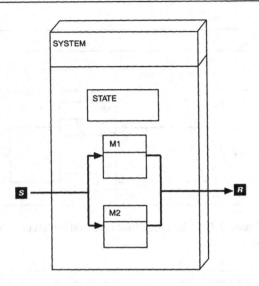

Figure 7.6   The clear box concurrent structure (shown with two machines).

expansion. As shown in figure 7.7, it is a derivation task to deduce a black box from a state machine or to deduce a state machine from a clear box, whereas it is an expansion task to induce a state machine from a black box or to induce a clear box from a state machine. That is, a black box derivation from a state machine produces a *state-free* description, and a state machine derivation from a clear box produces a *procedure-free* description. Conversely, a state machine expansion of a black box produces a *state-defined* description, and a clear box expansion of a state machine produces a *procedure-defined* description. The expansion step does not produce a unique product because there are many state machines that behave like a given black box and many clear boxes that behave like a given state machine. The derivation step does produce a unique product because there is only one black box that behaves like a given state machine and only one state machine that behaves like a given clear box.

In summary, black box, state machine, and clear box expansions provide behaviorally equivalent views of an information system or subsystem at increasing levels of internal visibility. This equivalence relationship is depicted in figure 7.8.

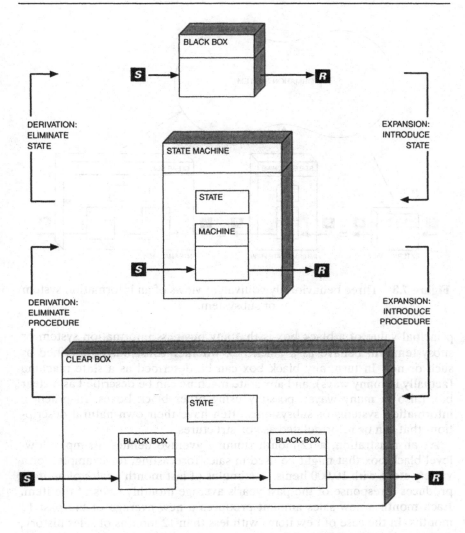

Figure 7.7 Box structure derivation and expansion (shown with sequence clear box).

A box structure illustration

Although the concept of box structures is easy to grasp, its use in actual business systems requires business knowledge. In fact, box structures provide forms in which to describe business knowledge in a standard way. The

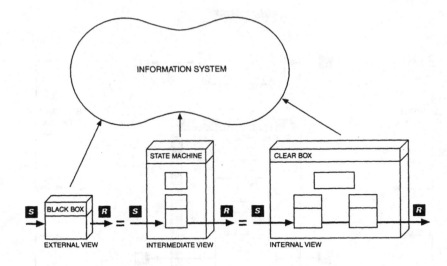

Figure 7.8   Three behaviorally equivalent views of an information system or subsystem.

principal value of a black box is that any business information system or subsystem will behave as a black box whether consciously described as such or not. In turn, any black box can be described as a state machine (actually in many ways), and any state machine can be described as a clear box (also in many ways), possibly using other black boxes. In practice, information systems or subsystems often have their own natural descriptions that can be reformulated as box structures.

As an illustration, a 12-month running average defines a simple, low-level black box that might be used in sales forecasting, for example, for a variety store with 10,000 items. A stimulus of last month's sales of an item produces a response of the past year's average monthly sales of the item. Each month a new sales amount produces a new average of the past 12 months. In the case of new items with less than 12 months of sales history, the response can be the average of sales to date. If i is the age of an item in months, then the number of months to average is *min* $(i,12)$, the minimum of i and 12, no matter how long the sales history is.

Figure 7.9 shows the Running Average black box where for an item of age i, $S.1 = S$ is last month's sales, $S.2$ is the next previous month's sales, and so on. The symbol ":=" means that the term on the left side (R) is assigned the value of the expression on the right side.

One possible state machine with the same behavior as this black box would store the previous *min* $(i,12)$ monthly sales $S.1, S.2, \ldots$ in state vari-

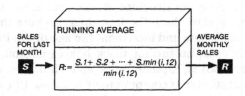

Figure 7.9 Running Average black box.

ables *S1*, *S2*, ..., and item age *i* in state variable *I*. Then, with each new stimulus *S*, there is sufficient information to calculate the response and update the state. The state variable *I* must be initialized, say to 1, and incremented with each stimulus. The state variables *S1*, *S2*, ... will be initialized as the first 12 months of sales materialize.

Figure 7.10 shows the corresponding Running Average state machine. The multiple assignments are to be understood as concurrent. That is, all expressions on the right sides use the data available at the beginning of the transition, not data computed in assignments above them.

Note a distinction between *S.1*, *S.2*, ..., which are monthly sales and *S1*, *S2*, ..., which are state variables. The values are the same (at the end of each transition), but unless *S.1*, *S.2*, ... are recorded in *S1*, *S2*, ..., they will be lost to the state machine because it does not access stimulus history, as does the black box. The assignments made to *S2*, *S3*, ... before *S1*, *S2*, ... are initialized reference undefined values, but do no harm because they are not used in *R*.

A clear box will describe how the response and new state are computed

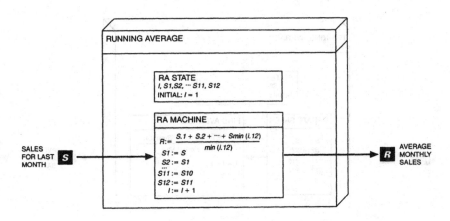

Figure 7.10 Running Average state machine.

in a sequential or concurrent structure of other black box uses. One possible design is to first update the sales data, then compute the running average from the new state data and increment the age of the item, as shown in figure 7.11. In this case, no further black box expansion will be needed because both black boxes, Update Sales and Find Average, require no more than their last stimuli to compute their response [they can be defined as mathematical functions from stimuli (not stimulus histories) to responses]. Of course, the stimuli on which they operate include the state variables of Running Average.

Note that many other state machine and clear box designs could have been chosen to implement the Running Average black box. For example, after the value of I exceeds 11, the state data could be stored as monthly sales values divided by 12. The running average would then be found by adding all the state data.

A Running Average black box is a simple sales forecaster. However, if sales are seasonal or have definite trends, a more suitable black box may be required. Such a forecaster will differ in details, but can still be described in a black box/state machine/clear box structure.

Box structure verifications

In the foregoing example, we began with an informal description of a black box ("12-month running average"), then formalized it into an assignment from stimulus histories to responses,

$$R := \frac{S.1 + S.2 + \ldots + Smin(i,12)}{min(i,12)},$$

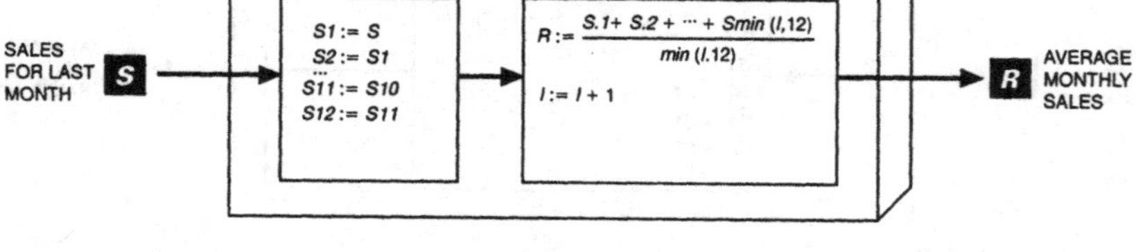

Figure 7.11   Running Average clear box.

accounting for new items with less than 12 months of sales history. Next, we expanded this black box into one of many possible state machines, as in figure 7.10, then expanded the state machine into one of many possible clear boxes, as in figure 7.11. These two expansions were simple and direct, because the black box itself is quite simple. Even so, these designs are possibly faulty, and in more complex cases the probability of faulty designs increases, even with the greatest of care.

Fortunately, there is a direct and rigorous way to check these designs: Independently derive the state machine of the final clear box expansion and compare it with the intended state machine designed above. If the intended state machine is recovered by derivation, the expansion into the clear box has been verified. Next, we can independently derive the black box from the verified state machine and compare it with the intended black box formulated initially.

We call this rederivation and comparison process a *box structure verification*. It works on the same principle used in division to check that the division has been done correctly, that is, a multiplication of quotient and divisor added to the remainder to independently derive the dividend.

Box structure verification defines an objective, rigorous process for self-checking and peer inspections. Even though people are fallible, this fallibility can be reduced dramatically by such inspections based on an objective, rigorous foundation.

In this example, beginning with the clear box of figure 7.11, the first task is to eliminate the procedurality – in this case the sequence of Update Sales and Find Average – to obtain the black box machine of the derived state machine. In Find Average, the expression for R references $S1, \ldots,$ $Smin (I, 12)$, which were updated in Update Sales, where $S1$ was assigned S, $S2$ assigned $S1, \ldots,$ and $S12$ assigned $S11$. Therefore, in terms of the stimulus and original state at the beginning of the transition, the assignment to R is

$$R := \frac{S + S1 + \ldots + Smin(I - 1,11)}{min(I,12)} ,$$

Also, in Find Average, the expression for I references only I which is not changed in Update Sales, so this assignment remains as before.

$$I := I + 1$$

Since Update Sales is the first black box used, its assignments are from the stimulus and original state, so those assignments remain the same. The result of collecting all these assignments into a single black box machine results in the derived state machine shown in figure 7.12.

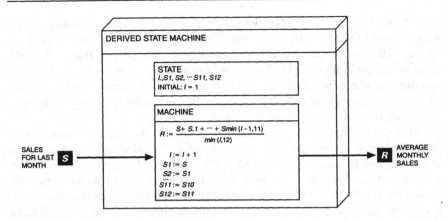

Figure 7.12   Derived state machine.

Now we can compare the derived state machine of figure 7.12 with the Running Average state machine as shown in figure 7.10. They are not identical, line by line, but they differ only in the placement of the line $I := I + 1$ in the multiple assignments. But since these multiple assignments are concurrent, the order of placement of $I := I + 1$ has no effect on the responses of these two machines. So they are identical in effect in returning a response and updating the state of the state machines. With this derivation and comparison, the Running Average clear box of figure 7.11 has been verified to be a correct (and complete) expansion of the Running Average state machine of figure 7.10.

Now that the Running Average clear box has been verified, we can turn our attention to the verification of the Running Average state machine, by the independent derivation of its black box, to be compared with the original Running Average black box of figure 7.9.

Each value in the state of the Running Average state machine is the cumulative result of its initial value and all subsequent transitions to date. Our objective is to determine the value assigned to R, which is

$$R := \frac{S + S1 + \ldots + Smin(I - 1, 11)}{min(I, 12)},$$

not in terms of stimulus and state data, but in terms of stimulus history data instead.

First, at age i of the item, we observe that $I = i$ at the beginning of the transition, because at age 1, $I = 1$ by initialization, and I is incremented by 1 at each transition. Therefore, at age i, by direct substitution of i for I in the assignment above,

$$R := \frac{S + S1 + \ldots + Smin(i - 1,11)}{min(i,12)},$$

Furthermore, at the beginning of the transition at age i, the state variables $S1$, $S2$, ..., $Smin$ $(i - 1,11)$ will contain the sales values $S.2$, $S.3$, ..., $Smin$ $(i,12)$ for the following reason.

At age 1 of the item, all values of $S1$, $S2$, ..., $S12$ are uninitialized, but $S1 = S.1$ after the transition at age 1. At age 2, $S2$ is assigned the value of $S1$, which is the value of $S.1$ at age 1, but is renamed $S.2$ at age 2, so $S2 = S.2$, and $S1$ is assigned $S.1$. Continuing, at age i, $S1$, $S2$, ..., $Smin$ $(i - 1,11)$ are assigned $S.1$, $S.2$, ..., $Smin$ $(i - 1,11)$ after the transition. But at the beginning of the next transition, these sales values will have all aged one month. So, in fact, at the beginning of the transition at age i, the state variables $S1$, $S2$, ..., $Smin$ $(i - 1,11)$ will contain the sales values $S.2$, $S.3$, ..., $Smin$ $(i,12)$.

Finally, we observe that $S = S.1$, the last sales value, so we can complete the substitution of sales values for state values in the calculations for R in the assignment above, to get the derived black box shown in figure 7.13.

The derived black box of figure 7.13 is identical to the Running Average black box of figure 7.9. With this derivation and comparison, the Running Average state machine of figure 7.10 has been shown to be a correct (and complete) expansion of the Running Average black box of figure 7.9.

The joint result of these two verifications is the verification that the Running Average clear box of figure 7.11 is a correct (and complete) expansion of the Running Average black box of figure 7.9.

INFORMATION SYSTEMS DEVELOPMENT WITH BOX STRUCTURES

The box structure concepts presented in the previous section can be expanded into a complete methodology for information systems develop-

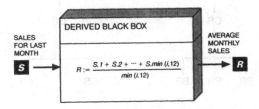

Figure 7.13 Derived black box.

ment. The first step is to describe an information system as a multilevel usage hierarchy wherein each node is a box structure expansion of an independent system part. We then demonstrate how fundamental principles of system development can be applied in the box structure hierarchy.

Box structure hierarchies

A box structure hierarchy, as shown in figure 7.14, provides an effective means of control for managing and developing complex information systems. By identifying black box subsystems in higher levels of the system, state data and processing are decentralized into lower-level box structures. Each subsystem becomes a well-defined, independent module in the overall system. Although the progression from black box to state machine to clear box at any point in the hierarchy may appear to be a triplication of effort, this is not the case. Each subsystem can be initially described in its most natural form, with the other forms determined as necessary for analysis and design.

The concept of hierarchies is crucial in system and program development. Top-down programming is based on the principle of stepwise refinement of program modules in a hierarchy. Similarly, usage hierarchies of system modules allow a top-down discipline of system specification and implementation.

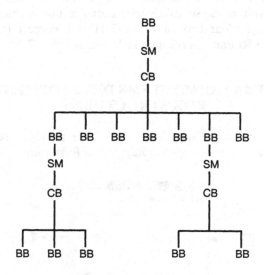

Figure 7.14   A box structure hierarchy.

The box structure hierarchy, in particular, provides for the systematic application of four essential principles of system development. These principles, called referential transparency, transaction closure, state migration, and common services, are discussed next.

Referential transparency

The box structure hierarchy provides a formal method for defining system modules while preserving referential transparency between levels. Referential transparency is a guiding principle for forming system hierarchies.

Principle of referential transparency
In the delegation of any system part for design and implementation, all requirements should be specified explicitly and independently, so that no further communication or coordination is logically required to complete the system part.

The principle of referential transparency provides a crisp discipline for management delegation and assignment of responsibility. The lack of referential transparency can lead to management nightmares where nothing works and no one is to blame.

The kinds of system parts required to make the principle possible are data abstractions. The specification of such a part must be defined at the stimulus/response level (i.e., black box) for each access to the part, and account for the effect of any previous access to the part. Popularized system development methods that use plausible ideas such as HIPO charts,[28] structure charts,[15] or data flow diagrams[16] can still lose vital information and thus make referential transparency impossible. It takes the right kinds of system parts to defer details without losing them.

The clear box view of a system provides the key abstraction that ensures referential transparency in a box structure hierarchy. The procedurality of the clear box makes precise the control flow and data flow into and out of all embedded black boxes. At the next level of the system hierarchy, each black box can be designed and implemented independently of its surroundings in a system, so accountability is achieved in the delegation. Flexibility is achieved in the delegation because a black box can be redesigned with different state machines and clear boxes as required. As long as the new black box behavior is identical to that of the original, the rest of the system will operate exactly as before. Such black box replacement may be required or desirable for purposes of better performance, changing hardware, or even changing from manual to automatic operations.

When designers and implementers are required to discuss and coordinate details of separate parts after their assignment of responsibilities, gamesmanship becomes an important part of a day's work, in addition to system development. It's only sensible, with ill-defined responsibilities, to cover one's bets and tracks with activities and documents designed as much to protect as to illuminate.

Even with the best of intentions, extensive communication and coordination with respect to design and implementation details opens up many more opportunities for misunderstandings and errors. Such errors are always written off as human fallibilities (nobody is perfect), but errors of unnecessary communication and coordination should be charged to the methodologies that require them, not to the people forced to do the unnecessary communication and coordination.

Transaction closure

Principle of transaction closure
The transactions (transitions) of a system or system part should be sufficient for the acquisition and preservation of all its state data, and its state data should be sufficient for the completion of all its transactions. In particular, system integrity as well as user function should be considered in achieving transaction closure.

The principle of transaction closure can forestall many surprises and afterthoughts in specifying and designing systems. A common mistake for amateur (and not so amateur) analysts and designers is concentrating so much on primary user transactions that the secondary transactions to make primary user transactions available and reliable become awkward or impossible. For example, if system security or recovery requirements are not identified up front, an ideal user system (imagined in a perfect world of hardware and people) may end up with data structures that make security or recovery difficult or impossible. Therefore, transactions provided for security and recovery need to be defined as early as user transactions, and as carefully.

The principle of transaction closure defines a systematic, iterative specification process, in ensuring that a sufficient set of transactions is identified to acquire and preserve a sufficient set of state data. The iteration begins with the transactions for the primary users, and the state data needed for those transactions, then considers the transactions required for the acquisition and preservation of those state data, then identifies the state data needed for those transactions, and so on. Eventually, no more transactions will be required in an iteration, and transaction closure will have been achieved.

The concept of system integrity plays a special role in transaction closure. Transaction closure assuming perfect hardware and people is not enough; many transactions can only be defined once specific hardware and people are identified for system use. For example, an information system using an operating system with automatic checkpoint and restart facilities will not need checkpoint and restart transactions, but one without them will. The problem of system security provides a classic example. Many operating systems and database systems in wide use today cannot be retrofitted for high-level multilevel security because they were conceived and specified before such security requirements were identified.

In simplest terms, information systems integrity is the property of the system fulfilling its function while handling all of the system issues inherent in its implementation. For example, systems are expected to be correct, secure, reliable, and capable of handling their applications. These requirements may not be explicitly stated by managers, users, or operators, but it is clear that the designed system must have provisions for such properties. Questions of system integrity are largely independent of the function of the system, but are dependent on its means of implementation, manual or automatic. Manual implementations must deal with the fallibilities of people, beginning with their very absence or presence (so backup personnel may be required), that include limited ability and speed in doing arithmetic, limited memory capability for detailed facts, lapses in performance from fatigue or boredom, and so on. Automatic implementation must deal with the fallibilities of computer hardware and software, beginning with their total lack of common sense, that include limited processing and storage capabilities (much larger than for people, but still limited), hardware and software errors, security weaknesses, and so on.

The process of transaction closure is essential in the development of a top-level black box for any system. A useful beginning of this search for a top-level black box begins with the most obvious users of the system but seldom ends there. These most obvious users often interact with the system daily, even minute by minute, in entering and accessing data (for example, a clerk in an airline reservations system). Usually, however, the data they use are provided in part by other users who enter and access data less frequently, such as those entering flight availability information. And other users even more distant from the obvious users enter and access data even less frequently (for example, users who add route schedule information). All the while, an entirely different group, the operators of the system, is entering and accessing system control data that affect the users in terms of more or less access to the system because of limited capacity or availability.

The top-level black box must accommodate the transactions of all these users and operators, not just the most obvious ones. A cross-check can be made between the top-level black box and its top-level state machine. Every item of data in the top-level state must have been loaded with the original system or acquired by previous black box transactions. Are there any items not so loaded or acquired? It is easy, in concentrating on one set of transactions, to assume the existence of data to carry them out. A comprehensive scrutiny of these needed data items can discover such unwarranted assumptions early.

State migration

Principle of state migration

System data should be decentralized to the smallest system parts that do not require duplicating data updates. If, for geographic or security reasons, system data should be decentralized to smaller system parts, the system should be designed to ensure correctly duplicated data updates.

The principle of state migration eliminates the need for instant decisions (often faulty) about how data should be structured and how the data should be stored in a system. Instead, it permits the definition of system data at a conceptual level, and permits the concrete form and location of the data to be worked out interactively with the system design and decomposition into system parts. As better design ideas emerge, system data can be relocated effectively to accommodate such ideas, all the while maintaining correct function as required in the system transactions.

When system data need to be decentralized to smaller system parts than allowed by the principle of state migration, the smallest system defined by this part must be redesigned to accommodate correct duplicate updating. In this case, it is a different system and should be recognized as such from the outset. The problem of incorrect updating of duplicated data is a well-known burden of faulty system designs.

System data in a box structure hierarchy are distributed into the states of their component box structures. State migration through the box structure hierarchy is a powerful tool in managing system development. It permits the placement of state data at the most effective level for its use. Downward migration may be possible when black boxes are identified in a clear box; state data used solely within the state machine expansion of one black box can be migrated to that state machine at the next lower level of the hierarchy. The isolation of state data at proper levels in the system hierarchy provides important criteria for the design of database and file systems. Upward migration is possible when duplicate state data are updated in identical ways in several places in the hierarchy. These data can be migrated up to the common parent state machine for consistent update at one location.

Common services

Principle of common services

System parts with multiple uses should be considered for definition as common services. A corollary principle is to create as many opportunities as possible for reusability within and between system parts.

Operating systems, data management and database systems, network and terminal control systems are all illustrations of common services between systems. It is axiomatic in today's technology to seek as much reuse of common services as possible to multiply productivity and increase reliability. These common services must satisfy the principle of referential transparency in their use, so their specifications are as important as their implementations. On a smaller scale, effective system design seeks and creates commonality of services and identifies system parts for widespread multiple uses within a system.

When several black boxes of a clear box expansion access or alter a common state part, it is generally inadvisable to migrate the state part to those lower levels. But it may be advisable to define a new box structure hierarchy to provide access to or to alter this common state part for these several black boxes. Such a new box structure must be invoked in the clear box expansions of these black boxes. This new box structure thereby provides a common service to these several black boxes. Such a common service structure in effect encapsulates a state part, by providing the only means for accessing or altering it in the box structure hierarchy.

State encapsulation requires a new box structure whose state will contain the common state part and whose transactions will provide common access to that state part for multiple users. In essence, state encapsulation permits state migration to be carried out in another form, with the provision that the only possible access to the migrated state is by invoking transactions of the new box structure that encapsulates it.

Common service box structures are ubiquitous in information systems. For example, any database system behaves as a common service box structure to the people and programs that use it. As a simple illustration, consider a clear box expansion of a master file update state machine. Such a clear box would contain a number of black boxes which operate on the master file, for example, to open, close, read, and write the file, as well as black boxes to access transaction files, directory and authorization information, etc. The master file of the clear box state cannot be migrated to these lower-level black boxes without duplication. However, the master file can be encapsulated, without duplication, in a new box structure that provides the required transactions to open, close, read, and write the file. These transactions can then be invoked from the original box structure hierarchy as required. The new box structure can be designed to ensure the integrity of the master file and all access directed to it. In fact, when the master file is migrated to this common service, it is protected from faulty access by the box structure in an effective way.

THE SPIRAL DEVELOPMENT PROCESS

In information systems development, the box structure methodology defines a set of limited, time-phased *activities* to decompose and manage the work required. A formal *development plan* defines and schedules the specific activities required to address a specific problem. The development plan represents long-range planning for information system development; the activity plans represent short-range planning. As each activity is completed, the entire development plan is updated to account for the current situation.

Although the activities of a development plan are always specific to a particular system development problem, they can be categorized into three general classes: *investigation*, *specification*, and *implementation*. An investigation is a fact-finding, exploratory study, usually to assess the feasibility of an information system. For example, such a study may define the black box behavior of a projected information system. A specification is more focused to define a specific information system and its benefits to the business. For example, a specification activity may result in definition of state data and high-level clear boxes of a projected information system. An implementation converts a specification into an operational system. For example, implementation may elaborate the black boxes of high-level clear boxes into box structure hierarchies of their own, eventually arriving at human and computer procedures in user guides and software, respectively.

The system development spiral

Many current methods of information systems development reflect appearances rather than principles. One of the obvious appearances in information systems is the system development life cycle. It is certainly apparent that information systems go through various stages of conception, specification, design, implementation, operation, maintenance, modification, and so on. But although these terms are suggestive, real information systems do not pass through these stages in any simple or straightforward way.

In contrast to a fixed life cycle, the box-structured system development process is defined by a set of time-phased activities that are initiated and managed dynamically on the basis of the outcome of previous activities in the development. This progression of activities is conveniently represented in a flexible *system development spiral* that reflects the actual progress of a development effort in terms of box structure analysis and design tasks.

The time-phased set of activities in a spiral can be strictly sequential or may have concurrent parts. If a development is sequential, it can be pictured, in prospect or retrospect, as shown in figure 7.15. In this example the activity sequence is a straightforward progression of

- investigation
- specification
- implementation

with a management approval to enter each activity and to end the entire development. Such a progression for developing a system is ideal, but is not necessarily possible or even desirable.

It may not be possible because the business problem is too complex and needs several investigation activities to arrive at a solution. It may not be possible because the system development problem is too complex and needs several specification and implementation activities in an incremental development. It may not be desirable because the business problem is too acute and a less-than-best implementation is called for as soon as possible. It may not be desirable because the happy outcome of the first investigation activity is the discovery of an existing implementation to meet the business need.

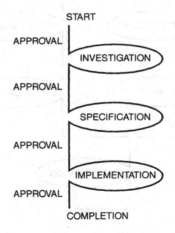

Figure 7.15 A system development spiral.

If a development is concurrent, it can be pictured in a network of spirals, as in the example of figure 7.16. In this network, activity dependencies are shown by the approval lines ("A" lines here). For example, Investigation 1 enables both Specification 1 and Investigation 2, whereas both Implementation 1 and Specification 2 must be completed before Implementation 2 can be started. The specific network pictured might, for example, represent the concurrent development of a database system (Implementation 1) and an application system (Implementation 2) that uses it.

Managing spiral development

The system development process generates limited, time-phased activities of investigation, specification, and implementation that must be managed. Formal stages of *planning, performance,* and *evaluation* in each activity define an orderly process for this management. The box structure method-

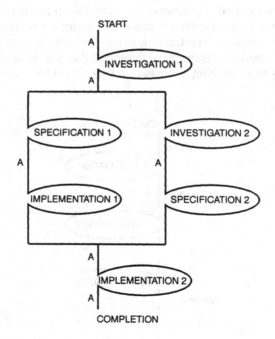

Figure 7.16   A system development spiral with concurrent activities.

ology provides a great deal of commonality across these activities for the analysis and design work that is required. The management problems are also very similar. As the names imply, the most challenging stages for management are planning and evaluation, whereas the performance stage is the most challenging for technical professionals.

Planning
There are three basic results from the planning stage of any activity:

(1) *Activity objective.* A statement of what the activity is to produce.
(2) *Activity statement of work.* A statement of how the activity will achieve its objective.
(3) *Activity schedule.* An assignment of work items in the Statement of Work to professionals together with agreed-on completion dates.

With such a plan, each member of the entire development team understands the objectives, Statement of Work, and the individual responsibilities for making good on the work objectives and schedule. Such a plan not only requires the agreement of the professionals, but also requires their direct participation in the planning process. But the planning process must be led by managers to address the proper questions and problems for the activity in the overall development plan.

Performance
If plans are well made, performance is focused and predictable. The management job in performance is to assess and track progress against the Statement of Work and schedules. Management must identify unexpected problems and help professionals decide how to meet them, and must identify unexpected windfalls in solutions that can free up people and resources. It is here that good understandings and agreements on assignments and schedules pay off.

Evaluation
Evaluation is both a closing out of one activity and a basis for selecting and commencing one or more following activities. The objectives and results of performance can be compared and related to the business and its situation. Even if objectives are not met, the lessons learned may be useful. If the objectives are met, so much the better, and the expected next activities can be initiated. In particular, the evaluation stage is the point where the development plan for future activities can be assessed and modified.

These activities and stages can be organized in tabular form, as shown in table 7.1, which indicates typical tasks in systems development. A detailed discussion of these tasks is found in Mills et al.[7]

Table 7.1 Stages in activities: typical tasks

Activities	Stages		
	Planning	Performance	Evaluation
Investigation	Activity objective Statement of work Scheduling	Business process and objectives Requirements analysis System prototype	Feasibility assessment Review and acceptance Development plan update
Specification	Activity objective Statement of work Scheduling	Systems analysis and design Operations analysis and design	Design verification Review and acceptance Development plan update
Implementation	Activity objective Statement of work Scheduling	Resource acquisition Systems integration Operations education	System testing Review and acceptance Development plan update

CONCLUDING REMARKS

The box structure methodology provides a rigorous approach for information systems analysis and design. The black box, state machine, and clear box present three different, yet complementary, views of an information system and any of its subsystems. The methodology provides formal techniques for relating these structures and constructing box structure hierarchies.

The correctness of box structure designs can be verified in stepwise fashion from clear boxes by systematically deriving their actual state machine and black box behaviors, and comparing them to their intended behaviors.

Box structures permit application of specific principles of information systems development that help ensure complete and well-structured designs. Referential transparency permits precise delegation of black box expansions once their clear box connections have been designed. Transaction closure ensures complete system behavior for users and complete state definitions for developers. State migration avoids data flow jungles in systems by decentralizing data storage and access into box structure subsystems. Common service design permits migration of widely used data into new box structure hierarchies that provide all required data access.

Box structures permit a flexible management process of spiral development, in contrast to a fixed life cycle. Spiral development is characterized by steps of investigation, specification, and implementation of box structures that can be dynamically sequenced and managed to best capitalize on the current progress and remaining resources of a development effort.

References

1 O. Dahl, E. Dijkstra, and C. A. R. Hoare, *Structured Programming*, Academic Press Inc., New York (1972).
2 A. B. Ferrentino and H. D. Mills, "State machines and their semantics in software engineering," *Proceedings of COMPSAC 1977*, Chicago (November 1977), pp. 242–251.
3 R. C. Linger, H. D. Mills, and B. I. Witt, *Structured Programming: Theory and Practice*, Addison-Wesley Publishing Company, Inc., Reading, MA (1979).
4 H. D. Mills, D. O'Neill, R. C. Linger, M. Dyer, and R. E. Quinnan, "The management of software engineering," *IBM Systems Journal* 19, No. 4, 414–477 (1980).
5 M. B. Carpenter and H. K. Hallman, "Quality emphasis at IBM's Software Engineering Institute," *IBM Systems Journal* 24, No. 2, 121–133 (1985).
6 M. Schaul, "Designing using software engineering principles: Overview of an educational program," *Proceedings 8th International Conference on Software Engineering*, London (1985), pp. 201–208.

7   H. D. Mills, R. C. Linger, and A. Hevner, *Principles of Information Systems Analysis and Design*, Academic Press, Inc., New York (1986).

8   F. T. Baker, "Chief programmer team management of production programming," *IBM Systems Journal* **11**, No. 1, 56–73 (1972).

9   F. T. Baker, "System quality through structured programming," *AFIPS Conference Proceedings Fall Joint Computer Conference* **41**, 339–343 (1972).

10   A. J. Jordano. "DSM software architecture and development," *IBM Technical Directions* **10**, No. 3, 17–28 (1984).

11   D. Parnas, "A technique for software module specification with examples," *Communications of the ACM* **15**, No. 5, 330–336 (May 1972).

12   J. Guttag and J. Horning, "The algebraic specification of abstract data types," *Acta Informatica* **10** (1978).

13   G. Booch, "Object-oriented development," *IEEE Transactions on Software Engineering* **SE-12**, No. 2, 211–221 (February 1986).

14   D. L. Parnas, "Designing software for ease of extension and contraction," *IEEE Transactions on Software Engineering* **SE-5**, No. 3, 128–138 (March 1979).

15   E. Yourdon and L. Constantine. *Structured Design Fundamentals of a Discipline of Computer Programs and System Design*, 2nd Edition, Yourdon Press, New York (1978).

16   T. DeMarco, *Structured Analysis and System Specification*, Yourdon Press, New York (1979).

17   W. P. Stevens, *Using Structured Design*, John Wiley & Sons, Inc., New York (1981).

18   W. P. Stevens, "How data flow can improve application development productivity," *IBM Systems Journal* **21**, No. 2, 162–178 (1982).

19   B. Liskov, A. Snyder, R. Atkinson, and C. Schaffert, "Abstraction mechanisms in CLU," *Communications of the ACM* **20**, No. 8, 564–576 (August 1977).

20   D. Bjørner and C. Jones, "The Vienna Development Method: The Meta-Language," *Springer-Verlag Lecture Notes in Computer Science* **61**, Springer-Verlag, New York (1978).

21   D. Bjørner, "On the use of formal methods in software development," *Proceedings 9th International Conference on Software Engineering* (1987), pp. 17–29.

22   K. Levitt, P. Neumann, and L. Robinson, "The SRI Hierarchical Development Methodology and its application to the development of secure software," *Proceedings of Software Engineering Applications*, Capri (1980).

23   J. Guttag, J. Horning, and J. Wing, *Larch in Five Easy Pieces*, Technical Report, Digital Equipment Corporation Systems Research Center, Maynard, MA (1985).

24   D. L. Parnas and W. Bartussek, *Using Traces to Write Abstract Specifications for Software Modules*, UNC Report TR 77-012, University of North Carolina, Chapel Hill, NC 27514 (1977).

25   C. A. R. Hoare, "Some properties of predicate transformers," *Journal of the ACM* **25**, No. 3, 461–480 (July 1978).

26   B. Liskov and S. Zilles, "Specification techniques for data abstraction," *IEEE Transactions on Software Engineering* **SE-1**, No. 3, 114–126 (March 1975).

27 M. Shaw, "Abstraction techniques in modern programming languages," *IEEE Software* **1**, No. 4 (October 1984).
28 H. Katzen, *Systems Design and Documentation: An Introduction to the HIPO Method*, Van Nostrand Reinhold, New York (1976).

Further reading

R. Burstall and J. Goguen, "An informal introduction to specifications using CLEAR," in Boyer and Moore, editors, *The Correctness Problem in Computer Science*, Academic Press Inc., New York (1981).
L. Robinson and O. Roubine, *SPECIAL – A Specification and Assertion Language*, Technical Report CSL-46, Stanford Research Institute, Stanford, CA (1977).

8   Stepwise Refinement and Verification in Box-structured Systems

H. D. MILLS

INTRODUCTION

System design begins in problem domains, usually with considerable informality, and ends in computer domains in completely formal languages for programmers and users. Ideally, the system specification should be defined formally first, and the system designed accordingly. However, there are few systems of any size where this is practical. Even if a designer could do it, the sponsors and users would be hard pressed to understand the formal specification.

I propose that the formality of specifications and designs be developed together in box structures with many sponsor and user interfaces. Box structures allow the stepwise refinement and verification of hierarchical system designs from their specifications at formal and informal levels.

Long division in place notation is an example of a stepwise refinement and verification process that produces a quotient and remainder from a dividend and divisor. Each major step produces the next digit of the quotient by a creative estimate of its value followed by an immediate verification of its correctness. If the verification fails, a new estimate is provided and verified. The minor steps are digit-by-digit arithmetic operations with no further invention beyond estimating the next digit of the quotient. Using the fundamental mathematical discoveries that made long division possible, a skilled school child can solve problems beyond the capability of Euclid and Archimedes.

© 1988 IEEE. Reprinted, with permission, from *IEEE Computer*, vol. 21, no. 6, pp. 23–36, June 1988.

Box-structured system design[1] is a stepwise refinement and verification process that produces a system design from a specification. Such a system design is defined by a hierarchy of small design steps that permit the immediate verification of their correctness, just as the next digit can be verified immediately in long division. Three basic principles underlie the box-structured design process:

1   All data to be defined and stored in the design is hidden in data abstractions.[2] Even program variables define simple data abstractions with entries for, say, set and query; the set entry with a value ensures that any query entry preceding another set returns that value.

2   All processing is defined by sequential and concurrent uses of data abstractions. For example, the simple assignment statement $x := y$, where x and y name program-variable data abstractions, can be considered as the sequence of a query of y followed by a set of x using the value returned by y.

3   Each use of a data abstraction in the system occupies a distinct place in the usage hierarchy.[3] For example, a data abstraction for the assignment $x := x + y$ would use the data abstraction for x in two distinct ways and show the uses in its usage hierarchy.

These three principles unify the distinctions between system design and program design. In particular, Parnas' usage hierarchy[3] provides a powerful place notation for creating, documenting, and inspecting software designs.

Program variables and assignment statements are especially simple data abstractions. Stacks and queues are more elaborate, requiring tens or hundreds of program declarations and statements. Entire systems, such as information or database systems containing thousands or millions of lines of program source code, are also data abstractions, whether consciously developed as such or not.

Defining a data abstraction in three forms reduces the size of steps required to define its structure and use in system design. These forms are called the *black box*, *state box*, and *clear box*. The black box gives an external description of data abstraction behavior in terms of usage. The state box gives an intermediate description in terms of an internal state and the use of an internal data abstraction. The clear box gives an internal description by replacing the state box's internal data abstraction with the sequential or concurrent usage of other data abstractions.

Each major step in box-structure design expands a black-box description into a state box and then into a clear box. An immediate verification of correctness follows each substep. If a verification fails, a new expansion is required. Two points of creative invention are required in each major step: (1) the encapsulation of usage histories into a state box and (2) the decomposition of state-box transitions into a clear-box process. The verification steps are analytic and repeatable without invention.

USAGE HIERARCHIES AND BLOCK DIAGRAMS

Block diagrams, such as those found in data-flow diagrams, coalesce the uses of each data abstraction in the usage hierarchy into a single node and coalesce the usage relations among data abstractions into arcs between nodes. Such diagrams irreversibly summarize hierarchical information. Mappings from usage hierarchies to block diagrams are from many to one and mappings from block diagrams to usage hierarchies are from one to many.

Block diagrams used in descriptions summarize system structure to aid general understanding of a system's parts and data flow among the parts. The parts can be decomposed into block diagrams and parts hierarchies for a general perspective of system structure.

Block diagrams used in design are conceptions about data flow among modules to be designed. Since the mapping from block diagram to complete design is from one to many, only one or a few designs that satisfy a block diagram will be correct. Consequently, if the sequential or concurrent use of modules shown in block diagrams is left as programming details for later expansions, then the design process is inherently error-prone because the correctness of use among modules cannot be immediately verified. Correct detailed program design is even more difficult when block diagrams are expanded into hierarchies of more-detailed block diagrams without defining sequential and concurrent uses at each level.

BOX STRUCTURES OF DATA ABSTRACTIONS

There is a direct relationship between object-oriented development and box-structured design in the implementation of data abstractions as "objects."[4] In fact, box-structured design represents a systematic process for creating object-oriented designs.

Object-oriented development also uses inheritance to describe objects or data abstractions. As data abstractions become more complex and usage hierarchies become deeper, inherited properties can dramatically improve the precision of descriptions. Such property hierarchies, combined with formal methods of axiomatic and algebraic description,[2] are needed to deal with substantial systems in an orderly way.

Black-box descriptions

Stepwise refinement and verification of system design describes system behavior entirely in data abstractions. Parnas' principle of information hiding distinguishes between concrete, visible data storage in a system with persistent information and the system's external behavior.[3] Parnas describes system behavior by its traces with no reference to stored data.[5] Hoare also uses traces to define system behavior for networks of communicating processes.[6] These ideas lead to a direct, mathematical description of system behavior.

Any realized data abstraction exists in real time, whether it performs a so-called real-time function or not. Various uses are initiated at various entries, possibly concurrently. It is useful to classify each initiation (defined by the entries and any data required) as a stimulus to the abstraction and each return (defined by the exits and any data produced) as a response by the abstraction. Each response is determined uniquely by the stimuli it has previously received and accepted. That is, for each realized data abstraction, there is a mathematical function from its stimulus histories to its next response.

Many abstractions do not require specific real-time behavior, even though each realization exists in real time. In such cases, the function is defined for sequentially ordered stimuli. For example, a finite-stack data abstraction is usually described as a sequential process rather than a real-time process.

Figure 8.1 shows a black box, with a stimulus (possibly through multiple concurrent entries) producing a response (possibly through multiple concurrent exits). Let S be the set of possible stimuli and R be the set of possible responses. The black-box description is a mathematical function f from the set of sequences on S (call it S^*) to R of type

$$f: S^* \to R$$

For especially simple data abstractions, f can be given in closed mathematical notation. For large abstractions, it may be necessary to give f in the

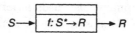

Figure 8.1   Black box.

natural language of a problem domain, often a mixture of formal and informal language. Whatever the notation, the black-box description is a function.

A specification for a data abstraction can be given as a set of traces[6] consisting of every acceptable sequence of interleaved stimuli and responses. If two subsequences are identical until a stimulus produces different responses in each, then the specification defines a mathematical relation rather than a function. Mathematical relations can also be used as black boxes to describe data abstractions with nondeterministic behavior.

In programming languages that permit program variables to be declared but not initialized, data abstractions of the variables have nondeterministic behavior up to the first set stimulus, but deterministic behavior after. In programming languages that require variable initialization, these data abstractions are deterministic.

State-box descriptions

The term "data abstraction" implies the possibility of storing data between stimuli to respond to the effects of previous stimuli. For example, in a finite-stack abstraction, a push provides a data item that may be required as a response for some later copy-top operation. The principle of information hiding requires that any such data be regarded as part of an abstract state of the data abstraction, which may be implemented in various ways but always provides a correct description of behavior.

There is a simple mathematical way to guarantee the existence of such a state and the correct behavior of an abstraction with it. Regard the stimulus history itself as the state. Then, for each stimulus, use the black-box function to compute the response from the stimulus history, including the stimulus just received. Finally, compute the new state by appending that stimulus to the previous state. This construction defines a state machine, but not a finite-state machine because stimulus histories are not bounded. Of course, most interesting data abstractions have a function mapping the unbounded set of stimulus histories to a finite set of new state representations that let a finite-state machine provide the black-box behavior.

However, the classical-state machine, in which the state machine transition is a mathematical function from stimuli and old states to responses and new states, has one serious deficiency in elaborating system behavior in a hierarchical structure. Such a transition function forces all state data into the state machine's state, terminating the hierarchy of state data storage. In fact, the implementations of complex data abstractions typically contain several levels, with information hidden at each level.

A state box – a simple generalization of the idea of a state machine –

allows such implementations. A state box uses a data abstraction to determine the next state and response for each stimulus. The abstract state can then be distributed in any way desired between the state and the transition behavior of the state box. A state box is pictured in figure 8.2, which shows an internal black box whose stimulus arrives concurrently from the external stimulus and the internal state, and whose response departs concurrently to the external response and new internal state.

Let T be a set of states. The behavior of the state box is given by an initial state t in T and function g of the type

$$g: S^* \times T^* \to R \times T$$

that is, a black-box function from stimulus and state histories to the next response and state. Each pair $\langle t, g \rangle$ uniquely defines a black-box function f through the elimination of intermediate states by repeated substitution.

For example, given $\langle t, g \rangle$ with ith stimulus $s.i$, stimulus history $sh.i = \langle s.1, s.2, \ldots, s.i \rangle$, ith response $r.i$, state $t.i - 1$, state history $th.i - 1 = \langle t, t.1, \ldots, t.i - 1 \rangle$, and $g = \langle gr, gt \rangle$ then

$$r.i = gr(sh.i, th.i - 1)$$

and

$$t.i = gt(sh.i, th.i - 1)$$

Define the state history function gth such that

$$gth(sh.i, th.i - 1) = \langle t, gt(sh.1,\langle t \rangle), \ldots, gt(sh.i, th.i - 1) \rangle$$

By substitution, if $i > 1$,

$$r.i = gr(sh.i, gth(sh.i - 1, th.i - 2))$$

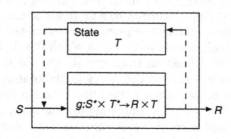

Figure 8.2   State box.

If $i > 2$,

$$r.i = gr(sh.i, gth(sh.i - 1, gth(sh.i - 2, th.i - 3)))$$

and, continuing i substitutions,

$$r.i = gr(sh.i, gth(sh.i - 1, \ldots, gth(sh.1, \langle t \rangle) \ldots))$$

which is a value of a function of type f with parameter t. That is, for each state box there is a unique black box. Given black-box functions of type F, state-box functions of type G, and states of type T, there exists a mathematical function d of type

$$d: T \times G \to F$$

The values of function d are called the black-box derivatives of state boxes. To verify that a state box has been designed correctly to provide black-box behavior, the derived black box need only be compared to the intended black box.

Clear-box descriptions

The theorems and experiences of structured programming lead to a direct definition of four kinds of clear boxes: three sequential forms for sequence, alternation, and iteration, and one concurrent form. In each case, a particular form of sequential or concurrent usage of data abstractions is defined to replace the internal data abstraction of the state box. Alternation and iteration use special data abstractions called *conditions* in which the stimulus is directed out through one of multiple exits. In each use, a regular data abstraction (not a condition) accesses and updates the state.

The definitions in sequential usage are familiar. In concurrent usage, the definitions are novel to ensure referential transparency in concurrent and sequential usage. The definitions in concurrent usage provide an ordered set of new states and responses from each concurrent data abstraction, with the requirement that a new data abstraction, called Resolve, be defined to resolve discrepancies among the responses into a single response.

The four kinds of clear boxes are pictured in figures 8.3–8.6. Their function semantics can be derived directly from the semantics of their states and black boxes. As in the case of mapping a state box into a black box, there is a derivative function mapping any clear box into a unique state box. To verify that a clear box has been designed correctly to provide state-box behavior, the derived state box need only be compared with the intended state box. These verifications can be carried out by substitution and case analyses to eliminate sequential and concurrent process.

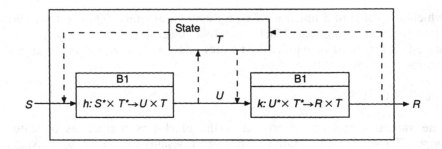

Figure 8.3   Sequence Clear Box. The response from B1 becomes the stimulus to B2.

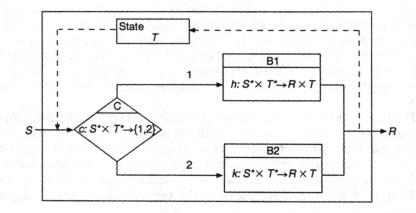

Figure 8.4   Alternation Clear Box. The condition black box C directs its stimulus to B1 or B2.

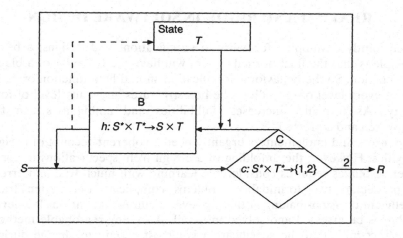

Figure 8.5   Iteration Clear Box. The condition black box C directs its stimulus to B or the external response of the clear box. The response from B becomes the stimulus to C.

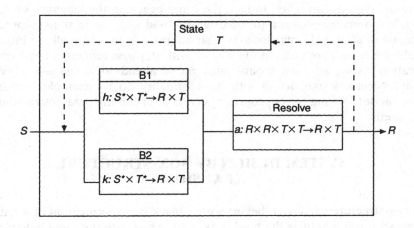

Figure 8.6   Concurrent Clear Box. The external stimulus is directed to both B1 and B2. The responses from B1 and B2 together become the stimulus to Resolve.

REALISM AND RIGOR IN SOFTWARE DESIGN

When jointly developing formality in specifications and designs, a basic principle is that the final, formal system will have the behavior of a black box function. So the behavioral specification should be a function or relation at every level of formality. The box structures allow any level of formality. As formality increases, fallibilities and ambiguities can be discovered and corrected.

Sponsors and implementers urgently need a coherent account of design activities. However, the unfolding of a design from specifications to computer resources requires considerable learning with much trial and error. In particular, two formidable problems complicate the design trail. Intelligent decision-making at the top level requires that various low-level problems be assessed and solved in detail. Also, any reasonable method must recognize that the specification is almost certain to change during development. To deal with such problems, Parnas advocates a usage hierarchy of modules, each hiding certain secrets, by a joint study of the specification in the problem domain and the available computing resources, with the probability of change explicitly recognized.[3]

Box-structured design leads to the same goal as Parnas' usage hierarchy. Let's assume that the top of a mountain is a formal description and that farther down its slopes the descriptions are more and more informal (with more and more fallibility). I propose a spiral approach to the top through several levels of formality. In fact, the climb begins in the language of the problem domain – often a lot of English – and ends up in the computer domain of entirely formal code. Box structures, whether formally or informally described, are used on the way up with stepwise refinement and verification. Also, advance scouts must move ahead to assess and solve problems in low-level details with more formality. So, for example, Parnas' ideas about looking for appropriate secrets in upcoming data abstractions are useful.

SYSTEM DESIGN BY BOX-STRUCTURE EXPANSION

A box-structure expansion begins with a black-box specification of a data abstraction. It identifies the black box, a state box with the same behavior as that of the black box, and a clear box with the same behavior as that of the state machine, using data abstractions at the next level with their own black-box behavior. Although the theory can be given entirely in function theoretical terms with abstract states and functions, a practical design process must use concrete design and programming languages to describe data abstractions and their uses. This shift from theory to practice involves only a change in syntax, not in semantics. A design or program is a rule for a function, and data descriptions and program structures are means for facilitating expression of such rules.

Each expansion of a box structure is a step in designing internal state data and internal sequential or concurrent process. These steps can require considerable invention. It helps to break each expansion into smaller steps, leaving design trails that permit more objective engineering inspections. For this purpose, I define the following 11-step box-structure expansion process:

Define the black box
  (1) Define black-box stimuli
         Determine all possible stimuli for the black box.
  (2) Define black-box behavior
         For each possible stimulus, determine its complete response in terms of its stimulus history.

Design the state box
  (3) Discover state data requirements
         For each response to be calculated, encapsulate its stimulus history into a state data requirement.
  (4) Define the state
         Select a subset of the required state data items to encapsulate stimulus histories.
  (5) Design the state box
         For the selected state, determine the internal black box required for the state box.
  (6) Verify the state box
         Verify the correctness of the state box with respect to the required black-box behavior.

Design the clear box
  (7) Discover state data accesses
         For each item of state data and each possible stimulus, determine all possible accesses of the item.
  (8) Define data abstractions
         Organize state data into data abstractions for effective access.
  (9) Design the clear box
         Define sequential or concurrent uses of the data abstractions defined to replace the internal black box of the state box.

(10) Verify the clear box
     Verify the correctness of the clear box with respect to the state-box behavior.

Continue the process
(11) Repeat stepwise expansion until design completion
     For each new data abstraction, repeat steps 1–10 until suitable data and program specifications are reached.

The inventions required in this process are strictly contained in steps 4, 5, 8, and 9 and labeled there. The other steps are analytic and repeatable. This process isolates and embeds the creative design steps, allowing design reviews in canonical cases and automatically developing relevant information while leading up to each step. For example, step 3 provides enough background to carry out step 4 and review it objectively.

In contrast, heuristic approaches often skip these analytic steps and leap to networks of sources, processes, stores, and sinks. However, in large problems, it is difficult and sometimes painful to determine if a leap was inspired or flawed. The complexity and the number of design alternatives make it risky to leap that discontinuity without a lot of engineering analysis.

A NAVIGATION AND WEATHER BUOY CASE STUDY

Booch uses the problem of a navigation and weather buoy to illustrate a data-flow approach to object-oriented architecture and design.[4] The problem was redone in box structures as shown below. (I subsequently learned that this problem was originally suggested by Chmura et al.[7] with a solution in terms of a set of information-hiding modules. The solution below was developed without knowledge of Chmura's solution.) Booch gives the following statement of the problem.

The Host at Sea system is a group of free-floating buoys that provide navigation and weather data to air and ship traffic. The buoys collect data on air and water temperature, wind speed, and location through sensors. Each buoy can have a different number of sensors and can be modified to support other types of sensors.

Each buoy is also equipped with a radio transmitter (to broadcast weather and location information as well as an SOS message) and a radio receiver (to receive requests from passing vessels). A sailor can flip a switch on the buoy to initiate an SOS broadcast and some buoys are equipped with a red light that can be activated by a passing vessel during search operations. Software for each buoy must:

- Maintain current average wind, temperature, and location information. Wind speed readings are taken every 30 seconds, and temperature and location readings are taken every 10 seconds. Wind and temperature values are kept as a running average.
- Broadcast wind, temperature, and location information every 60 seconds.
- Broadcast wind, temperature, and location information from the past 24 hours in response to requests from passing vessels. This takes priority over the periodic broadcast.
- Activate or deactivate the red light based on a request from a passing vessel.
- Continuously broadcast an SOS signal after a sailor engages the emergency switch. This signal takes priority over all other broadcasts and continues until reset by a passing vessel.

On the basis of this problem statement, Booch invented a data-flow diagram and identified objects, attributes, and operations for an object-oriented architecture for such a buoy.[4] However, the 11-step expansion process outlined above yields a different architecture.

Preliminary black-box analysis

The data-flow approach jumps right in with various internal flows and processes to solve the problem. The box-structure approach focuses first on defining the problem as a real-time transformation of stimuli to responses. The problem statement identifies the following general types of stimuli:

- clock data (various references to time)
- wind data
- temperature data
- location data
- request to broadcast 24 hours of weather data
- request to activate or deactivate a red light
- request to start or stop continuous sos broadcast

Members of these stimulus types may arrive concurrently in various combinations to make up a stimulus.

The problem statement further identifies possible responses to these stimuli as:

- start or stop continuous sos broadcast
- activate or deactivate the red light
- start a broadcast of 24 hours of weather data
- start a broadcast of current weather data

Since there is only one transmitter, starting a broadcast means stopping any other broadcast currently under way.

The rest of the problem statement generally indicates which response should follow any possible stimulus. The response depends on the stimuli accumulated to the moment, through references to running averages. So the buoy's black box will require histories of certain stimuli covering more than 24 hours (for example, a 24-hour-old running average will require data more than 24 hours old).

Data must be encapsulated in any state box for this black box. References to running averages of wind and temperature data suggest that new data abstractions can greatly simplify the necessary computations and data management. However, before rushing into architecture and design decisions on internal data flows and processes, it is worthwhile to focus more attention on the problem.

Questions about the problem statement

This preliminary black-box analysis shows that the problem statement is far from a specification. Many additional decisions are needed to remove ambiguities, ensure completeness and consistency, and provide a solution without unpleasant surprises for the buoy's sponsors and users. Such problems should be tackled at the black-box level before plunging into state-box and clear-box expansions.

Obviously absent from the problem statement is how the buoy is to be operated. While the buoy could be developed as an expendable device that is deployed and left alone, whoever is responsible for its operation might want more control (for example, to monitor system integrity, security, or correctness through testing or diagnostics). If so, additional types of stimuli and responses must be defined.

This example assumes the buoy is expendable. However, note that a focus on immediate users, to the exclusion of secondary users such as operators and maintainers, usually leads to faulty designs that can only be patched up enough to become poor designs.

Also absent from the problem statement are questions involving initialization:

- Is the periodic weather broadcast (every 60 seconds) tied to Greenwich

Mean Time (GMT) or to an internal clock that will appear random in real time to its users?

- What is expected if a 24-hour-weather broadcast is requested before enough data have been collected since the start (or restart) of the buoy's operation?
- Can the operators restart the buoy (for example, after moving it to another location in an emergency situation)?
- How are the running averages to be initialized?

The problem statement mentions that sos broadcasts and 24-hour-weather broadcasts have priority, but that raises more questions:

- Does a lower-priority broadcast abort when a higher-priority one is requested, or does it finish first?
- Can a 24-hour request abort another 24-hour request?

Other questions to be addressed at this stage include:

- What is the exact content of a current-weather broadcast? Of a 24-hour-weather broadcast?
- How many samples are needed for running averages, and can that parameter be controlled by the operators?
- Is the running average of wind a vector average?

Completing the problem statement

A black-box analysis forces the identification of every possible stimulus of the buoy and every acceptable response in terms of the stimulus history. The principle of transaction closure[1] requires that any information needed to produce a response be provided by some previous stimulus. For example, a weather broadcast requires previous wind and temperature data.

A black box is a formal specification that is complete, unambiguous, and consistent because it is a mathematical function or relation from all possible stimulus histories to responses, whether it is represented in mathematical notation, English, or a mixture of the two in the problem domain. Completion of a black-box analysis and description usually requires many interactions with sponsors and users. However, getting a good specification is far less expensive over the life cycle than launching into design and implementation without knowing what the sponsors had in mind or the users needed.

In this case study, let us assume the following resolutions to the previous questions:

- The buoy clock and sensors are restarted at the next GMT minute mark after the moment of restart.
- The phrase "24-hour-weather broadcast" means "weather-since-restart broadcast" if restart was less than 24 hours ago.
- A buoy can be restarted or shut down at any time by the use of a password, with restart conditions for its location and running-average parameters. The password can be changed by use of the current password; the initial password is "buoy." The password is unchanged by a restart or shutdown.
- A request for SOS broadcast preempts and aborts any other broadcast.
- A periodic weather broadcast is cancelled if any other broadcast is under way.
- A request for 24-hour-weather broadcast is ignored if an SOS broadcast is under way. It is queued to follow a periodic current-weather broadcast or 24-hour-weather broadcast if one of these is already under way. Otherwise, it is granted immediately.
- The exact content of a current-weather broadcast is the current location, running average of wind, and running average of air and water temperatures. A 24-hour-weather broadcast contains the current-weather broadcasts for each of the previous 24 GMT hour marks (or all GMT hour marks if restart was less than 24 hours ago).
- The number of samples in running averages for wind and temperature is defined by integer parameters set at restart or by default. The term "running average" means "average since restart."
- The running average of wind is the running average of the wind vector.

In practice, these resolutions should be further scrutinized by sponsors, users, and analysts, and the entire problem statement/black box should be cast into a more systematic problem-domain statement for formal review and concurrence by sponsors and users.

The result is a mathematical function or relation from all possible stimulus histories to responses, in which transaction closure is obtained. This function or relation must deal specifically with the response to the first stimulus, the second, the third, and so on, even though it is tempting to focus on steady-state operations far removed from initial conditions.

STEPWISE BOX-STRUCTURE EXPANSION OF THE BUOY PROBLEM

Step 1: define black-box stimuli

The second round of the problem statement analysis gave the buoy a restart capability that obviates all history except the current password. Such a restart capability is usually needed for operational control, no matter how well the device was thought out.

The physical media for stimulus types include clock and sensor connections, radio receptions, and mechanical switches. Let us suppose the buoy has a basic internal clock that polls the digitized information and is accurate enough to deal with the sensors and the radio transmitter and receiver. Let us also assume that a "start broadcast" command is available and that the transmitter returns a "broadcast terminated" signal.

Because of the need to maintain GMT, let us suppose the clock is synchronized to GMT by means outside the scope of this study and that the basic periodic clock pulse generated is present in every stimulus. The possible stimulus types are:

- clock pulse
- restart command and data
- shutdown command
- change password command and data
- wind data
- air temperature data
- water temperature data
- location data
- request to broadcast 24 hours of weather data
- request to activate a red light
- request to deactivate a red light
- request to start continuous sos broadcast
- request to stop continuous sos broadcast
- broadcast terminated

Thus, there are 14 possible stimulus types present in every stimulus. The clock pulse is always present and the others are present independently of each other. Seven of these types contain data, but seven do not.

Some types conflict in their effects. For example, a vessel may send a request to stop continuous sos broadcast due to its handling of one emergency at the same time a sailor pushes the switch to start an sos broadcast for another emergency. The black box must describe the response to this presumably unusual case. In fact, the information developed in the interaction between sponsors, users, and analysts must determine the response from every possible stimulus history, whether expected frequently or infrequently.

Step 2: define black-box behavior

As derived above, the domain for the black box (function) is the set of all possible histories of stimuli with 1 to 14 members of these stimulus types. That is an infinite domain, but with a simple structure. Fortunately, the interactions between these stimulus types are also simple.

The function mapping from these stimulus histories to responses is simple enough to decompose the effects of stimulus types to a few cases, many quite autonomous for the stimulus type involved. This is shown in figure 8.7, where the response required is denoted by R. The response required

1. clock pulse
    R: IF no shutdown command since last restart
        command
       THEN
          IF no broadcast is under way AND a
          24-hour-weather broadcast has been
          requested
          THEN form and start 24-hour-
             weather broadcast
       ELSE
          IF GMT is at the minute mark
          THEN form and start current-
             weather broadcast.

2. restart command and data
    R: IF password correct
       THEN confirm restart.

3. shutdown command
    R: IF no shutdown command since last restart
        command
       THEN
          IF password correct and no restart
          command
          THEN confirm shutdown.

4. change password command and data
    R: IF no shutdown command since last restart
        command
       THEN
          IF password correct and no restart or
          shutdown command
          THEN confirm password change.

5. wind data
    R: acknowledge data.

6. air temperature data
    R: acknowledge data.

7. water temperature data
    R: acknowledge data.

8. location data
    R: acknowledge data.

9. request to broadcast 24 hours of weather data
    R: IF no shutdown command since last restart
        command
       THEN
          IF no broadcast is under way
          THEN form and start 24-hour-
             weather broadcast.

10. request to activate red light
    R: activate red light.

11. request to deactivate red light
    R: If no request to activate red light
       THEN deactivate red light.

12. request to start continuous SOS broadcast
    R: start continuous SOS broadcast.

13. request to stop continuous SOS broadcast
    R: IF no request to start SOS broadcast
          THEN stop continuous SOS broadcast.

14. broadcast termination
    R: acknowledge termination.

Figure 8.7 Black-box responses for buoy.

for each stimulus type is given in Box Description Language[1] for readability by sponsors, users, and analysts. The outer syntax is formal (denoted in figure 8.7 in uppercase characters), but the inner syntax is informal for now.[8] The informal expressions in inner syntax should be replaced by more formal expressions as the design progresses.

Note that the responses in figure 8.7 are described entirely in terms of stimulus histories. The phrase "broadcast is under way" looks suspiciously like a status, but is used as shorthand for "broadcast previously started with no subsequent broadcast termination stimulus." "Broadcast has been requested" is shorthand for "broadcast previously requested with no subsequent broadcast started." It is sometimes convenient to use response history (such as broadcast started) as proper shorthand in a black-box description because any such response can be determined from previous stimulus history.

The actions in figure 8.7 are limited to responses without presuming internal activity. For example, statement 9, in response to a request to broadcast 24 hours of weather data, responds only if no broadcast is under way. If a broadcast is under way, one might expect some internal action to note the request for later response, but statement 9 takes no such action. However, statement 1 deals with this situation by checking stimulus histories for requests that can be responded to at each clock pulse. The principle is to deal only with responses specified by stimulus histories, not to begin inadvertently inventing internals.

Note that several stimulus types are accepted during shutdown, namely restart command and data, request to activate or deactivate red light, request to start or stop sos broadcast, all sensor stimuli, and broadcast termination. These are decisions about specifications as well as design if they have not been explicitly defined. In fact, the black box will define a specification that the sponsors and users should understand in confirming previous agreements on what is required of the system.

Step 3: discover state data requirements

The next step is to determine the information needed to encapsulate stimulus histories to be maintained from one stimulus to the next, so no previous stimulus is required to determine the response. There is a simple necessary and sufficient condition for this encapsulation:

- The responses define the necessary information to be maintained in the state box.
- The history of stimuli contains sufficient information for the state box.

That is, a satisfactory encapsulation of history into the state and internal black box of the state box can be derived directly from the black box.

To provide a convenient design trail for engineering inspections of the buoy, I expand the listing of stimulus types and responses in figure 8.7 into state data that encapsulates the necessary histories, as shown in figure 8.8. The encapsulation follows directly from an examination of the responses and their dependency on stimulus histories.

For example, in the clock pulse stimulus type, the condition "no shutdown command since the last restart command" must be encapsulated because it depends on stimulus history. Let us encapsulate it in "buoy

1. clock pulse
   R: IF no shutdown command since last restart
      command
      THEN
         IF no broadcast is under way AND a
            24-hour-weather broadcast has been
            requested
            THEN form and start 24-hour-
               weather broadcast
         ELSE
            IF GMT is at the minute mark
               THEN form and start current-
                  weather broadcast.
   E: buoy status, broadcast status, broadcast-
      request status, 24-hour weather history, clock
      time, location, wind history, air temperature
      history, water temperature history

2. restart command and data
   R: IF password correct
      THEN confirm restart.
   E: password, restart state.

3. shutdown command
   R: IF no shutdown command since last restart
         command
      THEN
         IF password correct and no restart
            command
            THEN confirm shutdown.
   E: password, shutdown state

4. change password command and data
   R: IF no shutdown command since last restart
         command
      THEN
         IF password correct and no restart or
            shutdown command
            THEN confirm password change.
   E: password

5. wind data
   R: acknowledge data.
   E: none

6. air temperature data
   R: acknowledge data.
   E: none

7. water temperature data
   R: acknowledge data.
   E: none

8. location data
   R: acknowledge data.
   E: none

9. request to broadcast 24 hours of weather data
   R: IF no shutdown command since last restart
         command
      THEN
         IF no broadcast is under way
            THEN form and start 24-hour-
               weather broadcast.
   E: broadcast status, 24-hour weather history

10. request to activate red light
    R: activate red light.
    E: none

11. request to deactivate red light
    R: If no request to activate red light
          THEN deactivate red light.
    E: none

12. request to start continuous SOS broadcast
    R: start continuous SOS broadcast.
    E: none

13. request to stop continuous SOS broadcast
    R: IF no request to start SOS broadcast
          THEN stop continuous SOS broadcast.
    E: none

14. broadcast termination
    R: acknowledge termination.
    E: none

Figure 8.8   Derivation of encapsulated data for buoy.

status," an invented term for a derived requirement, and suppose that buoy status is on only if there has been no shutdown command since the last restart command. Similarly, the condition "no broadcast is under way" can be encapsulated in "broadcast status," and "24-hour-weather broadcast has been requested" can be encapsulated in "broadcast-request status." In figure 8.8, encapsulated data is denoted by E.

Note that these state data requirements are derived from the responses of the black box, not the stimuli. For example, the stimulus types for wind and temperature data require only acknowledgment of such data, not retention. The need to encapsulate wind and temperature data in the state box comes from the response "form and start current-weather broadcast." In summary, the encapsulated data requirements are:

- buoy status
- broadcast status
- broadcast-request status
- 24-hour weather history
- clock time
- location
- wind history
- air temperature history
- water temperature history
- password
- restart state, and
- shutdown state

Step 4: define the state

The identification of state data requirements is a first design step. However, all such data are candidates for migration into lower-level box structures. For example, the four history types in the above list appear to be logical candidates for migration, since they will each require considerable storage and processing to meet the buoy's needs. Also, restart state and shutdown state are candidates for migration because each appears in only one statement. The remaining data items are scalar and can make up the state for the buoy state box. Decisions on the migration of encapsulated data are reversible if further analysis uncovers a better strategy.

Step 5: design the state box

Steps 3 and 4 derive state data from the black box by rewriting the responses in figure 8.7 in terms of state data and appending the state transitions required for the state box. These responses and transitions are shown in figure 8.9. For each stimulus type, the response and transition is denoted by *RT*. In Box Description Language, CON/NOC brackets concurrent statements separated by commas.

1. clock pulse
    *RT:*IF buoy status on
        THEN
            CON
                update clock,
                IF broadcast status off AND
                    broadcast-request status on
                THEN
                    CON
                        form and start 24-hour-
                            weather broadcast,
                        set broadcast status on,
                        set broadcast-request status
                            off
                    NOC
                ELSE
                IF clock time is at the minute mark
                THEN
                    CON
                        form and start current-
                            weather broadcast,
                        set broadcast status on
                    NOC
            NOC

2. restart command and data
    *RT:*IF password in stimulus = password
        THEN confirm restart

3. shutdown command
    *RT:*IF buoy status on
        THEN
            IF password in stimulus = password
                AND no restart command
            THEN confirm shutdown

4. change password command and data
    *RT:*IF buoy status on
        THEN
            IF password in stimulus = password
                AND no restart or shutdown
                command
            THEN
                CON
                    confirm password change,
                    update password
                NOC

5. wind data
    *RT:*acknowledge data

6. air temperature data
    *RT:*acknowledge data

7. water temperature data
    *RT:*acknowledge data

8. location data
    *RT:*CON
            acknowledge data,
            update location
        NOC

9. request to broadcast 24 hours of weather data
    *RT:*IF buoy status on
        THEN
            IF broadcast status off
            THEN
                CON
                    form and start broadcast,
                    set broadcast status on
                NOC
            ELSE
                set broadcast-request status on

10. request to activate red light
    *RT:*activate red light

11. request to deactivate red light
    *RT:*IF no request to activate red light
            THEN deactivate red light

12. request to start continuous SOS broadcast
    *RT:*IF broadcast status not SOS
        THEN
            CON
                start continuous broadcast,
                set broadcast status on
            NOC

13. request to stop continuous SOS broadcast
    *RT:*IF no request to start SOS broadcast
        THEN
            CON
                stop SOS broadcast,
                set broadcast status off
            NOC

14. broadcast termination
    *RT:*CON
            acknowledge termination,
            set broadcast status off
        NOC

Figure 8.9   State-box responses and transitions for buoy.

Note the internal action in statement 9 that turns broadcast-request status on if the response is to be handled later, in contrast with statement 9 of the black box.

Step 6: verify the state box

To verify the state box, the state data must be eliminated to obtain a derived black box, which then must be compared with the intended black box. The derivation for this state box is quite direct at the level of description given.

For example, the clock pulse *RT* statement in figure 8.9 begins

IF buoy status on

while the clock pulse *R* statement in figure 8.7 begins

IF no shutdown command since last restart command

which must be verified as equivalent. In this case, figure 8.9 shows that buoy status is set only by the restart command and shutdown command. Since the restart command only sets buoy status on and the shutdown command only sets buoy status off, eliminating the state data in the condition "buoy status on" reduces to any stimulus history in which "no shutdown command since last restart command" holds. Therefore, the two IF statements from the black box and state box begin with equivalent conditions.

Broadcast status and broadcast-request status can be treated similarly to buoy status. The systematic elimination of state data in figure 8.9 to derive a black box to compare with figure 8.7 may seem like a rather detailed effort at this point, but it builds a solid foundation for continuing the design, even on an informal basis such as this.

The alternative to this detailed analysis is to leave the high-level control properties defined by these three state items to later programming details, which cannot be verified as design decisions, and leave the actual design to people who may not comprehensively understand the system requirements. However, in system design, every level of decomposition must be controlled by a few details that should be identified and verified immediately.

Figure 8.9 should contain enough information to verify the correct use of state data to meet the requirements of black-box behavior in figure 8.7. If this verification cannot be carried out, even informally, the state box is not completely defined.

In a completed design in a formal language, the derivation will take on the character of a formal engineering analysis of the designed state box to determine the derivative black box for comparison with a formal black-box specification. This engineering analysis is defined in the function theoretical proof that a state box has a unique black-box derivative. But even at the informal level described here, the outline of the verification can be a reminder and guide for the formal design and verification.

Step 7: discover state data accesses

The previous lists and figures 8.7, 8.8, and 8.9 can be used to cross reference all possible accesses to this data in various stimulus types. For example, buoy status data will be captured in certain stimuli and the analysis shows the necessity of their retention in state data. These cross references are given in figure 8.10. For each state data requirement item, every stimulus type that could or should access it is listed. For each such type, every

1. buoy status
   - in clock pulse
     use to test if buoy on
   - in restart command and data
     update as part of restart state
   - in shutdown command
     use to test if buoy on
     update as part of shutdown state
   - in change password command and data
     use to test if buoy on
   - in request to broadcast 24 hours of weather data
     use to test if buoy on
   - in broadcast termination
     use to test if buoy on

2. broadcast status
   - in clock pulse
     use to test if no broadcast under way
     update at start 24-hour-weather broadcast
     update at start current-weather broadcast
   - in restart command and data
     update as part of restart state
   - in request to broadcast 24 hours of weather data
     update at start 24-hour-weather broadcast
   - in request to start continuous SOS broadcast
     update at start continuous broadcast
   - in request to stop continuous SOS broadcast
     update at stop continuous broadcast
   - in broadcast termination
     update at broadcast termination

3. broadcast-request status
   - in clock pulse
     use to test if 24-hour broadcast has been requested
     update at start 24-hour-weather broadcast

   - in restart command and data
     update as part of restart state
   - in request to broadcast 24 hours of weather data use to test if broadcast is under way
     update at start 24-hour-weather broadcast

4. clock time
   - in clock pulse
     update every clock pulse
     use to test if GMT is at the minute mark
     use to test if GMT is at the hour mark
   - in restart command and data
     update as part of restart state

5. location
   - in clock pulse
     use in current-weather broadcast
   - in restart command and data
     update as part of restart state
   - in location data
     update with location data

6. password
   - in start command and data
     use to test if password correct
   - in shutdown command
     use to test if password correct
   - in change password command and data
     use to test if password correct
     update with new password

Figure 8.10   Encapsulated data analysis table for buoy.

type of action related to the items is also listed. For convenience, I identify each access as an update or use. Data must be updated before being used, so further study is indicated if analysis shows no update.

Step 8: define data abstractions

Access and storage of the 12 data items listed in Step 3 have been represented explicitly in the state or in data abstractions at lower levels. Figure 8.8 shows every access by every stimulus type, providing a basis to derive the black boxes required for a clear-box design at this level. Six of these objects represent scalar variables in the state:

- buoy status
- broadcast status
- broadcast-request status
- clock time
- location
- password

while four represent histories to be migrated as common services to new data abstractions:

- 24-hour weather history
- wind history
- air temperature history
- water temperature history

and two are complete buoy states to be migrated down in the clear box to be designed:

- restart state
- shutdown state

The response requirements on these common data abstractions determine their forms. For example, "24-hour weather history response" is a sequence of current-weather records, each consisting of a GMT hour mark, location, wind average, air temperature average, and water temperature average, with a maximum of 24 elements in the list. However, the only use of wind average and air and water temperatures (in current-weather broadcast) calls for a running average, so these histories can be migrated and encapsulated into abstractions whose only data responses are running averages.

Step 9: design the clear box

The clear-box expansion of the state machine is quite direct at this point. The responses and transitions in figure 8.9 lead directly to a clear box of 14 concurrent black boxes – one for each stimulus type – in which each black box recognizes its own stimulus type in the current complex stimulus and responds accordingly. Certain black boxes must also recognize other stimulus types. For example, the shutdown-command black box must check for the absence of a restart command before shutting down the system. Also, the clock-pulse black box must identify the stimulus type "request to broadcast 24 hours of weather data." These 14 concurrent black boxes are shown as part of figure 8.9.

The Resolve black box required for this concurrent clear box must resolve possible conflicts in the broadcast responses and the values set for buoy status, broadcast status, and broadcast-request status. In this case, the conflicts can be resolved as follows:

R: accept any response of change in state data except for response
        broadcasts, buoy status, broadcast status, and broadcast-request
        status, which are to be resolved as follows:
            response broadcast:
                select in priority order – sos broadcast, 24-hour-weather
                broad-cast, current-weather broadcast, no broadcast
            buoy status: on
            broadcast status: based on response broadcast
            broadcast-request status: on

Step 10: verify the clear box

To verify the clear box, the sequential and concurrent process must be eliminated to obtain the derived state box, which then must be compared with the intended state box. The derivation is quite direct for this clear box because its concurrent black boxes respond to different stimulus type values. The Resolve black box defines the priorities and conflict resolutions among the concurrent black boxes as already identified. Immediate verification again provides direct control over the eventual behavior of the system.

One possible issue here is the responses to other stimulus types at restart or shutdown. The derived state box will provide responses to sensors and various requests for service that may be counter to the spirit of the problem. For example, if a shutdown command and a request to broadcast 24 hours of weather data arrive concurrently, the derived state box may both confirm a shutdown and form and start the broadcast, possibly a questionable response. A review of the intended state box shows that this clear-box behavior meets the state-box requirements. So, the state box itself should be questioned, which leads back to the black box from which the expansion began. In fact, this may be a desirable way to shut down, but it should be resolved and documented in black-box behavior. The stepwise refinement and verification process leaves a design trail for such reconsiderations, with enough documentation to maintain consistency between specifications and design.

Step 11: repeat stepwise expansion until design is complete

The new common services – 24-Hour Weather History, Wind History, Water Temperature History, and Air Temperature History – are also subject to systematic design with the stepwise box-structure expansion process.

For example, in order to relocate weather data into a new abstraction called 24-Hour Weather History, its black-box stimuli and responses must be determined. The abstraction's main purpose is to return a 24-hour weather history on demand for the 24-hour-weather broadcast. Consequently, a query stimulus is needed. Also, weather data including GMT, location, wind average, and air and water temperature averages must be acquired hourly. Call this a data stimulus. And, because the buoy can be restarted, a restart stimulus is also needed. This information is captured formally as follows:

Black-box stimulus types
1 restart
2 data (GMT, location, wind average, air temperature average, water temperature average)
3 query

Black-box responses
1 restart
   R: acknowledge restart.
2 data (GMT, location, wind average, air temperature average, water temperature average)
   R: acknowledge data.
3 query
   R: last 24 or fewer records of weather data received since last restart stimulus.

If this expansion were continued, the state data required for the state box would be derived using the necessary and sufficient condition for the encapsulation of history into state. As before, the listing of stimulus types and responses would be expanded one more step. The expansion is simple in this case, but it provides a design trail for engineering inspections as part of the overall design of the buoy.

CONCLUSIONS

Stepwise refinement and verification in the box structures of data abstractions provides a systematic discipline for complex system design at any level of formality. Once the black box is understood as a mathematical function from stimulus histories to responses, the derivation of state data requirements becomes a very direct analysis process subject to rigorous engineering inspections. The identification of state boxes to encapsulate state data and processes at the next level is also a very direct process. Since data abstractions are used at the next level, their restatement as black boxes defines their behavior, from which state data and even lower-level box structures can be derived and inspected systematically. Unlike heuristic invention, this derivation is repeatable, allowing engineering inspections because the products and the steps in deriving them are familiar to the inspectors.

Acknowledgments

It is a pleasure to acknowledge stimulating discussions with Richard Cobb, Alan Hevner, Richard Linger, and David Weiss in the preparation of this chapter. The reviewers of this chapter also contributed significantly to its quality.

References

1 H. D. Mills, R. C. Linger, and A. R. Hevner, "Box-Structured Information Systems," *IBM Systems J.*, Vol. 26, No. 4, 1987, pp. 395–413.
2 J. Guttag, J. Horning, and J. Wing, *Larch in Five Easy Pieces*, tech. report, DEC Systems Research Center, Palo Alto, 1985.
3 D. L. Parnas, "On a 'Buzzword': Hierarchical Structure," *Proc. IFIP Congress 74*, North Holland, 1974, pp. 336–339.
4 G. Booch, *Software Components with Ada*, Benjamin/Cummings, 1987.
5 D. L. Parnas and W. Bartussek, *Using Traces to Write Abstract Specifications for Software Modules*, University of North Carolina technical report, UNC TR77-012, 1977.

6   C. A. R. Hoare, *Communicating Sequential Processes*, Prentice Hall, 1985.

7   L. Chmura et al., *Software Engineering Principles*, course notebook, Naval Research Laboratory, 1981.

8   R. C. Linger, H. D. Mills, and B. I. Witt, *Structured Programming: Theory and Practice*, Addison-Wesley, 1979.

9 Correctness Verification: Alternative to Structural Software Testing

M. DYER AND A. KOUCHAKDJIAN

INTRODUCTION

Testing is accepted as that step in the software development process where errors introduced during the design and implementation steps can be isolated and removed through the execution of the implemented product. Structural testing is performed by the software developer to uncover implementation errors and validate the product structure. Functional testing is performed by groups other than the developer to assure correct implementation of product requirements and to gain confidence in user acceptance of the delivered product.

Recent experience with formal software design methods has shown that software of significantly improved quality can be produced without the traditional developer test step. The basis for this improvement comes from the use of correctness verification in the construction and subsequent inspection of the software design. Improved software quality could be anticipated with the use of verification, but the accompanying productivity gains could not. This productivity bonus prompted further examination of the interplay between software test and verification methods, as discussed in this chapter.

The formal design methods that are defined in the Cleanroom software development process[1] were used for these software developments. These methods are based on structured programming theory and use a limited set of design constructs to elaborate software logic and data structure. The design constructs are the building blocks for a stepwise refinement of software requirements into verified designs.

A functional approach[2] to correctness verification is an integral part of the design methods and is based on demonstrating an equivalence between required function and elaborated design at each refinement step. In the Cleanroom approach to software development, the software design and corresponding correctness proofs are built simultaneously and become interleaved so that software error prevention is integral to the design process.

In this chapter, these formal methods and the functional verification model are reviewed and their use illustrated, to provide the basis for comparison with testing methods. Their impact on product quality is considered both in terms of software error rates and potential for error prevention. Their productivity impact is discussed as an alternative method to the structural testing performed by the software developer. Sample data from recent software developments are used to compare formal verification methods against accepted approaches to structural software testing.

FORMAL DESIGN PROCESS

Structured programming provides a framework for creating software designs with conviction about their correctness and confidence in their solution to a set of requirements. A design process[3] based on structured programming practice is discussed, which uses formal methods for improving precision and completeness of design recording and which supports the verification of design correctness. This process differs from traditional software practice as correctness verification is woven into each step of the design elaboration and not limited to inspection and review points. As will be discussed, inspections in this context are used to confirm design correctness but exhibit many similarities with the design and code inspections[4] found in current software practice.

The specific process employs a systematic and stepwise decomposition of requirements into levels of design logic and subrequirements. Verification is performed to assure that at every stage the design addresses the intended requirements and that the integrity of the requirements is preserved throughout the decomposition.

The objective is to develop a design in concert with its correctness proof where the proof can vary from a simple mental conviction to an extended symbolic analysis. Designs that can be easily verified are favoured and ones that are difficult to verify should be considered suspect and redone for simplicity. A reasonable rule of thumb would be that when reading a design becomes difficult and the correctness arguments are not obvious, then it is time for a simpler design.

DESIGN REFINEMENT PROCEDURE

In organizing any software product design, a reasonable outline of the software architecture should be formulated and basic details on data representation and processing algorithms thought out. Design refinement starts at the software product level with product requirements reexpressed as sets of intended functions. The designer abstracts the major software function(s) from the total requirements and identifies the product data required for function execution(s).

As refinement proceeds, these product-level functions are broken down into equivalent structures of lower-level subfunctions, each of which addresses some part of the original requirements but is individually more specific (simpler) than the original functions. Subfunctions are themselves subdivided and respecified as lower-level functions, with the process repeated until all product requirements are resolved. Throughout, the software designer looks only far enough ahead to be comfortable with the decomposition. If a function is familiar, added thought and elaboration might be unnecessary. If it is not familiar, it should be refined to a point where an obvious solution is apparent.

In the decomposition process, design logic must be created to connect subfunctions and control their interaction. The design constructs of the structured programming-based process[3] are essential in organizing this logic.

A point should be made on the difficulty of specifying functions for the refinement process, which is really a question of the required formality (level of precision and completeness) in a specification. If these specifications are to be used to drive verification systems that generate code from specifications (ongoing research direction), they must be absolutely precise and complete and documented with a formal notation. If the specifications are to be used in an automated process that allows for human intervention, then less formal specifications could be introduced with a relaxation on the need for absolute precision and completeness.

At one extreme, automation to drive semantic analyses in support of human verification would need a reasonably precise and complete specification. At the other, automation that drives the analysis of the design structure and not the specification semantics could support even further relaxation in specification formality. No automated analysis still makes further relaxation acceptable. In each of these last three cases, human intervention compensates for a relaxation in the need for absolute precision and completeness and the use of formal notation. In this chapter, verification supported by analysis at the design-structure level is envisioned, which seems to strike a reasonable compromise with the difficulty in formulating specifications and the thoroughness of their verification. Targeting for rigorous but not overexacting levels of specification formality increases the chances for acceptance and use of the formal design process.

DESIGN REFINEMENT EXAMPLE

To demonstrate refinement, the design for a triangle solver program, which appears in most articles on software test, is used. Requirements for this program are that it inputs a triple of data values from some external storage, decides if the three arbitrary inputs constitute the sides of a triangle, and, if so, classifies the type of triangle (i.e., equilateral, isosceles, or scalene) and in all cases prints the results of each triple analysis. Either this requirements statement or more mathematical notation could be used to specify the program function. In either case, the input characteristic should be spelled out. For this example, three arbitrary numeric values are acceptable, but restrictions (e.g., positive integers) could have been imposed to constrain the program logic further.

At the first refinement, two subfunctions are a reasonable choice; namely, get the input triples and classify the triangle type. Input sources, termination logic, etc. would be specified for the first subfunction, while classification algorithms, presentation of results, etc. would be appropriate for the second. The designer must ensure that all program requirements (stated and implied) and their elaboration are covered in one or the other.

At the next refinement, specifying the classification algorithm would be appropriate. Here, different strategies could be selected, such as eliminating non-triangle cases before classifying, classifying with non-triangle cases as the exception, or a mixture of the two. The subfunction at this next level would specify the strategy selected and define a complete and unambiguous classification algorithm.

A flowchart for one solution[5] to this program is shown in figure 9.1 and the corresponding design refinement with the function–subfunction elaboration in figure 9.2. Note that English is used, where appropriate, which reflects a designer's decision about the function content and illustrates the point that there is no one correct way (nor should there be) to decompose requirements for software design.

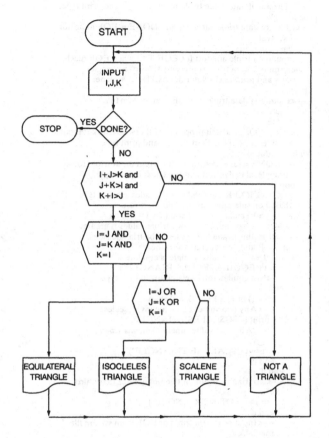

Figure 9.1 Flowchart description of triangle solver problem.

CORRECTNESS VERIFICATION PROCEDURE

In this chapter, software correctness is defined as the correspondence between a requirement and the design logic that purports to satisfy that requirement. Functions, subfunctions, and design constructs are introduced to hypothesize solutions. Verification is introduced to validate the hypotheses.

Functional verification is organized around correctness proofs, which are defined for the design constructs used in a software design. The proof for a construct is applied in exactly the same way, wherever that construct

```
 1.    --<Determine if data value triple forms triangle and print type.        >
 2.    proc triangle
 3.    --<I,J,K are data triple variables and DONE is EOF indicator.           >
 4.    var i,j,k: Real
 5.        done: Boolean
 6.    --<Input data triple and test for EOF. Exit when EOF reached.
 7.        Determine if data triple represents sides of a triangle,
 8.        classify and print as equilateral, isosceles or scalene.           >
 9.    begin
10.    --<Input first data triple or EOF from system file.                    >
11.    read i,j,k
12.    read done
13.    --<When EOF read exit procedure; otherwise check if inputs
14.        are sides of triangle, then classify and print type.              >
15.    while (    done)
16.        --<DONE = false: determine if current input triple forms
17.            triangle, classify/print and read next input triple.          >
18.        loop
19.        --<Check if I,J,K are valid triangle sides, classify type
20.            based on side relationships and print results.                >
21.        if (i + j > k) and (j + k > i) and (k + i > j) then
22.            --<Test that sum of any two triple values is greater
23.                than third value for values to be triangle sides.         >
24.            if (i = j) and (j = k) and (k = i) then
25.                --<I = J = K means triangle is equilateral.               >
26.                print ('EQUILATERAL TRIANGLE')
27.                --<Not equilateral, so check further for type.            >
28.            else
29.                if (i = j) or (j = k) or (k = i) then
30.                    --<Any two values equal means isosceles.              >
31.                    print ('ISOSCELES TRIANGLE')
32.                    --<All three values unequal means scalene.            >
33.                else
34.                    print ('SCALENE TRIANGLE')
35.                end if
36.            end if
37.            --<No triangle if sum of two not greater than third.          >
38.            else
39.                print ('NOT A TRIANGLE')
40.            end if
41.        --<Input next data triple or EOF from system file.                >
42.        read i,j,k
43.        read done
44.    end loop
45.    end
```

Figure 9.2   Process design language description of triangle solver
problem.

is used in a design. In the identified design process verification is performed twice: first by the software designer in constructing a design and then by other software engineers when inspecting that design. The designer must establish the correctness of the design for the current level of refinement before proceeding, which also ensures the soundness of the subfunction specifications for the next level of refinement.

Independent inspections check the designer's approach to correctness and confirm the correctness of a design. This is a decidedly different role for software inspections, which are no longer limited to finding errors in designs and code. In the verification context inspections are an audit of the designer's correctness proofs, which suggests a positive quality focus (i.e., yes/no on correctness). Current practice provides more of a yardstick from inspections, which is useful for the comparison of error rates across different software developments.

CORRECTNESS VERIFICATION EXAMPLE

To illustrate a use of the verification procedure, the sample design for the triangle solver program (see figure 9.2) is used. As can be seen, 45 lines of design language record the design in terms of design constructs such as sequence, while–loop, and if–then–else. The value-add of this design description comes from the elaboration of function specifications at each level in the design. These are recorded as the commentary, enclosed in angle brackets on lines 1, 3, 6, 10, 13, etc. in figure 9.2. The content of the commentary (function specification) is chosen by the designer and, as shown, can be a mix of English and/or symbolic text. The only obligation

1. Does the combination of behavior specs on lines 3 and 6 satisfy the intended function on line 1?
2. Does the combination of behavior specs on lines 10 and 13 satisfy the behavior spec on line 6?
3. Is loop termination guaranteed for any argument on the predicate on line 15 (i.e. $\neg$DONE)?
   AND
   Does the behavior spec on line 13 equal the behavior spec on line 16 followed by the behavior spec on line 13 when the predicate on line 15 (i.e. $\neg$DONE) is true?
   AND
   Does the behavior spec on line 13 equal identity when the predicate on line 15 (i.e. $\neg$DONE) is false?
4. Does the combination of behvior specs on lines 19 and 41 satisfy the behavior spec on line 16?
5. Does the behavior spec on line 22 satisfy the behavior spec on line 19 when the predicate on line 21 (i.e. $(i + j > k)$ AND $(j + k > i)$ AND $(k + i > j)$) is true?
   AND
   Does the behavior spec on line 37 satisfy the behavior spec on line 19 when the predicate on line 21 (i.e. $(i + j > k)$ AND $(k + i > j)$) is false?
6. Does the behavior spec on line 25 satisfy the behavior spec on line 22 when the predicate on line 24 (i.e. $(i = j)$ AND $(j = k)$ AND $(k = i)$) is true?
   AND
   Does the behavior spec on line 27 satisfy the behavior spec on line 22 when the predicate on line 24 (i.e. $(i = j)$ AND $(j = k)$ AND $(k = i)$) is false?
7. Does the behavior spec on line 30 satisfy the behavior spec on line 27 when the predicate on line 29 (i.e. $(i = j)$ OR $(j = k)$ OR $(k = i)$) is true?
   AND
   Does the behavior spec on line 32 satisfy the behavior spec on line 27 when the predicate on line 29 (i.e. $(i = j)$ OR $(j = k)$ OR $(k = i)$) is false?

Figure 9.3 Correctness proof for triangle solver problem.

on the designer is to make the content rigorous enough to support verification. The designer may elect not to provide specifications for anything that is considered an obvious function, so that in this case commentary as in lines 3, 25, 30, 32, and 37 might not be included. The important point is that the designer makes the conscious decision on the need for a specification before it is discarded.

As the design evolves, the designer should organize a correctness proof such as shown in figure 9.3. The particular proof systematically steps through the program logic based on the hierarchical structure of the design constructs used for the refinement. These same proof steps would be subsequently revisited during inspection to obtain an independent confirmation on the design correctness. With problems the size of the triangle solver problem, the complete design can be inspected at one time. For larger problems, a series of inspections might be required as pieces of the design evolved. A reasonable rule of thumb is to inspect each 200–250 lines of the design, which is acceptable for maintaining the inspector's concentration and for constraining the extent of the redesign when correctness cannot be verified.

CORRECTNESS VERIFICATION AS ALTERNATIVE TO STRUCTURAL TEST

This review of formal design and verification strategies was given to provide background for the examination of an alternative to the traditional software testing strategies. In software development two testing strategies are generally employed. The first concentrates on validating the internal structure of the software and is labelled as "whitebox" or structural test. The second considers the software as a complete product and validates the function, performance, and quality that is provided to the user. This is labelled "blackbox" or functional test.

Software developers are generally responsible for structural testing and other test or engineering groups for functional testing. In practice both strategies are used to varying degrees by each group, but the responsibility split tends to hold. A functional approach to correctness verification focuses on the structure of a software design, so verification would be expected to satisfy the same objectives as structural test. Because of the systematic allocation of requirements during a formal design process, the same verification methods could also address many functional test objectives, but this is not considered in this chapter. Rather the focus is on the overlap between correctness verification and structural test methods and on their relative impacts on software quality and development process productivity.

QUESTION OF SOFTWARE QUALITY

Table 9.1, which is taken from published data[6] on trends in software quality, projected the impact of design, test, and management processes on software quality. More recently published data[7,8] confirm that the average rate of 50 defects per 1000 lines of source code (ksloc) is still being experienced, particularly when modern development methods are not used.

These same published data also confirm that modern design methods can reduce error rate to the 20–40 defects per ksloc range. Published data from Cleanroom software projects[9] indicate that error rates in the 0–20 defects per ksloc range are realized when formal design and correctness verification methods are used.

Most defects (some 80%) are introduced during the design and coding steps.[6] Table 9.2 profiles the effectiveness of inspections and testing in removing defects for a sample of recent IBM software. These data correlate with published data that typically report 50–60% of software defects to be uncovered during inspections. The 40–50% remaining defects (i.e., defect leakage from inspections) are left for discovery during test, with half found through developer (structural) test. Functional tests by independent groups attempt to drive the defect number to zero to assure delivery of high-quality products.

Table 9.1 Software quality trends

	Defect rates (defects/1000 lines of code)	
	Total development	At delivery
Traditional practice	50–60	15–18
Bottom-up design		
Unstructured code		
Removal through testing		
Modern practice	20–40	2–4
Top-down design		
Structured programming		
Design/code inspections		
Incremental releases		
Future improvements	0–20	0–1
Formal design practice		
Correctness verification		
Reliability measurement		

Table 9.2   Profiles of defect removal efficiencies

Defect removal step	Software product									
	1	2	3	4	5	6	7	8	9	10
Inspection	0.50	0.60	0.58	0.66	0.60	0.57	0.70	0.46	0.52	0.52
Testing										
Structural	0.25	0.24	0.21	0.17	0.19	0.20	0.15	0.24	0.22	0.24
Functional	0.25	0.16	0.21	0.17	0.21	0.23	0.15	0.30	0.26	0.24
Defect leakage from inspection	0.50	0.40	0.42	0.34	0.40	0.43	0.30	0.54	0.48	0.48

The significant software-quality benefit from using the verification methods is improved defect removal, working in concert with simpler (more defect-free) software designs. As a software designer must verify designs as they are constructed and expose them to subsequent independent reverification, the normal strategy is to solve problems with simple and straightforward solutions. Reported experience[9] points out this "right the first time" trend and describes a changed character in defects, which tend to be easier to find and fix.

Because of the similar orientation of verification with inspection and structural test, verification might be expected to uncover 75–80% of the total software defects. Even better detection results are reported,[9] however, with less than 10% of defects persisting into the test step. Developing software where essentially all defects (90+%) are found and eliminated before any execution of code explains the quality of the delivered code.

QUESTION OF PROCESS PRODUCTIVITY

The generally accepted model for software development has a 40–20–40 split in a developer's effort for design, coding, and test (basically structural). Correctness verification would have a real productivity impact if it could offset all or part of this test effort. To look at the productivity impacts, a comparison was made of the correctness verification and structural test methods. The underlying premise is that verification considers the same logic and data executions that would be examined by discrete cases during test, so that the effort involved in each approach could be compared.

Structural testing theory[10,11] suggests the use of more than one test method, each of which would contribute to the total validation of a software product. Statement and branch testing are basic to all testing strategies. They are used to check that each coded statement and each leg of a branch could be executed, whenever reached in the processing. They provide minimal validation and must be augmented by path testing to obtain reasonable confidence in the correctness of a software implementation.

Path testing is viewed as a more complete method for structural test but is also recognized as impractical for software of any complexity or significant size. Complete path testing requires a combinatorial addressing of all logic nesting based on dataflow dependencies and the execution of all values within expected data domains. As this is clearly an impossible task, a commonly adopted compromise strategy is to test subsets of the possible paths to reach some confidence in the design in lieu of confirming design correctness.

To study the productivity question, a randomly selected set of 100 software design segments was examined. These segments comprised some 6,500 design statements and were used to address a variety of application areas (e.g., language processing, avionics, and manufacturing). To determine the structural test requirements, these design segments were analysed for the logic structures that would trigger test selections for the resultant code (statement sequences, procedure/function calls, branches and loops). Data on the number of such structures in each segment are shown in table 9.3.

To compare the two methods, a working hypothesis was formulated that assumed that the effort required for selecting and executing tests was comparable to working through a correctness verification step. This may be too liberal as the software designer's effort in organizing a correctness proof and the subsequent inspection of that proof can, on average, be measured in minutes whereas the work involved in defining/executing a test case and analysing execution results tends to be measured in at least tens of minutes.

A second hypothesis was needed to translate the summaries on logic structures into comparable counts of required test cases. For this conversion, it was assumed that one discrete test would be required for each statement sequence and for each procedure/function call but that two discrete tests would be required for each branch and loop structure.

The loop assumption provides for one test of execution without loop iteration and a second test of execution with some iteration through the

Table 9.3   Analysis of design segments sample

Design segment	Stmt count	Proof		Logic forms				
		Steps	Topics	Loop	Branch	Call	Sequence	Total
1	55	9	17	—	5	2	3	10
2	51	5	8	1	3	—	—	4
3	127	23	50	1	2	15	—	17
4	54	4	9	2	2	—	4	8
5	52	7	12	1	2	1	1	7
6	55	8	15	2	2	1	2	8
7	57	11	20	1	6	—	2	9
8	56	9	16	—	4	2	2	8
9	55	21	38	—	7	10	1	18
10	50	11	19	—	1	7	2	10
11	54	16	30	—	4	8	1	13
12	59	5	8	—	3	—	4	7
13	56	8	14	1	4	—	2	7
14	54	23	38	1	7	8	—	16
15	55	10	18	1	4	3	1	9
16	57	9	18	2	3	2	3	10
17	57	14	25	1	4	5	4	14
18	54	5	10	1	2	1	—	4
19	54	7	14	2	3	—	1	6
20	55	7	13	—	5	1	1	7
21	54	8	18	2	1	4	—	7
22	56	16	29	1	5	6	1	13
23	54	8	15	1	3	2	1	7
24	54	10	17	1	3	2	2	8
25	54	4	12	—	4	1	—	5
26	55	6	11	1	2	1	3	7
27	57	8	15	1	2	3	3	9
28	54	6	11	2	2	1	1	6
29	54	5	9	1	2	—	—	3
30	55	8	14	1	2	2	2	7
31	67	16	28	1	2	10	3	16
32	129	1	1	—	—	—	1	1
33	70	17	25	—	8	—	9	17
34	122	25	39	—	14	—	11	25
35	107	27	43	—	13	—	14	27
36	70	17	27	—	7	—	10	17

Table 9.3 – *continued*

Design segment	Stmt count	Proof		Logic forms				
		Steps	Topics	Loop	Branch	Call	Sequence	Total
37	68	13	21	—	5	—	8	13
38	66	8	14	—	2	—	6	8
39	59	7	12	—	5	—	2	7
40	51	2	3	—	1	—	1	2
41	50	5	7	—	2	—	3	5
42	48	5	7	—	2	—	3	5
43	39	4	7	—	1	—	3	4
44	64	16	28	1	3	10	2	16
45	40	8	12	—	4	—	4	8
46	34	6	10	—	1	—	5	6
47	91	14	23	—	7	—	7	14
48	35	5	7	—	2	—	3	5
49	48	7	12	—	5	—	2	7
50	57	13	21	—	5	—	8	13
51	56	11	19	—	2	5	3	10
52	57	11	20	1	4	4	1	10
53	54	4	8	1	2	—	2	5
54	52	16	30	—	—	14	1	15
55	58	12	22	—	5	5	1	11
56	59	15	28	2	3	6	2	13
57	72	7	20	—	6	—	—	6
58	58	9	14	1	2	3	2	8
59	55	8	11	3	3	—	—	6
60	61	5	12	4	—	1	4	9
61	85	2	3	—	—	1	2	3
62	53	9	17	1	4	2	1	8
63	59	8	13	—	2	3	3	8
64	61	11	20	—	3	5	3	11
65	57	11	18	2	2	5	1	10
66	58	14	25	2	4	5	2	13
67	62	7	11	2	2	—	4	8
68	54	10	21	3	2	3	3	11
69	57	12	21	2	3	4	4	13
70	54	8	13	1	3	2	—	6
71	54	11	21	—	1	8	—	9
72	51	3	7	2	—	—	3	5

Table 9.3 – *continued*

Design segment	Stmt count	Proof		Logic forms				
		Steps	Topics	Loop	Branch	Call	Sequence	Total
73	55	15	27	—	7	4	—	11
74	58	6	12	1	2	2	2	7
75	56	8	17	—	5	1	1	7
76	56	11	21	2	4	2	1	9
77	54	3	5	—	2	—	2	4
78	57	12	23	1	5	4	3	13
79	54	8	14	—	3	3	2	8
80	56	9	18	1	2	5	1	9
81	60	5	7	—	2	—	3	5
82	35	7	10	—	3	—	4	7
83	35	7	10	—	3	—	4	7
84	37	4	7	—	1	2	1	4
85	42	8	16	—	8	—	—	8
86	62	17	37	—	6	9	2	17
87	64	13	20	—	5	—	8	13
88	37	4	8	—	1	1	2	4
89	81	11	18	2	3	—	6	11
90	85	12	20	—	4	3	4	11
91	81	4	6	—	—	2	2	2
92	68	7	11	—	1	2	4	7
93	154	35	56	1	6	16	11	34
94	71	21	39	—	6	11	5	22
95	61	18	32	—	5	9	4	18
96	69	6	10	—	2	2	1	5
97	105	19	44	—	2	15	1	18
98	279	73	122	—	16	34	23	73
99	290	52	88	—	16	20	15	51
100	97	17	31	—	14	—	2	16
Totals	6,575	1,123	1,993	65	375	331	308	1,079
Averages	65.8	11.2	19.9	0.7	3.8	3.3	3.1	10.8

loop. This assumption offers minimum loop validation where more typically a minimum of four tests would be considered for reasonable validation, using structured path testing techniques.[10] Applying these assumptions against the table 9.3 data on the 100 design segments, an average of 15.4 tests would be required to provide a minimal structural test of the particular design segments.

To make a productivity comparison, correctness verification of this set of software (table 9.3) would require an average of 11.2 steps for a complete correctness examination. Though the absolute numbers are not crucial, the trends in the table 9.3 data are. They indicate that correctness proofs are typically compact and use a small number of steps (e.g., the seven steps in the proof for the triangle problem). This is not the case with structural testing, where the preferred method (path testing) is considered impractical in terms of complete coverage, forcing the use of arbitrary test subsets to accommodate the schedule/cost objectives of the development effort.

To support the comparison conclusion further, the triangle problem is again used to illustrate the difficulties in defining structural tests. Whereas formal verification uses a seven-step proof that also addresses the iteration case, some 16 tests are suggested,[12] in a set of 14 self-assessment questions, as an adequate but incomplete check on one pass through the design. The indicated tests consider both valid and invalid input sequences, which is exactly what is examined at each validation step, where the legality of the input domain is continually checked. An additional point is made[12] that experienced software testers tend to define only half (7, 8) of the suggested tests, which reinforces the point that defining structural tests even for small programs is nontrivial.

This productivity difference between verification and structural testing methods tends to hold across software applications and suggests the potential for overall cost and schedule savings. The time and cost connected with more careful design and implementation are more than offset by the savings from substantially eliminating the structural testing within a development. Thus a net reduction can be realized in the cost of the software development. The experience with Cleanroom methods[9] identifies a minimal role for structural testing, as software with exceptional quality was produced without any developer testing.

Additional study is required and planned to confirm that correctness verification methods scale-up for any size and application type and to demonstrate that similar cost efficiencies can be realized with their application. The payoff, if the indicated trends hold, will be that more defect prevention can be introduced into the software process and that overall lower costs can be realized in development.

References

1 Dyer, M., "Designing software for provable correctness", *Inf. Soft. Technol.* Vol. 30, No. 6 (July/August 1988) pp. 331–340.

2 Mills, H. D., "The new math of computer programming," *Commun. ACM* Vol. 18, No. 1 (January 1975).

3 Linger, R. C., Mills, H. D., and Witt, B. I., *Structured programming: theory and practice*, Addison-Wesley, Reading, MA (1979).

4 Fagan, M. E., "Design and code inspections to reduce errors in program development," *IBM Syst. J.* Vol. 17, (1978).

5 Hennell, M. A., *Testing for the achievement of software reliability*, Pergamon Infotech Ltd, Oxford (1986).

6 Knight, B. M., "On software quality and productivity," *IBM Tech. Directions* No. 2 (1978).

7 NSIA, *Proc. NSIA Software Reliability Conf.* (March 1988), pp. 70, 209, 335, 591.

8 Grady, R. B., "Role of software metrics in managing quality and testing," in *Proc. Sixth Int. Software Testing Conf.* (May 1989).

9 Linger, R. C., and Mills, H. D., "Case study in Cleanroom software engineering," in *COMPSAC '88 Proc.* (October 1988).

10 Ntafos, S. C., "A comparison of some structural testing strategies," *IEEE Trans. Soft. Eng.* Vol. 14, No. 6 (June 1988).

11 Prather, R. E., "Theory of program testing – an overview," *Bell Syst. Tech. J.* Vol. 62 (December 1983).

12 Myers, G. J., *The art of software testing*, John Wiley, New York (1979).

10 Reuse and Cleanroom

E.-A. KARLSSON

1 INTRODUCTION

The purpose of this chapter is to present how the development process used in Cleanroom Software Engineering[1] can be adapted to incorporate reuse. We use the general guidelines and techniques for object oriented reuse developed in the ESPRIT project REBOOT,* which are adaptable to initially non-object oriented development processes. In addition we argue that the Cleanroom concept has many aspects which are advantageous for reuse.

The rest of this chapter is organized as follows:

- Section 2 gives a short overview of Cleanroom Software Engineering and summarizes the practices in Cleanroom which support reuse.
- Section 3 provides an overview of what we have adapted in Cleanroom to support reuse.
- Sections 4–6 go into more detail on the adaptations of the different models, activities and documents in the Cleanroom process.

This contribution was first published in the *Proceedings of the First Annual European Industrial Symposium on Cleanroom Software Engineering (EISCSE)*, held in Copenhagen, Denmark, on October 26–27, 1993, and is reprinted with the permission of Q-Labs.

* REBOOT (REuse Based on Object-Oriented Techniques) is a 4 year, 124 man years, ESPRIT-2 Project #5327/#7808 that started in September 1990. The partners are Bull S.A. (prime, France), Cap Gemini Innovation (France), LGI at IMAG (France), SEMA GROUP S.A.E. (Spain), Siemens A.G. (Germany), Q-Labs and Frameworks (Sweden), TXT (Italy) and SINTEF/NTH (Norway).

2   OVERVIEW OF CLEANROOM SOFTWARE ENGINEERING

In this section we briefly discuss the basic models and practices of the Cleanroom development process, which we will later adapt to development for reuse.

This section is not intended as a Cleanroom tutorial, but to give a short explanation of the concepts, so that the adaptations can be put in perspective. For a more thorough discussion of the Cleanroom process and concepts we refer to reference 1.

2.1   Model and process overview

Models are used to analyse, design and implement the software system, and one of the main tasks in adapting a process to development for reuse is to understand the models in the process, and how to represent variability in them. The Cleanroom software development is based on models shown in figure 10.1.

The purposes of these models are as follows:

- The Mission is a textual representation of the requirements as stated by the customer and refined by the developers. It contains both functional requirements as well as how the system is to be delivered.
- The User reference manual is a description of the interface of the system. If the system is to be incorporated in a larger system it is the application programmer's interface. The User reference manual is used to validate the requirements towards the customer. The User Reference Manual also contains information on how to configure, compose, build and install the system.

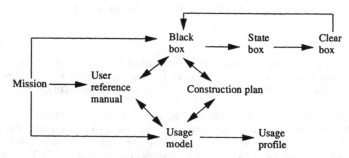

Figure 10.1   The models of Cleanroom Software Engineering.

- The (top level) Black box is the formalized specification of the system expressed as stimuli histories and responses. The State box is a transformation of the Black box where we have represented selected stimuli histories as state data. The Clear box is a further refinement where we have identified lower level Black boxes to which we propagate stimuli. The development from a top level Black box to code is formalized by steps of invention, transformation and verification in the Box Structure Algorithm. The Black box can be considered as the system viewed from inside and out, i.e. we describe the responses the system gives based on the stimuli which the system can get.
- The Usage model represents the behaviour of the users of the system, usually expressed as a state machine. The Usage model is the system seen from the outside and in, i.e. we describe the users of the system, the stimuli they give and how they affect each other. The Usage profile assigns probabilities to the transitions in the Usage model; this gives a Markov model. The Markov model is used to generate tests from which we can estimate the reliability of the system under normal operation, i.e. MTTF.
- The Construction plan divides the development of the system into vertical increments instead of the traditional horizontal breakdown into subsystems. This gives Cleanroom a touch of spiral model, but in contrast to the original spiral model it is only the realization which is broken into increments, not the analysis. The Construction plan must take into consideration that it shall be possible to add each increment to the previous, and test the sum of increments according to parts of the Usage model.

A typical Cleanroom development project can be illustrated as shown in figure 10.2.

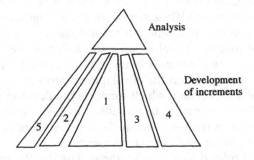

Figure 10.2 Cleanroom development in increments.

Here Analysis includes all the specification models: Mission, User reference manual, Black box, Usage model and Construction plan. It is important to notice that the increments can be developed partly in parallel as long as they are only dependent on already finished increments to be executable. In figure 10.2 we could envisage the following dependencies: 2 and 3 depend on 1, 5 depends on 2, and 4 on 3. Then increment 2 and 3 could be developed in parallel.

2.2   Sound engineering practices supporting reuse

Most of the successes of Cleanroom techniques can be traced back to sound engineering practices which are enforced and supported by the process. We will here discuss those which we find most important, and their connection to reuse:

- Ample time on analysis and well defined specification models. In an average Cleanroom project 50–60% of the time is used in the initial analysis, i.e. developing the specification models (User reference manual, top level Black box, Usage model and Construction plan). The specification models are also well defined, giving a clear media of communication. In development for reuse it is important to get all the requirements from all possible reusers before we make any design decisions, and this is supported by the long analysis time.
- Several independent specification models: User reference manual, Black box, Usage model and Construction plan. There are several – partly overlapping, partly giving different views – specification models of the system. This improves the quality and completeness of the specification which is important for development for reuse where the requirements incorporate variability.
- A well defined development algorithm. When development of the increments starts, Cleanroom has a well defined Box structure algorithm to transform the top level Black box to code. This algorithm makes it easier to adapt the process to development for reuse, as it is clear which activities we must modify. It is also easier to verify that we are incorporating all the different requirements in our design, as we have a larger degree of intellectual control over the development process.
- Incremental development which supports the development of invariant functionality in the earlier increments which can then be reused as is. Later reusers can then start from these increments and add their specific functionality as additional increments.
- Well defined roles during development. The development team is split into three subteams: specification, construction and certification. The

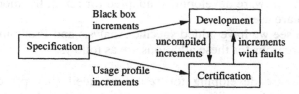

Figure 10.3 Cleanroom teams and interfaces.

interfaces between the teams are illustrated in figure 10.3.

In development for reuse the role of the certification team may need to be extended to incorporate also the validation of the reusability of the components and its documentation. The separate specification team can also be a safeguard that all the reuse requirements are realized in the development.

- Team work and frequent reviews. All work is done in teams, and in the Box structure algorithm there are frequent reviews and verifications which are done in teams. The different specification models are also verified against each other before construction starts. In development for reuse frequent reviews will ensure that we do not neglect some requirements, and that our solution really is reusable for all potential reusers.
- Focus on quality by doing it right the first time, and discover mistakes as early as possible. This is achieved by all the previous five points, and is particularly important for reusable components which are supposed to be reused in several applications.

3   WHAT HAS BEEN ADAPTED

Adapting a software process to development for and with reuse means to adapt the three components of the process:

- The models used to analyse the problem and express the solution have to be extended to incorporate variability in the problem and generality in the solutions.
- The activities have to be extended with specific reuse steps where we take into account reuse, both development for and with reuse.
- The documents have to be extended to record the reuse potential of the components, so that they can be reused later. We also have to prepare so that the documentation of reused components can be incorporated into our design (development with reuse).

In Cleanroom software development adapted for reuse, the models shown in figure 10.4 are used.

As we can see we have added specific Analysis and Preliminary design models. The reasons for these additions are as follows:

- When we are developing for reuse we need to capture different requirements from different customers (reusers). Not all of these requirements are profitable to incorporate in this system. For this reason we need models to capture the requirements and examine different solution strategies.
- When developing with reuse we need to investigate potential components which can be reused in this system. This investigation is supported by the preliminary design model.
- In Cleanroom it is recommended to use 50–60% of the time in the analysis and specification phase, investigating the problem and solution domain. This will be even more important when we incorporate reuse, and what we have done is to introduce models to investigate the problem (analysis) and solutions (preliminary design).

The other models have the same purposes as in original Cleanroom development, but are adapted to handle variability in requirements (problems) and generality in design (solution). The new analysis models and the adaptations of the existing models are described in the following sections.

Analysis involves iteration among the Mission where the textual requirements are stated, the Analysis model where we use an object oriented approach and the Preliminary design model which is a set of collaborating black boxes.

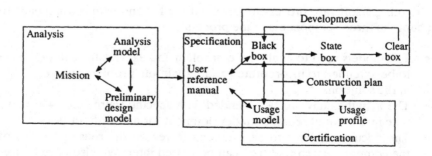

Figure 10.4   Adapted Cleanroom models.

4 ANALYSIS

4.1 Models and reuse activities

The analysis step is the first activity in Cleanroom development. The initial input to the analysis is a description of the requirements in the form of a Mission written by the customer, describing in general the system to be developed related to the Original problem space. The analysis will clarify the specification in a form that both the customer and the developer can agree upon. This is done with the help of the analysis model, which formalizes the requirements in the mission. The analysis activity has several purposes.

- The main purpose is to capture the customer requirements, the problem domain. As mentioned earlier the customer has written a mission, but the information it provides is usually not enough to precisely specify the system. The initial mission is detailed and clarified in the analysis activity.
- The second purpose is to create an understanding of the system to be developed, the solution domain. This gives the opportunity to evaluate different solution strategies, and gives a better understanding of the problem. These solutions will provide input to the construction planning and development phases.
- The last purpose is to serve as a basis for reuse analysis. This includes both development for and with reuse.

The analysis activity incorporating reuse considerations is depicted in figure 10.5.

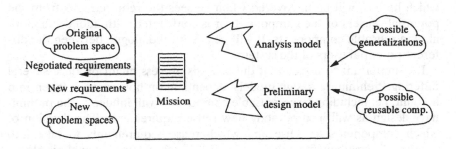

Figure 10.5 The analysis phase.

Reuse influences the analysis process in several ways:

- New requirements have to be taken into account from potential customers (reusers). These new customers have a problem space which is slightly different from the one of the original customer, and these differences have to be identified and analysed. We have also to assure that we can represent these differences in the preliminary design model. The identification of conflicts between the old and the new requirements can lead to a negotiation of the total set of requirements to provide the optimal solution.
- When doing an analysis or a preliminary design potential generalization opportunities will arise. These can be used to improve the reusability of the system, and can also serve to discover hidden requirements in one of the considered problem spaces. The reuse opportunities can be on any level of the system, e.g. the entire system can be reused with some generalizations, or some of the possible subsystems have a large reuse potential. The potential generalizations are input to search for potential customers which will provide new requirements.
- The investigation of potential components which can be reused in this system will provide opportunities for both adding new functionality, or negotiating the original requirements so that the reused component can be utilized. It is important to start the investigation of potential components to reuse as early as possible, as large reusable components can influence the analysis and functionality of the system to a large extent, and they are hard to incorporate late in the process.

The mission is refined in this process, and should then be presented to the customers as a validation of correctness of the requirements.

This process of extending the requirements may seem costly, but experience has shown that it also has the advantage of stabilizing the requirements for the original customer. Thus many of the unknown requirements which he has, will be uncovered when he sees the requirements from the potential reusers of the component, or is confronted with added functionality in reusable components. It will be a fruitful dialogue between the different potential users of the system.

It is important to notice that the analysis process might produce several differing Preliminary design models, depending on how reuse is taken into account, i.e. including large reusable components will influence the preliminary design as will incorporating new reuse requirements. The decision of which components to reuse and which reuse requirements to take into account is a cost/benefit analysis which will be taken after the analysis phase.

The rest of this section describes techniques and processes to use in the analysis phase.

4.2 Analysis process

The OO-analysis can be organized in several ways. The most common is let one or several analysts read the mission and interview the different people involved in the development, including also the customers and users. Thereby the analysts get an overview of the different views of the system. They then gather these views into a model that has to be accepted by all people involved. This approach can be both inefficient and time-consuming. It also demands a skilled analyst, who has to create a model that satisfies all people involved in the analysis.

Another way to organize the analysis phase is to use a group dynamic analysis (GDA) technique[2] to capture the requirements. Here a brief summary of the technique is given.

GDA is an interactive technique where customers, future users, domain experts, designers, and others with interest in the system, are gathered to capture the requirements. The modelling session is very dynamic, and to support this the walls in the analysis room are covered with plastic sheets so that they can be used for drawing. The modelling language used is simple, and consists of the following parts:

- goals, subgoals and problems (requirements)
- concepts, relations and messages (object model)
- interaction scenarios (message sequence charts)

The session usually takes two consecutive half days, and is led by a GDA expert who has studied the problem to some extent in advance. The role of the GDA expert is crucial. His mission is to keep everyone active, and to help resolve problems and inconsistencies between the participants. To ensure that everyone takes active part in the analysis there are no chairs in the analysis room. The aim of GDA is to reach a consensus of what the problem is and to agree upon terminology. GDA can be used both to capture the requirements in an analysis model as well as making the preliminary design model.

Development for reuse can be incorporated in this step by including potential reusers in the modelling group. Potential for reusing existing objects (submodels) will also be identified, and should be noted.

4.3 Analysis techniques

There are many object-oriented analysis methods available on the market that can be used. These methods focus on different aspects of the system and will be more or less usable depending on the system or the subsystem to be analysed.

The methods all have a common goal, however, which is to reach an object model of the system as depicted in figure 10.6.

Three methods which we have found useful under different circumstances are as follows:

- OORAM[3] which focuses on roles and their interactions. The atomic roles are then composed into objects in a bottom-up manner.
- Objectory[4] which focuses on use cases, which are user scenarios. These use cases involves actors and domain objects. In the later design phase the intelligence in the use case is distributed to different kinds of objects: control objects representing the remaining functionality in the use cases, objects representing the domain objects and interface objects representing the actors.
- OMT[5] has three different models: an object model, a dynamic model and a functional model.

Several methods should be mastered by analysts, as they provide different ways to attack the problem.

5 SPECIFICATIONS

The input to the specification activity is the analysis model and the selected preliminary design model. At the end of the analysis step we have decided which reuse requirements we are to incorporate in the specification, and which reusable components we will incorporate in our design. The purpose of the specification phase is to make a precise user documen-

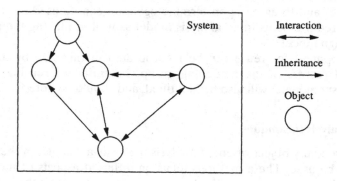

Figure 10.6   System object model.

tation and specification of the external properties of the system. The variability in the requirements and the analysis model must now be correctly captured and represented in the specification models.

An important issue to consider when making the specification is the representation of generality. There are several ways to do this:

- Isolation, where we isolate the variability in a part of the specification.
- Parameterization, where we provide parameters to customize the specification, e.g. everything from binary parameters, through scalar parameters, to functional parameters.
- Inheritance – narrowing, where we organize the specification in an inheritance hierarchy, the invariant parts as the abstract specification.
- Inclusion – widening, where we include all the functionality in one specification.
- Configuration, where we let the specification consist of several smaller specifications which can be composed in different ways to give variability on the system level.
- Generator, where we make a dedicated language to specify systems.

The choice as to how to represent the variability in the requirements is a design decision which will affect the specification and construction of the system, and these different possibilities should be investigated in the Preliminary designs, which are input to the specification phase. When we have decided how to represent the variability in the top level specification, this has to be reflected in the three specifications, User reference manual, Black box and Usage model, and in the construction plan. In the rest of this section we briefly discuss the influences on the different specifications and the construction plan.

5.1 User reference manual

The user reference manual has to incorporate all the different variability in the system. This also includes how the system is supposed to be reused, and how one can adapt the functionality of the system.

If the system is not one system, but covering a family of systems it might not be useful to try to make one User reference manual covering all the systems, but rather provide guidelines on how a user reference manual for one instantiation of the system should be.

5.2 Black box specification

Making one top level black box for a system with a large amount of variability might not always be cost effective or even possible, i.e. the different ways of configuring the systems (initiation stimuli) will change the behaviour of the system so that the black box function will be different for each configuration.

To cater for this it is possible to replace the top level black box specification with a set of interacting black boxes, which can be configured in different ways. It should be kept in mind that the splitting of the functionality of the system into several black boxes is a design decision. This decision is taken before absolutely necessary because the system is difficult to analyse due to the variability.

We will come back to the representation of variability with inheritance in the box structures later.

5.3   Usage modelling

The intention of making the Usage model reusable is to provide support for the reusers' test and certification of the reusable component. There are several aspects which have to be taken into account here:

- If the component is reused as is, the Usage profile might change. This means that we can reuse the Usage model, but that we must provide new transition probabilities for the Usage profile, and redo the certification.
- If the component is to be adapted we would like to reuse as much as possible of the Usage model. This means that the usage model should be adaptable the same way as the component itself.

5.4   Construction plan

The Construction plan supports development for and with reuse:

- Common invariant functionality can be allocated to earlier increments so that reusers can start with those increments and add their particular functionality.
- It serves as a help to divide the system into parts with reusable functionality, i.e. developing reusable components in separate increments.
- It helps when developing with reuse since the adaptations of the software can follow the Construction plan and thereby will ease the certification process.
- The justification will form a description of why the specific incremental division has been made.

It is not trivial to find the increments, but a good help is the Preliminary design made in the analysis phase.

When developing software using object-oriented methods, one faces problems when trying to make an incremental division of the system. Sometimes the functionality gathered in an object and the functionality in an increment are partly orthogonal, as depicted in figure 10.7.

This makes it harder to make an incremental division. We have found three approaches to handle this complication:

- Use subclassing as a basis for increments. The idea is to capture base functionality in a higher level object in the inheritance hierarchy. Functionality in later increments will then be added through subclassing. The increments will then follow the inheritance hierarchy derived for the system.
- Isolate functionality to groups of classes. This approach is to isolate the base functionality to a number of classes. These classes will then be the first increment in the system. The rest of the functionality will then be described as services associated to a class or a group of classes. Thereby it is possible that part of the functionality in an increment will not be used in the present configuration but still can be tested.
- Split classes which are on the border between increments in two.

As an example we have developed a Construction plan for the Fire Alarm System. A description of the system is shown in figure 10.8.

The different increments are as follows:

- Increment 1 contains the boxes for the Detector unit and the Actuator unit. The reason for this is that these units can be connected into a sys-

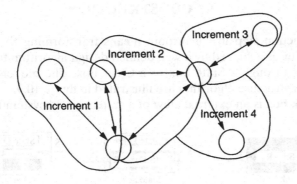

Figure 10.7 Increment contents vs. class contents.

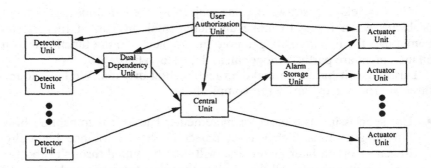

Figure 10.8   The fire alarm system.

tem that works and to some extent capture the base functionality of the
system.
- Increment 2 contains the box for the Central unit which makes it possible to connect several detectors and actuators in the same system.
- Increment 3 contains the box Dual dependency unit.
- Increment 4 contains the box Alarm storage unit.
- Increment 5 contains the box User authorization unit.

The motivation for this division is quite simple. Through this division we
capture the main functionality of the system and then increase the functionality by a number of added classes. Thereby it is simple to test and certify the functionality of the system. The incremental division of the system
is simple to make since through its design the system is easily re-configurable.

6   CONSTRUCTION

The construction step in Cleanroom means transforming the Black box
into code. This is achieved by a well defined design algorithm transforming
a Black box through a State box to a Clear box. The models developed
with the box structure algorithm are illustrated in figure 10.9.

The Black box is an external view of a system or subsystem that accepts

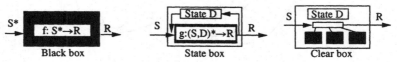

Figure 10.9   Black box, State box and Clear box.

stimuli and produces a response for each stimuli before accepting the next stimulus. The Black box omits all details of internal structure and operations and deals solely with the behaviour that is visible to its user in terms of stimuli and responses. Any Black box response is uniquely determined by the system's stimuli history.

The State box gives an intermediate system view that defines an internal system state, namely the data stored from stimulus to stimulus. Mathematically it can be established that every system described by a Black box can be described as a State box. One part of the State box is a Black box that accepts both external stimulus and the internal state as stimuli. It produces as a response both the external response and the new internal state which replaces the old state. The role of the State box is to open up the Black box one step at a time.

The Clear box opens up the State box one more step in an internal view that describes the processing of the stimulus and the state (stored data). The processing is described by sequence, alteration, iteration and concurrent. The Clear box can consist of several cooperating Black boxes that accept both stimuli and state as their stimulus. They produce both an external response and a new state as their response. Every system described as a State box can be described as a Clear box.

Note that even if we develop a system in vertical increments according to the Construction plan there is a hierarchical decomposition in lower level Black boxes within each increment.

7 CONCLUSIONS

In this chapter we have shown how to adapt the Cleanroom development process to incorporate reuse. To facilitate this we have extended it with an object oriented analysis phase, which is used in the initial specification phases. The thorough and formalized investigation of the problem and solution spaces are important to capture all the reuse opportunities. We have also discussed how to extend the Cleanroom models to incorporate the generality, and how to adapt the activities in the development process.

References

1   Harlan D. Mills, Michael Dyer and Richard C. Linger, "Cleanroom Software Engineering", *IEEE Software*, September 1987, pp. 465–484.
2   Kjell Scherlund, "Mot nya djärva språk – Modellering i gruppsamarbete med gemensam grafik", SISU report #14/90, SISU, Box 1250, 164 28 Kista, Sweden, 1990 (In Swedish).

3   Trygve Reenskaug et al., "OORASS: Seamless support for the creation and maintenance of object oriented systems", *Journal of Object Oriented Programming*, 5(6): 27–41, October 1992.
4   Ivar Jacobson et al., "Object-Oriented Software Engineering: A Use Case Driven Approach", Addison Wesley, 1992.
5   James Rumbaugh et al., "Object-Oriented Modelling and Design", Prentice Hall 1991.

11 Six-sigma Software Using Cleanroom Software Engineering Techniques

G. E. HEAD

INTRODUCTION

In the late 1980s, Motorola Inc. instituted its well-known six-sigma program.[1] This program replaced the "Zero Defects" slogan of the early '80s and allowed Motorola to win the first Malcolm Baldridge award for quality in 1988. Since then, many other companies have initiated six-sigma programs.[2]

The six-sigma program is based on the principle that long-term reliability requires a greater design margin (a more robust design) so that the product can endure the stress of use without failing. The measure for determining the robustness of a design is based on the standard deviation, or sigma, found in a standard normal distribution. This measure is called a capability index (C_p), which is defined as the ratio of the maximum allowable design tolerance limits to the traditional ±3-sigma tolerance limits. Thus, for a six-sigma design limit $C_p = 2$.

To illustrate six-sigma capability, consider a manufacturing process in which a thin film of gold must be vapor-deposited on a silicon substrate. Suppose that the target thickness of this film is 250 angstroms and that as little as 220 angstroms or as much as 280 angstroms is satisfactory. If as shown in figure 11.1 the ±30-angstrom design limits correspond to the six-sigma points of the normal distribution, only one chip in a billion will be produced with a film that is either too thin or too thick.

In any practical process, the position of the mean will vary. It is generally

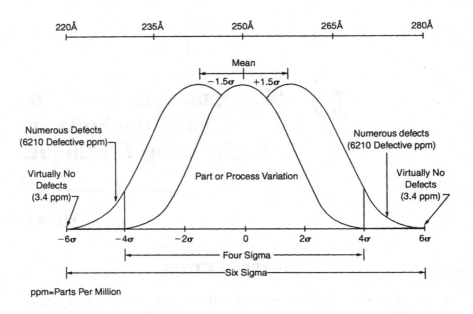

Figure 11.1   An illustration of a six-sigma design specification. A design specification of ±30 angstroms corresponds to a ±6-sigma design. Also shown is the ±1.5σ variation from the mean as a result of variations in the process.

assumed that this variation is about ±1.5 sigma. With this shift in the mean a six-sigma design would produce 3.4 parts per million defective. This is considered to be satisfactory and is becoming accepted as a quality standard. Table 11.1 lists the defective parts per million (ppm) possible for different sigma values.

At first the six-sigma measure was applied only to hardware reliability and manufacturing processes. It was subsequently recognized that it could also be applied to software quality. A number of software development methodologies have been shown to produce six-sigma quality software. Possibly the methodology that is the easiest to implement and is the most repeatable is a technique called Cleanroom Software Engineering, which was developed at ibm Corporation's Federal Systems Division during the early 1980s.[3] We applied this methodology in a limited way in a typical hp environment and achieved remarkable results.

When applied to software, the standard unit of measure is called *use*, and six-sigma in this context means fewer than 3.4 failures (deviations from

Table 11.1   Defective ppm for different sigma values

Sigma	ppm
1	697,700
2	308,733
3	66,803
4	6,210
5	233
6	3.4
7	0.019

specifications) per million uses. A use is generally defined to be something small such as the single transaction of entering an order or command line. This is admittedly a rather murky definition, but murkiness is not considered to be significant. Six-sigma is a very stringent reliability standard and is difficult to measure. If it is achieved, the user sees virtually no defects at all, and the actual definition of a use then becomes academic.

Cleanroom Software Engineering has demonstrated the ability to produce software in which the user finds no defects. We have confirmed these results at HP. This chapter reports our results and provides a description of the Cleanroom process, especially those portions of the process that we used.

CLEANROOM SOFTWARE ENGINEERING

Cleanroom Software Engineering ("Cleanroom") is a metaphor that comes from integrated circuit manufacturing. Large-scale integrated circuits must be manufactured in an environment that is free from dust, flecks of skin, and amoebas, among other things. The processes and environment are carefully controlled and the results are constantly monitored. When defects occur, they are considered to be defects in the processes and not in the product. These defects are characterized to determine the process failure that produced them. The processes are then corrected and rerun. The product is regenerated. The original defective product is not fixed, but discarded.

The Cleanroom Software Engineering philosophy is analogous to the integrated circuit manufacturing cleanroom process. Processes and environments are carefully controlled and are monitored for defects. Any defects found are considered to be defects in one or more of the processes. For example, defects could be in the specification process, the design methodology, or the inspection techniques used. Defects are not considered to be in the source file or the code module that was generated. Each defect is characterized to determine which process failed and how the failure can be prevented. The failing process is corrected and rerun. The original product is discarded. This is why one of the main proponents of Cleanroom, Dr Harlan Mills, suggests that the most important tool for Cleanroom is the wastebasket.[4]

LIFE CYCLE

The life cycle of a Cleanroom project differs from the traditional life cycle. The traditional 40–20–40 postinvestigation life cycle consists of 40% design, 20% code, and 40% unit testing. The product then goes to integration testing.

Cleanroom uses an 80–20 life cycle (80% for design and 20% for coding). The unexecuted and untested product is then presented to integration testing and is expected to work. If it doesn't work, the defects are examined to determine how the process should be improved. The defective product is then discarded and regenerated using the improved process.

NO UNIT TESTING

Unit testing does not exist in Cleanroom. Unit testing is private testing performed by the programmer with the results remaining private to the programmer.

The lack of unit testing in Cleanroom is usually met with skepticism or with the notion that something wasn't stated correctly or it was misunderstood. It seems inconceivable that unit testing should not occur. However it is a reality. Cleanroom not only claims that there is no need for unit testing, it also states that unit testing is dangerous. Unit testing tends to uncover superficial defects that are easily found during testing, and it injects "deep" defects that are difficult to expose with any other kind of testing.

A better process is to discover all defects in a public arena such as in integration testing. (Preferably, the original programmer should not be involved in performing the testing.) The same rigorous, disciplined processes would then be applied to the correction of the defects as were applied to the original design and coding of the product.

In practice, defects are almost always encountered in integration testing.

That seems to surprise no one. With Cleanroom, however, these defects are usually minor and can be fixed with nothing more than an examination of the symptoms and a quick informal check of the code. It is very seldom that sophisticated debuggers are required.

WHEN TO DISCARD THE PRODUCT

When IBM was asked about the criteria for judging a module worthy of being discarded, they stated that the basic criterion is that if testing reveals more than five defects per thousand lines of code, the module is discarded. This is a low defect density by industry standards,[5] particularly when it is considered that the code in question has never been executed even by an individual programmer. Our experience is that any half-serious attempt to implement Cleanroom will easily achieve this. We achieved a defect density of one defect per thousand lines of code the first time we did a Cleanroom project. It would appear that this "discard the offending module" policy is primarily intended to be a strong attention getter to achieve commitment to the process. It is seldom necessary to invoke it.

PRODUCTIVITY IS NOT DEGRADED

Productivity is high with Cleanroom. A trained Cleanroom team can achieve a productivity rate approaching 800 noncomment source statements (NCSS) per engineer month. Industry average is 120 NCSS per engineer month. Most HP entities quote figures higher than this, but seldom do these quotes exceed 800 NCSS.

There is also evidence that the resulting product is significantly more concise and compact than the industry average.[6] This further enhances productivity. Not only is the product produced at a high statement-per-month rate, but the total number of statements is also smaller.

NEEDED BEST PRACTICES

Cleanroom is compatible with most industry-accepted best practices for software generation. It is not necessary to unlearn anything. Some of these best practices are required (such as a structured design methodology). Others such as software reuse are optional but compatible.

As mentioned above, Cleanroom requires some sort of structured design methodology. It has been successfully employed using a number of

different design approaches. Most recently however, the Cleanroom originators are recommending a form of object-oriented design.[7]

All Cleanroom deliverables must be subject to inspections, code walk-
throughs, or some other form of rigorous peer review. It is not critical
what form is applied. What is critical is that 100% of all deliverables be
subjected to this peer-review process and that it be done in small quantities. For instance, it is recommended that no more than three to five pages
of a code module be inspected at a single inspection.

REQUIRED NEW FEATURES

In addition to the standard software engineering practices mentioned
above, there are a number of Cleanroom-specific processes that are
required or are recommended. These practices include structured specifications, functional verification, structured data, and statistical testing.
Structured specifications are applied to the project before design begins.
This strongly affects the delivery schedule and the project management
process. Functional verification is applied during design, coding, and
inspection processes. Structured data is applied during the design process.
Finally, statistical testing is the integration testing methodology of choice.
Figure 11.2 summarizes the Cleanroom processes.

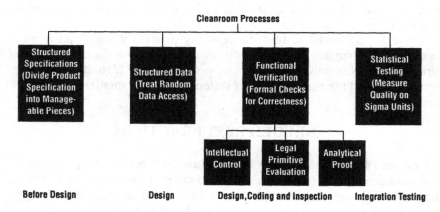

Figure 11.2   The processes recommended for Cleanroom Software
Engineering.

STRUCTURED SPECIFICATIONS

Structured specifications[8] is a term applied to the process used to divide a product specification into small pieces for implementation. It is not critical exactly how this division is accomplished as long as the results have the following characteristics:

- Each specification segment must be small enough so that it can be fully implemented by the development team within days or weeks rather than months or years.
- The result of implementing each segment must be a module that can be completely executed and tested on its own. This means that no segment can contain partially implemented features that must be avoided during testing to prevent program failure.
- The segments may not have mutual dependencies. For example, it is satisfactory for segment 4 to require the implementation of segment 3 to execute correctly. It is assumed that segment 3 will be implemented first and will exist to support the testing of segment 4. However, it is not satisfactory for segment 3 to require segment 4 to execute properly at the same time.

The structured specifications process is used by Cleanroom to facilitate control of the process by allowing the development team to focus on small, easily conceptualized pieces. A secondary but very important effect is that productivity is increased. Increased productivity is a natural effect of the team's being focused. Each deliverable is small and the time to produce it is psychologically short. The delivery date is therefore always imminent and always seems to be within reach. Morale is generally high because real progress is visible and is achievable.

Structured specifications also offer a very definite project management advantage. They serve to achieve the frequently quoted maxim that when a project is 50% complete, 50% of its features should be 100% complete instead of 100% of its features being 50% complete. Proper management visibility and the ability to control delivery schedules depend upon this maxim's being true.

Structured specifications are very similar to incremental processes described in other methodologies but often the purposes and benefits sound quite different. For instance, in one case the structured specifications process is called *evolutionary delivery*.[9] The primary benefit claimed for evolutionary delivery is that it allows "real" customers to examine early releases and provide feedback so that the product will evolve into something that really satisfies customer needs. HP supports this approach and has classes to teach the evolutionary delivery process to software developers.

From the description just given it would appear that each evolutionary release is placed into the hands of real customers. This implies to many people that the entire release process is repeated on a frequent (monthly) basis. Since multiple releases and the support of multiple versions are considered headaches for product support, this scenario is frowned upon. Cleanroom does not make it a priority to place each stage of the product into the hands of real customers.

Looking at the definition of a real customer in the evolutionary delivery process, you realize that a real customer could be the engineer at the next desk. In practice, the product cannot be delivered to more than a handful of alpha or beta testers until the product is released to the full market. This type of release should not occur any more often than normal. In fact, since Cleanroom produces high-quality products, the number of releases required for product repair is significantly reduced.

Another type of structured specifications technique, which is applied to information technology development, uses information engineering time boxes.[10] Time boxes are used as a means of preventing endless feature creep while ensuring that the product (in this case an information product) still has flexibility and adaptability to changing business requirements.

HP has adopted a technique called *short interval scheduling*[11] as a project management approach. Short interval scheduling breaks the entire project into 4–6-week chunks, each with its own set of deliverables. Short interval scheduling can be applied to other projects besides those involved in software development. This is an insight that is not obvious in other techniques.

All of these methods are very similar to the structured specifications technique. As different as they sound, they all serve to break the task into bite-sized pieces, which is the goal of the structured specifications portion of Cleanroom.

FUNCTIONAL VERIFICATION

Functional verification is the heart of Cleanroom and is primarily responsible for achieving the dramatic improvement in quality possible with Cleanroom. It is based on the tenet that, given the proper circumstances, the human intellect can determine whether or not a piece of logic is correct, and if it is not correct, devise a modification to fix it.* Functional veri-

---

* This tenet is also the definition of intellectual control.

fication has three levels: intellectual control, legal primitive evaluation, and analytical proof.

Intellectual control requires that the progression from specifications to code be done in steps that are small enough and documented well enough so that the correctness of each step is obvious. The working term here is "obvious." The reviewer should be tempted to say, "Of course this refinement level follows correctly from its predecessor! Why belabor the point?" If the reviewer is not tempted to say this, it may be advisable to redesign the refinement level or to document it more completely.

Legal primitive evaluation enhances intellectual control by providing a mathematically derived set of questions for proving and testing the assumptions made in the design specifications. Analytical proof[12] enhances legal primitive evaluation by answering the question sets mathematically. Analytical proof is a very rigorous and tedious correctness proof and is very rarely used.

We have demonstrated here at HP that intellectual control alone is capable of producing code with significantly improved defect densities compared to software developed with other traditional development processes. Application of the complete Cleanroom process will provide another two to three orders of magnitude improvement in defect densities and will produce six-sigma code.

Intellectual control

The human intellect, fallible though it may be, is able to assess correctness when presented with reasonable data in a reasonable format. *Testing is far inferior to the power of the human intellect.* This is the key point. All six-sigma software processes revolve around this point. It is a myth that software must contain defects. This myth is a self-fulfilling prophecy and prevents defect-free software from being routinely presented to the marketplace. The prevalence of the defect myth is the result of another myth, which is that the computer is superior to the human and that computer testing is the best way to ensure reliable software.

We are told that the human intellect can only understand complexities when they are linked together in close, simple relationships. This limitation can be made to work for us. If it is ignored, it works against us and handicaps our creative ability. Making this limitation work for us is the basis of functional verification.

The basis for intellectual control and functional verification is a structured development hierarchy. Most of us are familiar with a representation of a hierarchy like the one modeled in figure 11.3. This could be an illustration of how to progress from design specifications to actual code

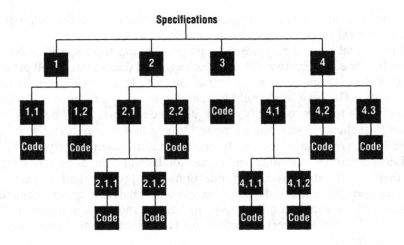

Figure 11.3   A typical representation of a hierarchical diagram. In this case the representation is for a software design.

using any one of the currently popular, industry-accepted best practices for design. Each of these practices has some form of stepwise refinement. Each breaks down the specifications into ever greater detail. The result is a program containing a set of commands in some programming language.

The difference between the different software design methods is reflected in the interpretation of what the squares and the connecting lines in figure 11.3 represent. If the developer is using structured design techniques, they would mean data and control connections, and if the developer is using object-oriented design, they would represent objects in an object-oriented hierarchy.

Functional verification does not care what these symbols represent. In any of these methods, the squares 1, 2, 3, and 4 are supposed to describe fully the functionality of the specifications at that level. Similarly, 4.1 through 4.3 fully describe the functionality of square 4, and the code of square 3 fully implements the functionality of square 3. Intellectual control can be achieved with any of them by adhering to the following five principles.

Principle 1

Documentation must be complete. The first key principle is that the documentation of the refinement levels must be complete. It must fully reflect the requirements of the abstraction level immediately above it. For instance, it must be possible to locate within the documentation of squares 1 through 4 in our example every feature described in the specifications.

If documentation is complete, intellectual control is nearly automatic. In the case described above, the designer intuitively works to make the documentation and the specifications consistent with each other. The inspectors intuitively study to confirm the correctness.

Note that it is not always necessary to reproduce the specifications word for word. It will often be possible to simply state, "This module fully implements the provisions of specification section 7-4b." The inspectors need only confirm that it makes sense for section 7-4b to be treated in a single module.

Other times it may be necessary to define considerably more than what is in the specifications. A feature that is spread over several modules requires a specific description of which portion is treated in each module and exactly how the modules interact with each other. It must be possible for the inspectors to look at all the modules as a whole and determine that the feature is properly implemented in the full module orchestration.

This principle is commonly violated. All industry-accepted best design processes encourage full documentation, but it is still not done because these design processes often lack the perspective and the respect for intellectual control that is provided by the principles of functional verification, or they are insufficiently compelling to convey this respect. The concept of intellectual control is often lost by many design processes because the main emphasis is on the mechanics of the specific methodology.

The result is that frequently the documentation for the first level of the system specifications is nothing more than the names of the modules (e.g., 1. Data Base Access Module, 2. In-Line Update Module, 3. Initialization Module, 4. User Interface Module). It is left to the inspectors to guess, based on the names, what portions of the specifications were intended to be in which module.

Even when there is an attempt to conform fully to the methodology and provide full documentation, neither the designer nor the inspectors seem to worry about the continuity that is required by functional verification. For example, a feature required in the design specification might show up first in level 4.1.2 or in the code associated with level 4.1.2 without ever having been referenced in levels 4 or 4.1. Sometimes the chosen design methodology does not sufficiently indicate that this is dangerous. Once again, this is the result of a failure to appreciate and respect the concept of intellectual control.

If proper documentation practices are followed, the result of each inspection is confidence that each level fully satisfies the requirements. For example, squares 1 through 4 in figure 11.3 fully implement the top-level specifications. Nothing is left out, deferred, undefined, or added, and no requirements are violated. Similarly, 4.1 through 4.3 fully satisfy the provisions of 4, and 4.1.1 and 4.1.2 fully satisfy 4.1.

With these conditions met, inspections of 4.1 through 4.3 should only require reference to the definition for square 4 to confirm that 4.1 through 4.3 satisfy 4. If 4.2 attempts to implement a feature of the specifications that is not explicitly or implicitly referenced in 4, it is a defect and should be logged as such in the inspection meeting.

Principle 2
A given definition and all of its next-level refinements must be covered in a single inspection session.

This means that a single inspection session must cover square 4 and all of its next-level refinements, 4.1 through 4.3. Altogether, 4.1 through 4.3 should not be more than about five pages of material. More than five pages would indicate that too much refinement was attempted at one time and intellectual control probably cannot be maintained. The offending level should be redone with some of the intended refinement deferred to a lower level.

Principle 3
The full life cycle of any data item must be totally defined at a single refinement level and must be covered in a single inspection.

This is the key principle that allows us to be able to inspect 2.1.1 and 2.1.2 and only be concerned about their reaction with each other and the way they implement 2.1. There is no need to determine, for example, if they interact correctly with 1.1 or 4.3.

This principle is a breakthrough concept and obliterates one of the most troublesome aspects of large-system modification. One seems never to be totally secure making a code modification. There's always the concern that something may be getting broken somewhere else. This fear is an intuitive acknowledgment that intellectual control is not being maintained.

Such "remote breaking" can only occur because of inconsistent data management. Even troublesome problems associated with inappropriate interruptability or bogus recursion are caused by inconsistent data management. Intellectual control requires extreme respect for data management visibility.

This visibility can be maintained by ensuring that each data item is fully defined on a single abstraction level and totally studied in a single inspection session. It should be clear:

- where and why the data item comes into existence
- what each data item is initialized to and why
- how and where each data item is used and what effects occur as a result of its use

- how and where each data item is updated and to what value
- where, why, and how each data item is deleted

Note that careful adherence to this principle contributes significantly to creating an object-oriented result even if that is not the intent of the designer. This principle is also one of the reasons why Cleanroom lends itself so well to object-oriented design methodologies.

Once the inspection team is fully satisfied that the data management is consistent and correct, there is no need to be concerned about interactions. For instance, the life cycle for data that is global to the entire module would be fully described and inspected when squares 1, 2, 3, and 4 were inspected. Square 2 then totally defines its own portion of this management and 2.1, 2.2, 2.1.1, and 2.1.2 need only be concerned that they are properly implementing square 2's part of this definition. Squares 1, 3, and 4 can take care of their own portion with no worry about the effects on 2.

Adherence to principle 3 means that it is not necessary to inspect any logic other than that which is presented in the inspection packet. There is no intellectually uncontrolled requirement to execute the entire program mentally to determine whether or not it works.

Principle 4
Updates must conform to the same mechanisms.

Since even the best possible design processes are fallible, it is likely that unanticipated requirements will later be discovered. Functional verification does not preclude this. For instance, it may be discovered that it is necessary to test a global flag in the code for 2.1.1 which in turn must be set in the code for 4.2. This is a common occurrence and the typical response is simply to create the global flag for 2.1.1 and then update 4.2 to set it properly. Bug found. Bug fixed. Everything works fine.

However, we have just destroyed the ability to make subsequent modifications to this mechanism in an intellectually controlled way. Future intellectual control requires that this new interface be retrofitted into the higher abstraction levels. The life cycle of this flag must be fully described at the square 1 through 4 level. In that one document, the square 2 test and the square 4 update must be described, and then the appropriate portions of this definition must be repeated and refined in 2.1, 2.1.1, and 4.2, and of course, all of this should be subject to a full inspection.

Principle 5
Intellectual control must be accompanied by bottom-up thinking.

These principles can lull people into believing that they have intellectual control when, in fact, intellectual control is not possible. Intellectual control is, by its nature, a top-down process and is endangered by a pitfall that threatens all top-down design processes: the tendency to postpone real decisions indefinitely. To avoid this pitfall, the designers must be alert to potential "and-then-a-miracle-happens" situations. Anything that looks suspiciously tricky should be prototyped as soon as possible. All the top-down design discipline in the world will not save a project that depends upon a feature that is beyond the current state of the art. Such a feature may not be recognized until very late in the development cycle if top-down design is allowed to blind the developers to its existence.

The key word is "obvious"

It must be remembered that these five principles are followed for the single purpose of making it obvious to the moderately thorough observer that the design is correct. Practicality must be sufficiently demonstrated, documentation must be sufficiently complete, the design must be tackled in sufficiently small chunks, and data management must be sufficiently clarified. All of these must be so obviously sufficient that the reviewer is tempted to say, "Of course! It's only obvious! Why belabor it?" If this is not the case, a redesign is indicated.

Our experience suggests that the achievement of such a state of obviousness is not a particularly challenging task. It requires care, but, if these principles are well understood, this care is almost automatic.

LEGAL PRIMITIVE EVALUATION

Legal primitive evaluation enhances intellectual control by providing a mathematically derived set of questions for each legal Dijkstra primitive (e.g., If-Then-Else, While-Do, etc.). For each primitive, the designers and the reviewers ask the set of questions that apply to that primitive and confirm that each question can be answered affirmatively. If this is the case, the correctness of the primitive is ensured.

A rigorous derivation of these questions can be found elsewhere.[13] There is insufficient space here to go through these derivations in detail, but we can illustrate the process and its mathematical basis by using a short, nonrigorous analysis of one of these sets, the While-Do primitive. Questions associated with the other primitives are given on pp. 249–250.

The While-Do construct is defined as follows:

```
S = [While A Do B;]
```

which means:

S is fully achieved by [While A Do B;].

The symbol S denotes the specification that the primitive is attempting to satisfy, or the function it is attempting to perform. The symbol A is the while test, and B is the while body.

As an example, S could be the specification: "The entry is added to the table." The predicate represented by A would then be an appropriate process to enable the program to perform an iteration and to determine if the operation is complete. B would be the processing required to accomplish the addition to the table. We have chosen to use a While-Do because, presumably, we think it makes sense. We may be intending to accomplish the entry addition by scanning the table sequentially until an appropriate insertion point is found and then splicing the entry into the table at that point. Whether or not this makes sense depends upon the known characteristics of the entry and the table. It also may depend upon the explicit (or implicit) existence of a further part of the specification such as "... within 5 ms."

To investigate whether it has been coded correctly, the following three questions are asked:

1   Is loop termination guaranteed for any argument of S?
2   When A is true, does S equal B followed by S?
3   When A is false, does S equal S?

When the answer to these three questions is yes, the correctness of the While-Do is guaranteed. The people asking these questions should be the designer and the inspectors.

These questions require some explanation.

1   Is loop termination guaranteed for any argument of S?

This means that for any data presented to the function defined by S, will the While-Do always terminate? For instance, in our example, are there any possible instances of the entry or the table for which the While-Do will go into an endless loop because A can never acquire a value of FALSE?

This would appear to be an obvious question: so obvious, that the reader may be tempted to ask why it is even mentioned. However, there is a lack of respect for While-Do termination conditions and many defects occur because of failure to terminate for certain inputs. A proper respect for this question will cause a programmer to take care when using it and will significantly help to avoid nontermination failures.

Respect for this question is justified because it is difficult to prove While–Do termination. In fact, it can be mathematically proven that, for the general case, it is impossible to prove termination.[14] To guarantee the correctness of a While–Do, it is therefore necessary to design simple termination conditions that can be easily verified by inspection. Complicated While–Do tests must be avoided.

2   When A is true, does S equal B followed by S?

This means that, when A is true, can S be achieved by executing B and then presenting the results to S again? This question is not quite so obvious.

Iterative statements are very difficult to prove. To prove the correctness of the while statement, it is desirable to change it to a noniterative form. We change it by invoking S recursively. Thus, the expression

$$S = [\text{While A Do B;}] \tag{1}$$

becomes

$$S = [\text{If A Then (B; S);}] \tag{2}$$

Expression 2 is no longer an iterative construct and can be more readily proven. Figure 11.4 shows the diagrams for these two expressions.

The equivalence of these two statements can be rigorously demonstrated.[15] A nonrigorous feeling for it can be obtained by observing that when A is true in [While A Do B], the B expression is executed once and then you start at the beginning by making the [While A] test again. If [While A Do B] is truly equal to S, then one could imagine that, rather than starting again at the beginning with the [While A] test, you simply start at the beginning of S. That changes the While–Do to a simple If–Then, and the predicate A is tested only once. If it is true, you execute B one time and then execute S to finish the processing.

The typical first reaction to this concept is that we haven't helped at all. The S expression is still iterative and now we've made it recursive making it seem that we have more to prove. The response to this complaint is that we don't have to prove anything about S at all. The specification (the entry is added to the table) is neither iterative nor recursive. We have simply chosen to implement it using a While–Do construct. We could, presumably, have implemented it some other way.

S is nothing more than the specification. In the general case, it may be a

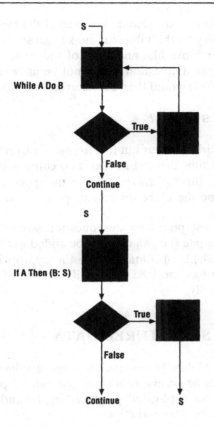

Figure 11.4 Diagrams of the primitives `While A Do B` and `If A Then` `(B,S)`.

completely arbitrary statement from any source. Whether the specification is correct or not is not our responsibility. Our responsibility is to implement it as defined.

Question 2 can therefore be restated as follows: If A is true, when we execute B one time and then turn the result over to whatever we've defined S to be, does the result still achieve S? An affirmative answer satisfies question 2.

In terms of our example, B will have examined part of the table. It will either already have inserted the new entry into the table or it will have decided that the portion of the table it examined is not a candidate for inserting of the entry. The unexamined portion of the table is now the new table upon which the construct must execute. This new instance of the table must be comparable to a standalone instance of the table so that the concept of adding an entry to the table still makes sense. If the resulting table fragment no longer looks like any form of the table for which the specification S was generated, question 2 may not be answerable affirmatively and the proposed code would then be incorrect.

3   When A is false, does S equal S?

This question seems fairly obvious but it is frequently overlooked. If A is found to be false the first time the While-Do is executed and therefore no processing of B occurs, is this satisfactory? Does the specification S allow for nothing to happen and therefore for no change to occur as a result of its execution?

In our example, the test posed by this question would likely fail. S requires something to happen (i.e., an entry to be added to the table). This would suggest that the While-Do may not be the appropriate construct for this S. We may never have noticed this fact if we hadn't been forced to examine question 3 carefully.

STRUCTURED DATA

The principle of structured data[16] recognizes that undisciplined accesses to randomly accessed arrays or accesses that use generalized pointers cause the same kind of "reasoning explosion" produced by the undisciplined use of GOTOs. For instance, take the instruction:

```
A[i] = B[j+k];
```

This statement looks innocent enough. It would appear to be appropriate in any well-structured program. Note, however, that it involves five variables, all of which must be accounted for in any correctness analysis. If the program in which this statement occurs is such that this statement is executed several times, some of these variables may be set in instructions that occur later in the program. Thus, this instruction all by itself creates a reasoning explosion.

Just as Dijkstra suggested that GOTOs should not be used at all,[17] the originators of Cleanroom suggest that randomly accessed arrays and pointers should not be used. Dijkstra recommended a set of primitives to use in place of GOTOs.

In the same way, Cleanroom recommends that randomly accessed arrays be replaced with structures such as queues, stacks, and sets. These structures are safer because their access methods are more constrained and disciplined. Many current object-oriented class libraries support these structures directly and take much of the mystery and the complexity out of mentally converting from random-array thinking.

Legal Primitive Evaluation

As described in the accompanying chapter, the process of doing legal primitive evaluation involves asking a set of mathematically derived questions about the correctness of basic programming primitives (e.g. If-Then-Else, For-Do, etc.) used in a program. The following is a list of the questions that must be investigated for each primitive.

In the following list S refers to the specification that must be satisfied by the questions asked about the referenced primitive.

```
Sequence             S = [A; B;]
Does S equal A followed by B?


For-Do               S = [For A Do B;]
    Does S equal first B followed by second B ...
    followed by last B?


If-Then              S = [If A Then B;]
    If A is true, does S = B?
    If A is false, does S = S?


If-Then-Else         S = [If A Then B Else C;]
    If A is true, does S equal B?
    If A is false, does S equal C?


Case                 S = [Case P part (C1)B1 ...
                          part (Cn)Bn Else E;]
    When p is C1, does S equal B1?

                 .

                 .

                 .

    When p is Cn, does S equal Bn?
    When p is not a member of set (C1, ..., Cn),
    does S equal E?


While-Do             S = [While A Do B;]
    Is loop termination guaranteed for any argument
    of S?
```

```
When A is true, does S equal B followed by S?
When A is false, does S equal S?

Do-Until            S = [Do A Until B;]
   Is loop termination guaranteed for any argument
   of S?
   When B is false, does S equal A followed by S?
   When B is true, does S equal A?

Do-While-Do         S = [Do₁ A While B Do₂ C;]
   Is loop termination guaranteed for any argument
   of S?
   When B is true, does S equal A followed by C fol-
   lowed by S?
   When B is false, does S equal A?
```

STATISTICAL TESTING

Statistical testing[8] is not really required for Cleanroom, but it is highly recommended because it allows an assessment of quality in sigma units. It does not measure quality in defects per lines of code. Measuring quality in sigma units gives users visibility of how often a defect is expected to be encountered. For instance, it makes no difference if there are 100 defects per thousand lines of code if the user never actually encounters any of them. The product would be perceived as very reliable. On the other hand, the product may have only one defect in 100,000 lines of code, but if the user encounters this defect every other day, the product is perceived to be very unreliable.

Statistical testing also clearly shows when testing is complete and when the product can safely be released. If the model is predicting that the user will encounter a defect no more often than once every 5000 years with an uncertainty of ±1000 years, it could be decided that it is safe to release the product. This is usually better than some industry-standard methods (e.g., when the attrition rate from boredom among the test team exceeds a certain threshold, it must be time to release, or "When is this product supposed to be released? May 17th. What's today's date? May 17th. Oh. Then we must be finished testing.").

Statistical testing specifies the way test scenarios are developed and executed. Testing is done using scenarios that conform to the expected user profile. A user profile is generated by identifying all states the system can be in (e.g., all screens that could be displayed by the system) and, on each one, identifying all the different actions the user could take and the relative percentage of instances in which each would be taken. As the scenario generator progresses through these states, actions are selected randomly with a weighting that corresponds to the predicted user profile.

For instance, if a given screen has a menu item that is anticipated to be invoked 75% of the time when the user is in that screen, the invocation of this menu item is stipulated in 75% of the generated scenarios involving the screen. If another menu item will only be invoked 1% of the time, it would be called in only 1% of the scenarios.

These scenarios are then executed and the error history is evaluated according to a mathematical model designed to predict how many more defects the user would encounter in a given period of time or in a given number of uses. There are several different models described in the literature.[18]

In general, statistical testing takes less time than traditional testing. As soon as the model predicts a quality level corresponding to a predefined goal (e.g., six sigma) with a sufficiently small range of uncertainty (also predefined), the product can be safely released. This is the case even when 100% testing coverage is not done, or when 100% of the pathways are not executed.

Statistical testing requires that the software to which it is applied be minimally reliable. If an attempt is made to apply it to software that has an industry-typical defect density, any of the statistical models will demonstrate instabilities and usually blow up. When they don't blow up, their predictions are so unfavorable that a decision is usually made to ignore them. This is an analytical reflection of the fact that you can't test quality into a program.

QUALITY CANNOT BE TESTED INTO A PRODUCT

Although it is the quality strategy chosen for many products, it is not possible to test quality into a product. DeMarco[19] has an excellent analysis that demonstrates the validity of this premise. This analysis is based on the apparent fact that only about half of all defects can be eliminated by testing, but that this factor of two is swamped by the variability of the software packages on the market. The difference in defect density between the best and worst products is a factor of almost 4,000.* Of course, these

---

* This factor is based on a defect density of 60 defects per KNCSS for the worst products and 0.016 defects per KNCSS for the best products. The factor difference between these two extremes is 60/0.016 = 3,750 or ~4,000.

are the extremes. The factor difference between the 25th percentile and the 75th percentile is about 30 according to DeMarco. No one suggests that testing should not be done – it eliminates extremely noxious defects which are easy to test for – but compared to the variability of software packages, the factor of two is almost irrelevant. What then are the factors that produce quality software?

Capers Jones[20] suggests that inspections alone can produce a 60% elimination of defects, and when testing is added, 85% of defects are eliminated. There is no reported study, but the literature would suggest that inspections coupled with functional verification would eliminate more than 90% of defects.[21] Remarkably enough, testing seems to eliminate most (virtually all) of the remaining defects. The literature typically reports that no further defects are found after the original test cycle is complete and that none are found in the field.[21] This was also our experience.

There is apparently a synergism between functional verification and testing. Functional verification eliminates defects that are difficult to detect with testing. The defects that are left after application of inspections and functional verification are generally those that are easy to test for. The result is that >99% of all defects are eliminated via the combination of inspections, functional verification, and testing. Table 11.2 summarizes the percentage of defect removal with the application of individual or combinations of different defect detection strategies.

OUR EXPERIENCE

We applied Cleanroom to three projects, although only one of them actually made it to the marketplace. The project that made it to market had Cleanroom applied all the way through its life cycle. The other projects were canceled for nontechnical reasons, but Cleanroom was applied as long as they existed. The completed project which consisted of a relatively

Table 11.2   Defect removal percentages based on defect detection strategies

Detection strategy	Defect removal (%)
Testing	50
Inspections	60
Inspections + testing	85
Inspections + functional verification	90
Inspections + functional verification + testing	>99

small amount of code (3.5 KNCSS), was released as part of a large Microsoft® Windows system. The project team for this effort consisted of five software engineers.

All the techniques described in this chapter except structured data and statistical testing were applied to the projects. All the products were Microsoft Windows applications written in C or C++. Structured data was not addressed because we never came across a serious need for random arrays or pointers. Although statistical testing was not applied, it was our intent eventually to do so, but the total lack of defects demotivated us from pursuing a complicated, analytical testing mode particularly when our testing resources were in high demand from the organization to help other portions of the system prepare for product release.

Design methodology

We applied the rigorous object-oriented methodology known as box notation.[7] This is the methodology recommended by the Cleanroom originators. We found it to be satisfyingly rigorous and disciplined.

Box notation is a methodology that progresses from functional specification to detailed design through a series of steps represented as boxes with varying transparency. The first box is a black box signifying that all external aspects of the system or module are known but none of the internal implementation is known. This is the ultimate object. It is defined by noting all the stimuli applied to the box by the user and the observable responses produced by these stimuli.

Inevitably, these responses are a function not only of the stimulus, but also of the stimulus history. For example, a mouse click at location 100,200 on the screen will produce a response that depends upon the behavior of the window that currently includes the location 100,200. The window at that location is, in turn, a function of all the previous mouse clicks and other inputs to the system.

The black box is then converted to a state box in which the stimulus history producing the responses of the black box is captured in the form of states that the box passes through. The response produced by a given stimulus can be determined not necessarily from the analysis of a potentially infinite stimulus history, but more simply by noting the state the system is in and the response produced by that stimulus within that state. The state box fully reveals this data. It contains an internal black box that takes as its input the stimulus and the current set of state data and produces the desired response and a new set of state data. The state data is fully revealed but the internal black box still hides its own internal processing.

The state box is then converted to a clear box in which all processing is visible. However, this processing is represented as a series of interacting black boxes in which the interactions and the relations are clearly visible but, once again, the black boxes hide their own internal processing. This clear box is the final implementation of the object. In this object, the encapsulated data and the methods to process it are clearly visible.

Each of these internal black boxes is then treated similarly in a stepwise refinement process that ends only when all the internal black boxes can be expressed as single commands of the destination language.

This process allows many of the pitfalls of object-oriented design and programming to be avoided by carefully illuminating them at the proper time. For instance, the optimum data encapsulation level is more easily determined because the designer is forced to consider it at a level where perspective is the clearest. Data encapsulation at too high a level degradés modularity and defeats "object orientedness," but data encapsulation at too low a level produces redundancies and multiple copies of the same data with the associated possibility of update error and loss of integrity. These pitfalls are more easily avoided because the designer is forced to think about the question at exactly that point in the design when the view of the system is optimum for such a consideration.

Inspections

We employed a slightly adapted version of the HP-recommended inspection method taught by Tom Gilb.[9] We found this method very satisfactory. Our minimal adaptation was to allow slightly more discussion during the logging meeting than Gilb recommends. We felt that this was needed to accommodate functional verification.

Functional verification

No attempt was made to implement anything but the first level of functional verification – intellectual control. This was found to be easily implemented, and when the principles were adequately adhered to, was almost automatic. Inspectors who knew nothing about functional verification or intellectual control automatically accomplished it when given material that conformed to its principles and, amusingly, they also automatically complained when slight deviations from these principles occurred.

Structured specifications

The project team called Cleanroom's structured specifications process evolutionary delivery because of its similarity to the evolutionary delivery methodology mentioned earlier and because evolutionary delivery is more like our HP environment. Structured specifications were developed in a defense-industry environment where dynamic specifications are frowned upon and where adaptability is not a virtue. However, evolutionary delivery assumes a dynamic environment and encourages adaptability. Regardless of the differences, both philosophies are similar.

At first, both marketing and management were skeptical. They were not reassured by the idea that a large amount of time would elapse before the product would take shape because of the large up-front design investment and because some features would not be addressed at all until very late in the development cycle. They were told not to expect an early prototype within the first few days that would demonstrate the major features.

Very quickly, these doubts were dispelled. Marketing was brought into the effort during the early rigorous design stages to provide guidance and direction. They participated in the specification structuring and set priorities and desired schedules for the releases. They caught on to the idea of getting the "juiciest parts" first and found that they were getting real code very quickly and could have this real code reviewed by real users while there was still time to allow the user's feedback to influence design decisions. They also became enthusiastic about participating in the inspections during the top-level definitions.

Management realized that the evolutionary staged releases were coming regularly enough and quickly enough that they could predict very early in the development cycle which stage had a high possibility of being finished in time to hit the optimum release window. They could then adjust scope and priority to ensure that the release date could be reliably achieved.

Morale

The Cleanroom literature claims that Cleanroom teams have a very high morale and satisfaction level. This is attributed to the fact that they have finally been given the tools necessary to achieve the kind of quality job that everyone wants to do. Our own experience was that this occurred surprisingly quickly. People with remarkably disparate, scarcely compatible personalities not only worked well together, they became enthusiastic about the process.

It appears that the following factors were influential in producing high morale:

- Almost daily inspections created an environment in which each person on the team took turns being in the "hot seat." People quickly developed an understanding that reasonable criticism was both acceptable and beneficial. The resulting frankness and openness were perceived by all to be remarkably refreshing and exhilarating.

- Team members were surprised that they were being allowed to do what they were doing. They were allowed to take the time necessary to do the kind of job they felt was proper.

Productivity

Productivity was difficult to measure. Only one project actually made it to the marketplace, and it is difficult to divide the instruction count accurately among the engineers that contributed to it. However, the subjective impression was that it certainly didn't take any longer. When no defects are found one suddenly discovers that the job is finished. At first this is disconcerting and anticlimactic, but it also emphasizes the savings that can be realized at the end of the project. This compensates for the extra effort at the beginning of the project.

CONCLUSIONS

The Cleanroom team mentioned in this chapter no longer exists as a single organization. However, portions of Cleanroom are still being practiced in certain organizations within Hewlett-Packard. These portions especially include structured specifications and intellectual control.

We believe our efforts can be duplicated in any software organization. There was nothing unique about our situation. We achieved remarkable results with less than total dogmatic dedication to the methodology.

The product that made it to market was designed using functional decomposition. Even though functional decomposition is minimally rigorous and disciplined, we found the results completely satisfactory. The project consisted of enhancing a 2-KNCSS module to 3.5 KNCSS.

The original module was reverse engineered to generate the functional decomposition document that became the basis for the design. The completed module was subjected to the intellectual control processes and the reviewers were never told which code was the original and which was modified or new code. A total of 36 defects were found during the inspection process for a total of 10 defects per KNCSS. An additional five defects were found the first week of testing (1.4 defects per KNCSS). No defects were encountered in the subsequent 10 months of full system integration testing and none have been found since the system was released.

It was interesting to note that the defects found during inspections included items such as a design problem which would have, under rare conditions, mixed incompatible file versions in the same object, a piece of data that if it had been accessed would have produced a rare, nonrepeatable crash, and a number of cases in which resources were not being released which would, after a long period of time, have caused the Windows system to halt. Most of these defects would have been very difficult to find by testing.

Defects found during testing were primarily simple screen appearance problems which were readily visible and easily characterized and eliminated. These results conform well to expected Cleanroom results. About 90% of defects were eliminated by inspections with functional verification. About 10% more were eliminated via testing. No other defects were ever encountered in subsequent full-system integration testing or by customers in the field. It can be expected on the basis of other Cleanroom results reported in the literature that at least 99% of all defects in this module were eliminated in this way and that the final product probably contains no more than 0.1 defect per KNCSS.

References

1 M. J. Harry, *The Nature of Six Sigma Quality*, Motorola Government Electronics Group, 1987.
2 P. A. Tobias, "A Six Sigma Program Implementation," *Proceedings of the IEEE 1991 Custom Integrated Circuits Conference*, p. 29.1.1.
3 H. D. Mills, M. Dyer, and R. C. Linger, "Cleanroom Software Engineering," *IEEE Software*, Vol. 4, no. 5, September 1987, pp. 19–25.
4 H. D. Mills and J. H. Poore, "Bringing Software Under Statistical Quality Control," *Quality Progress*, Vol. 21, no. 11, November 1988, pp. 52–55.
5 T. DeMarco, *Controlling Software Projects*, Yourdon Press, 1982, pp. 195–267.
6 R. C. Linger and H. D. Mills, "A Case Study in Software Engineering," *Proceedings COMPSAC 88*, p. 14.
7 H. D. Mills, R. C. Linger, and A. R. Hevner, *Principles of Information Systems Analysis and Design*, Academic Press, 1986.
8 P. A. Currit, M. Dyer, and H. D. Mills, "Certifying the Realiability of Software," *IEEE Transactions on Software Engineering*, Vol. SE-12, no. 1, January 1986, pp. 3–11.
9 T. Gilb, *The Principles of Software Engineering Management*, Addison-Wesley, 1988, pp. 83–114.
10 J. Martin, *Information Engineering Book III*, Prentice Hall, 1990, pp. 169–196.
11 *Navigator Systems Series Overview Monograph*, Ernst & Young International, Ltd., 1991, pp. 55–56.
12 R. C. Linger, H. D. Mills, and B. I. Witt, *Structured Programming: Theory and Practice*, Addison-Wesley, 1979, pp. 227–229.
13 Ibid., pp. 213–300.
14 H. D. Mills, V. R. Basili, J. D. Gannon, and R. G. Hamlet, *Principles of Computer Programming*, Allyn and Bacon, Inc., 1987, pp. 236–238.

15   R. C. Linger, H. D. Mills, and B. I. Witt, op. cit., pp. 219–221.

16   H. D. Mills and R. C. Linger, "Data Structured Programming: Program Design without Arrays and Pointers," *IEEE Transactions on Software Engineering*, Vol. SE-12, no. 2, Feb. 1986, pp. 192–197.

17   E. W. Dijkstra, "Structured Programming," *Software Engineering Techniques*, NATO Science Committee, 1969, pp. 88–93.

18   P. A. Currit, M. Dyer, and H. D. Mills, op. cit., pp. 3–11.

19   T. DeMarco, op. cit., p. 216.

20   Unpublished presentation given at the 1988 HP Software Engineering Productivity Conference.

21   R. C. Linger and H. D. Mills, op. cit., pp. 8–16.

Evolving Practice in Cleanroom Development

FORMALISM

Several efforts have been made to increase the formality of the Box Structure Method. The motivation for increased formality is to reduce the variability in design and presentation of design, to assure black-box completeness, consistency, and correctness, and to ensure that these black-box properties are not lost as the design develops through the state box and clear box. Additionally, formal expression of the BSM enables its comparison with other formal methods.

- "Using box structures with the Z notation" (D. T. Fetzer, M.S. Thesis, University of Tennessee, 1991) used Mills' Box Description Language (BDL) as outer syntax for box structures and Z as inner syntax. A summary of this work by Fetzer and Poore, "The Z notation with box structures," is published in the *Proceedings of the 25th Annual Hawaii International Conference on Systems Sciences* (IEEE, 1992).
- "An evaluation of integration of the Trace Assertion Method with the Box Structure Method for coding in C++" (A. L. Bangs, M.S. Thesis, University of Tennessee, 1993) used a C Design Language as outer syntax for box structures and Parnas' Trace Assertion Method (TAM) for representation and verification of function. Object-oriented methods and the C++ programming language were chosen for use in the study since they are increasingly used in industrial development environments.
- "The box-structure development method" (H. Mao, Ph.D. Dissertation, University of Tennessee, 1993) defines the formal syntax and semantics for the Box Structure Method. Mao's Box Development Method (BDM) specifies a "beta expansion" for stepwise refinement

that inherits all appropriate parts of previous design and preserves important theoretical properties as development proceeds. The division between mathematical inheritance and new inventive work is sharply defined. This work includes an especially thorough treatment of the mathematical issues associated with the state box and state migration.

- "Completeness and consistency in black box specification" (S. J. Prowell and J. H. Poore, University of Tennessee, in review) is an exploration of "sequence-based specification," i.e., black-box analysis via explicit enumeration of stimulus histories. This approach lends itself to considerable automated support, and yields specifications that are demonstrably complete and consistent. It is anticipated that this approach will appeal to safety-critical applications such as medical devices and nuclear power plant controls.

OBJECT-ORIENTATION

The most timely evolution in the Box Structure Method may be its treatment in relation to object-oriented methods. Some consider object-orientation to be a paradigm shift in software development, at odds with Cleanroom top-down functional decomposition. Others view object-orientation and Cleanroom to be complementary, with object identification and development naturally following black-box specification and naturally preceding state- and clear-box design. A third position is that boxes are objects, and the Box Structure Method is an object-oriented method.

- "Box structures with objects" (A. R. Hevner and H. D. Mills, *IBM Systems Journal*, 1993) takes this third position. The parallels between the properties of a box and those of an object are presented, and an example is used to demonstrate the key points.

The relationship between Cleanroom and object-oriented methods is not resolved. There are many forms of object-oriented methods, and these must be unified by a single mathematical characterization before comparison of the essential features of each approach will be possible.

CONCURRENCY

Modern-day computing environments are increasingly multi-user, multi-tasking, network-based, and distributed. System specification and design in an environment of such concurrency is an extremely complex matter. With growth in parallel computing, concurrency and complexity will be greater still. The Box Structure Method provides very little support for concurrency; it must evolve not only to meet the challenges of tomorrow, but also to cope with the present day.

PART IV

Cleanroom Certification

Current Practice in Cleanroom Certification

Cleanroom Certification treats software usage modeling, testing, and reliability estimation as a statistical experiment. In addition to its origin in Mills' ideas about statistical testing, Cleanroom certification has been heavily influenced by Ed Adams' study of failures in large IBM products and John Musa's work in software reliability engineering at AT&T. While Adams and Musa were not working within the Cleanroom framework, their contributions have directly advanced Cleanroom certification practice.

Two early works on Cleanroom certification, not included in this collection, were also influential on the road to current practice:

- "Certifying the reliability of software" (P. A. Currit, M. Dyer, and H. D. Mills, IEEE *Transactions on Software Engineering*, 1989), was the first paper to detail the motivation and techniques for statistical testing. The paper presents the mathematics of the Certification Model of reliability, which was developed to complement the Cleanroom development approach. Data for the second IBM Cleanroom project was presented and used in a simulation experiment based on the findings in the Adams data.
- "Statistical testing of software" (B. C. Sexton, M.S. Thesis, University of Tennessee, 1988) was the first full explication of software testing as a statistical experiment. The use of hypothesis testing in evaluating the statistical experiment is shown to provide reliability and confidence levels given k failures in n Bernoulli trials.

  Statistical testing of software is based on a usage model of the software specification. The structure of the usage model represents all possible user events, and probability distributions associated with the structure embody assumptions about usage. Usage models for statistical testing were first represented in stochastic grammars.

- "A Cleanroom test case generation tool" (Miller and Pleszkoch, 1995) describes the Statistical Test Case Generation Facility, a tool for writing detailed test case designs and generating both statistical and non-statistical test cases from the designs. Test case design (for traditional testing) or customer usage distribution (for statistical testing) is defined via a grammar that supports the use of variables and procedural processing. The chapter describes how grammars are used to define a usage distribution, gives examples of test designs, and reports on applications in which the tool has been used.

  Recent work in Cleanroom certification has treated software testing as a stochastic process and used the theory of Markov chains to model usage and the testing process. The capability of the software system is modeled by a set of states and transitions, while a specific usage environment is modeled by the transition probabilities. When software usage is modeled in this way, all the known properties and analytical power of the Markov chain become potentially meaningful upon interpretation in the application.

- "Markov analysis of software specifications" (Whittaker and Poore, 1993) describes the rationale and technique for representing a software usage model as a finite state, discrete parameter, time homogeneous Markov chain. Several standard analytical results for Markov chains are computed and given interpretations for software.

- "A Markov chain model for statistical software testing" (Whittaker and Thomason, 1994) recapitulates and extends the application of Markov theory to certification. Markov analysis of test plans and results are shown to yield coverage predictions and reliability estimates.

- "Statistical testing of software based on a usage model" (Walton, Poore, and Trammell, 1995) summarizes the state of usage modeling practice. Usage model structure is represented in a formal grammar, a graphical model, and a Markov matrix. Usage probabilities are derived from field data or informed estimates, or are given a uniform distribution. Variation in usage is discussed in terms of differences in users (e.g., hardware, software, and human users), uses (e.g., routine vs. non-routine use), and environments (e.g., platform or system load).

  Another usage modeling strategy draws on both Musa's high-level approach to operational profiles and the foregoing application of Markov chain ideas, to produce a hybrid model.

- "Certification of software components" (Wohlin and Runeson, 1994) introduces the State Hierarchy (SHY) model. Usage classes form the branches of the hierarchy, and usage behavior modeled as Markov chains represents the leaves. The SHY model was developed to characterize Ericsson Telecom's complex customer and product domain, and to facilitate reuse of model parts. The approach provides a unified model for random test generation, with hypothesis testing used for interpretation of test results. As the authors note, the SHY model is not a Markov chain, and should not be used as a source for the calculations given in the preceding papers.

Each of the foregoing approaches to usage modeling and testing has both advantages and disadvantages. Approaches that do not satisfy the probability laws of known and tractable stochastic processes have the common advantage of freeing the modeler from the strictures of any such process, but carry the disadvantage that one cannot reap the usual analytical benefits of such models. Certain types of software might best be modeled with grammars, might not easily conform to the probability law of the Markov chain, or might be satisfactorily represented by a simpler model than that represented by the Markov chain. The approaches may ultimately prove to be complementary, but such use has yet to be defined.

The validity of conclusions in statistical testing is not assured by the theory alone. The implemented protocol must also be consistent with the assumptions underlining the theory.

- "Experimental control in software reliability certification" (Trammell and Poore, 1994) identifies assumptions associated with a statistical experiment and their implications for statistical testing of software. Lessons learned in 15 Cleanroom projects at the University of Tennessee are used to show how small compromises in testing process control can threaten the validity of statistical inferences. Explicit policies are given for ensuring experimental control in statistical testing.

12 A Cleanroom Test Case Generation Tool

B. A. MILLER AND M. G. PLESZKOCH

INTRODUCTION

In 1991, the Cleanroom Software Technology Center (CSTC) set out to create a tool that would support statistical testing.[1] The intent was to randomly generate test cases from one or more customer usage distributions that reflect how the customer will use the software. At execution time, the test results would be recorded and fed into a statistical model. The statistics would reflect the reliability of the software with respect to the expected customer usage. However, the CSTC did not want to restrict the tool to only statistical testing, or to the CSTC view of statistical testing.

The following goals were defined for the design of the STGF:

- The STGF should perform the mechanical task of constructing the test cases, letting the testers spend most of their time on the creative task of determining what to test and how to test it. This would mean that the testers could spend time up-front specifying their test case design, just as Cleanroom developers create a rigorous black box specification. Once a test case design is written, it should be much easier to update for software specification changes than updating multiple test cases. Once a test case design is updated, new test cases can be generated.
- The STGF should be able to generate a set of test cases that present a rich combination of inputs to the software that would be very difficult to create via crafted test cases.

This contribution was first published in the *Proceedings of the Second European Industrial Symposium on Cleanroom Software Engineering (EISCSE'2)*, held in Berlin, Germany, on March 28–29, 1995, and is reprinted with the permission of Q-Labs.

- The STGF should be able to generate any type of test case: unit, function, system, coverage, statistical, etc. The type of test cases generated would be dependent upon the test case design written by the testers.
- The STGF should support the writing of customer usage specifications in as many different styles as possible, including Markov chains[2] and decision trees.[3]
- The STGF should be able to generate either scenarios that testers can follow or executable test cases. Therefore, a generated test case should consist of one or more files, containing any or all of the following:
  - the actual test case in one of the following formats:
    - overall test sequence which requires elaboration by the tester in order to perform the test
    - detailed test scenario for the tester to follow
    - an executable file for command oriented software; e.g., a DOS .bat file, a VM EXEC, an MVS CLIST, a UNIX shell script, etc.
    - input for a test execution tool
    - MVS or VSE JCL (Job Control Language)
    - source code to test an API (Application Program Interface)
  - generated data
  - expected results
- The tester should be able to write a test case design of any complexity. A simple design can always be evolved into a more complex design later.
- The tester should be able to generate random test cases that mimic existing crafted test cases. This is desirable when the existing test cases have proven to be effective.
- If a test tool is available for automatic execution of test cases, it should be possible to write the test case design to generate input for that test tool. This is one way to generate self-checking test cases. If the generated test cases are executable and at least partially self-checking, this allows a large number of test cases to be generated and executed.

The CSTC built the STGF and it satisfies these goals. In this chapter, we describe:

- the foundations of the grammar language that is used to define a test case design from which test cases can be generated
- experiences from the use of the STGF, including extractions of reports from two testers

USING GRAMMARS TO DEFINE A USAGE DISTRIBUTION

The Cleanroom Software Technology Center (CSTC) defined the Usage Distribution Language (UDL), which is used to define a usage distribution. Once a UDL grammar is written, the Statistical Test Case Generation Facility (STGF) is used to generate test cases from this grammar. The UDL is an extension of context-free grammars in which probabilities and variables are supported.

The following sections describe the fundamentals of context-free grammars, the extensions provided in the Usage Distribution Language (UDL), and how UDL grammars can be used to support both statistical and non-statistical testing.

Understanding context-free grammars

A context-free grammar is made up of the following parts:

- *Terminals.* A terminal is a literal in its final form that needs no further processing. In UDL, terminals can be integers, real numbers, or quoted character strings. In figure 12.1, the digits 0 thru 9 and the string "-" are terminals.
- *Nonterminals.* A nonterminal is a name enclosed in angle brackets (< >). It is an abstract name that has to be resolved to a resultant final form in each generated test case. In figure 12.1, the nonterminal names used include <phone_number>, <local>, <long_distance>, <collect>, <area_code>, <digit>, etc.
- *Production rule.* A production rule defines how the resultant final form will be generated by a nonterminal and is made up of the following parts:
  - Nonterminal name enclosed in brackets (< >)
  - ::=
    This is interpreted as "is defined as".
  - A grammar expression (body of production rule)
    An expression can be as simple as a quoted string, a nonterminal, or an arithmetic operation, or it can be a sequence of more complex expressions including list operations and conditional expressions.
  - ;
    Each statement in a UDL grammar is ended by a semicolon. A production rule is one of several kinds of statements in the UDL grammar.

The body (the expression to the right of ::=) of a production rule is typically expressed in one of the following ways:

- Alteration between two or more expressions (e.g., in <phone_number>, <digit>). The alternative expressions are separated by a "|" in the UDL.
- Sequence of one or more expressions (e.g., in <long_distance>, <local>, <extension>).
- Iteration of an expression (no examples in figure 12.1; see figure 12.4).

In figure 12.1, there are ten production rules. It is a complete context-free grammar, but it is not yet a complete UDL grammar. Although it specifies the set of valid phone numbers, it does not give any information on usage probabilities. (Also, it does not specify the name of the file in which to store the generated phone number.) The following subsections will expand on this grammar.

Alternation production type

In an alternation, there are two or more expressions to select from. In figure 12.1, the production rule for <phone_number> will return exactly one of the following expressions:

```
<local>
<long_distance>
<collect>
```

Note that the grammar in figure 12.1 does not indicate how to choose among the three alternatives. In figure 12.2, the probability for each alternative is specified along with the alternative. A local phone number is expected 40% of the time, a long distance phone number 30%, a collect call 30%. Note that the probabilities must total to 1.00 (100%) or the STGF will signal an error at test case generation time.

Sequence production type

In figure 12.1, the rule for <local> is a sequence of the following expressions which are evaluated in order:

```
<exchange>
"-"
<extension>
```

This rule generates a local phone number. Figure 12.3 shows a diagram of this sequence.

```
<phone_number>   ::= <local>
                 |  <long_distance>
                 |  <collect>
                 ;
<long_distance> ::= 1 "-" <area_code> "-" <local>
                 ;
<collect>        ::= 0 "-" <area_code> "-" <local>
                 ;
<area_code>      ::= <digit2_9> <digit0_1> <digit>
                 ;
<local>          ::= <exchange> "-" <extension>
                 ;
<exchange>       ::= <digit2_9> <digit> <digit>
                 ;
<extension>      ::= <digit> <digit> <digit> <digit>
                 ;
<digit>          ::= 0|1|2|3|4|5|6|7|8|9
                 ;
<digit2_9>       ::= 2|3|4|5|6|7|8|9
                 ;
<digit0_1>       ::= 0|1
                 ;
```

Figure 12.1 Context-free Grammar Example: <phone-number>. This grammar is not a valid UDL grammar as is. Figure 12.8 shows the grammar updated to be a valid UDL grammar based on the features in the following sections.

UDI PRODUCTION:

```
<phone_number>   ::=  <local>            [prob(.4)]
                 |    <long_distance>    [prob(.3)]
                 |    <collect>          [prob(.3)]
                 ;
```

DIAGRAM:

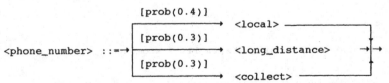

Figure 12.2 UDL alternation production example.

<local>::= ⟶ <exchange> ⟶ "-" ⟶ <extension> ⟶

Figure 12.3 Diagram for UDL sequence production example: <local>. The nonterminal <local> was taken from figure 12.1.

Iteration production type

Context-free grammars have an iteration operator (Kleene closure in reference 4) that indicates zero or more occurrences of the enclosed expression. In UDL grammars, the iteration operator must also be given the number of occurrences to generate, or a probability distribution for the number of occurrences. In the UDL, the symbol @ is used as the iteration operator. In figure 12.1, <extension> is <digit> explicitly replicated four times. In figure 12.4, the rule for <extension> has been rewritten to use iteration.

Variable iteration
To generate a variable number of occurrences, the appropriate probability distribution is utilized. For example, <unif_int> generates a uniform distribution of integer, values. Thus, the production rule in figure 12.5 iterates <command> from 1 to 14 times. Being a uniform distribution, it is just as likely to generate three occurrences as 14, or as any other number in the range 1–14.

Example:

```
    <extension>      ::=    4 @ <digit>;
```

Diagram:

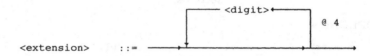

Figure 12.4   UDL iteration production example 1: Using @ operator.

Example:

```
    <test_case>  ::=  <unif_int>(1, 14) @ <command>;
```

Diagram:

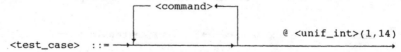

Figure 12.5   UDL iteration production example 2: using <unif_int>.

Iteration via recursion

Iteration can also be performed by using recursion, where a nonterminal calls itself. To generate zero or more commands, a combination of alternation and recursion can be used. For an example, see figure 12.6. Probabilistically, this turns out to be equivalent to the use of the geometric distribution[5] in figure 12.7.

File statement

The `<phone_number>` grammar in figure 12.1 was not a complete UDL grammar. Figure 12.8 shows a valid UDL grammar which uses the grammar features introduced above. This grammar includes the file statement which identifies the test case file name. Note that `tcnumber` is a UDL built-in variable that contains the number of the current test case. The file statement also identifies the contents of a test case via the name of the start nonterminal, the first nonterminal to be expanded.

As seen from the above examples, a usage grammar guides the construction of test cases from atomic test parts. Each test part can be of any granularity whatsoever, from a single token to a fairly sizable "canned" portion

EXAMPLE:

```
<test_case>  ::=  <:  :> /* empty */      [prob(0.1)]
             |    <command> <test_case>   [prob(0.9)]
             ;
```

DIAGRAM:

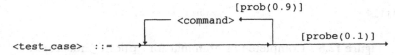

Figure 12.6 UDL iteration production example 3: recursion. This production rule can be replaced by the use of the geometric distribution. See figure 12.7.

Example:

```
<test_case>    ::=   <geom_dist>(.9) @ <command>;
```

Diagram:

```
                        ┌─── <command> ◄──┐
                        │                 │              @ <geom_dist>(.9)
<test_case>   ::= ──────┴─────────────────┴──────────────────────────────►
```

Figure 12.7 UDL iteration production example 4: geometric distribution. This production rule is equivalent to the one in figure 12.6.

```
file "PHON" tonumber ".TC" contents <phone_number>

<phone_number>         ::=      <local>              [prob(.4)]
                        |       <long_distance>      [prob(.3)]
                        |       <collect>            [prob(.3)]
                        ;

<long_distance>        ::=      1 "-" <area_code> "-" <local>
                        ;

<collect>              ::=      0 "-" <area_code> "-" <local>
                        ;

<area_code>            ::=      <digit2_9> <digit0_1> <digit>
                        ;

<local>                ::=      <exchange> "-" <extension>
                        ;

<exchange>             ::=      <digit2_9> <digit> <digit>
                        ;

<extension>            ::=      4 @ <digit>
                        ;

<digit>                ::=      <unif_int>(0, 9)
                        ;

<digit2_9>             ::=      <unif_int>(2, 9)
                        ;

<digit0_1>             ::=      <unif_int>(0, 1)
                        ;
```

Figure 12.8   Complete UDL grammar for <phone_number>.

of a test case. The appropriate test parts are selected and combined according to the instructions contained in the usage grammar productions, according to the specified usage probabilities.

Combination production type

As seen above, the body of a production rule can be written as an alternation, sequence, or iteration. Two or more of these types can be combined when writing the body of a production rule.

The grammar in figure 12.9 will generate 6–20 commands. An individual command will be "direct," having no operands, 40% of the time, while the command will have an operand 60% of the time.

EXAMPLE:
```
<commands>    ::=
  <unif_int>(6, 20) @
    ( <direct>                    [prob(.4)]
    | <indirect> <operand>        [prob(.6)]
    );
```

DIAGRAM:

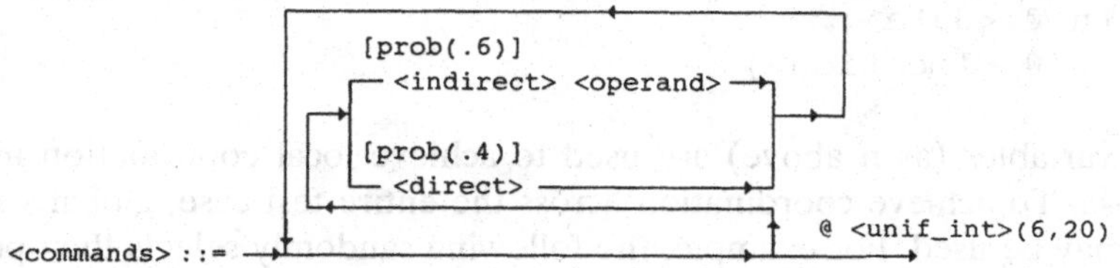

Figure 12.9   UDL combination production example.

Extending context-free grammars

It is very often the case that a pure context-free grammar is not sufficient to completely generate a consistent test case. For example, in generating a test case for a compiler, the grammar nonterminal for the programming language statement must (for a correctly compiling test case) choose among only those variables that have been previously declared in the test case. As another example, in generating a test case for a database, the grammar nonterminal for a table insert must (for a successfully executing test case) generate the appropriate number of data items of the appropriate type for the column definitions of the table. As a final example, in generating a self-checking test case, the grammar nonterminal for the expected results must generate the appropriate system response for the previously generated system input.

To accommodate these situations, the UDL grammar format has been extended to include several concepts from programming languages, including variables (both local and global), procedural processing, and aggregate data types (such as lists and maps).

Variables

Variables are useful for saving information that will be used later. Variables can only be updated via procedural code which must be within curly braces ({ }). There are several types of procedural code statements, but the most important one is the assignment statement.

The following example sets the variable x to a random number between 3.8 and 9.2:

```
{x := <unif_real>(3.8, 9.2)}
```

The following assignment statement sets the variable x to data items as result locations (this is known not to be context-free [3]):

```
<test_case>  ::=
    {n := <unif_int>(1,100)}
    (n @ <command>)
    (n @ <data>)
    (n @ <location>)
```

Local variables (as n above) are used to achieve local coordination in a test case. To achieve coordination across the entire test case, global variables may be used. For example, the following randomly selects the operating system to be booted for the generated test case. Various nonterminals in the usage grammar may access the value of test_platform to adjust probabilities, etc.

```
global test_platform := "DOS" [prob(.2)]
                      | "OS/2" [prob(.8)];
```

Global variables may also be updated by grammar nonterminals.

The type of data that a variable contains is determined by the expression to the right of the := operator. Like the programming language APL, the same variable can hold differently typed values at different times.

Procedural processing

Nonterminals may be defined to accept input data equivalent to programming language parameters. For example, the following nonterminal generates 1 to n commands:

```
commands>(n)  ::=
    <unif_int>(1,n) @ <command>;
```

The use of n is equivalent to inherited attributes of attribute grammars.

Statistical testing using UDL grammars

Markov chains

Because Markov chains[2] are equivalent to right-recursive context-free grammars, the STGF can easily accommodate usage specifications that have been developed in the form of Markov chains.

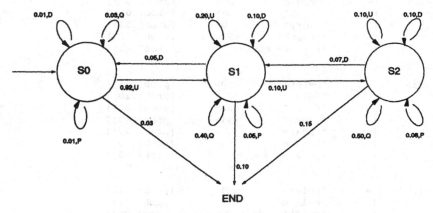

Figure 12.10   Example of a Markov chain.

Figure 12.10 shows an example Markov chain. The circles indicate states and the arrows indicate state to state transitions. The annotations by the arrows indicate what percentage of the time that transition occurs for that state and the command that causes the transition. This Markov chain is for a data base program. The command key used in this figure is:

- U = Update
- D = Delete
- Q = Query
- P = Print

The state key used for this figure is:

- S0 = database just starting to be loaded with required data
- S1 = database half loaded with required data
- S2 = database nearly fully loaded with required data

The following is a sample test case:

    S0 → Update → S1
       → Update → S1
       → Update → S1
       → Query → S1
       → Update → S2
       → Delete → S1
       → END

```
<S0>    ::=       "Delete"      <S0>      [prob(.01)]
        |         "Print"       <S0>      [prob(.01)]
        |         "Query"       <S0>      [prob(.03)]
        |         "Update"      <S1>      [prob(.92)]
        |         <: :> /* end */         [prob(.03)]
        ;

<S1>    ::=       "Delete"      <S0>      [prob(.05)]
        |         "Delete"      <S1>      [prob(.10)]
        |         "Print"       <S0>      [prob(.05)]
        |         "Query"       <S1>      [prob(.40)]
        |         "Update"      <S1>      [prob(.20)]
        |         "Update"      <S2>      [prob(.10)]
        |         <: :> /* end */         [prob(.10)]
        ;

<S2>    ::=       "Delete"      <S1>      [prob(.07)]
        |         "Delete"      <S2>      [prob(.10)]
        |         "Print"       <S2>      [prob(.08)]
        |         "Query"       <S2>      [prob(.50)]
        |         "Update"      <S2>      [prob(.10)]
        |         <: :> /* end */         [prob(.15)]
        ;
```

Figure 12.11   UDL grammar for Markov chain of figure 12.10.

There are many ways to express a Markov chain as a UDL grammar. One of the simplest is to make a nonterminal for each state as in figure 12.11

Nonstatistical testing using UDL grammars

By appropriate construction of the usage grammars, the STGF can be used to perform any kind of testing desired:

- customer usage test cases
- functional coverage test cases
- weird, off-the-wall test cases
- any kind of test cases desired

Functional coverage test cases are typically obtained by making all the probability distributions "flat," that is, by making all alternatives have equal probability. By creating an STGF global variable, the coverage obtained through the randomly generated test cases can be recorded, so that follow-on non-statistical testing need only test the uncovered items.

Off-the-wall test cases are typically obtained by greatly increasing the probabilities of unusual alternatives. These test cases are typically created to find obscure errors. They include combinations of features that would not normally be found in customer usage or functional coverage test cases.

STGF EXPERIENCE

Some test teams have used the STGF for traditional testing, while others have used it for Cleanroom certification (statistical testing). Some examples of projects that have used the STGF follow:

1   Statistical testing was performed on a CICS/IMS networking application of 65 thousand lines of code which was developed using Cleanroom. Over a thousand TPNS (TeleProcessing Network Simulator, an IBM program product) test cases were generated. The grammar was written to reflect typical network configurations and load patterns. The probabilities used in the grammar were based on usage information collected on the frequency of various network commands, various load patterns, etc. There were 7,400 lines of grammar written; 2,500 of these were global variable declarations. The global variables defined the testing environment and other characteristics such as IMS vs. CICS, number of simultaneous commands, etc.

2   The STGF was part of a test case environment set up to generate self-checking test cases for a print product. The test organization decided to use the STGF due to the extensive product specification changes being made. Five testers wrote over 15,000 lines of grammar. It took the testers approximately two weeks to learn the UDL on their own, without any education.

3   A 6,000-line usage grammar was written (by two people over a two month period) to test the file I/O portion (not Cleanroom developed) of a fourth-generation programming language interpreter/compiler. Based on general usage information, the usage grammar allowed the probability of the next I/O command and associated parameters to depend on the previous commands and the current contents of the file system. Over 100 automated, self-checking test cases were generated and executed. The list and map aggregate data types were extensively used to keep track of the current state of the file system in order to calculate the expected results of each I/O command generated. Each generated test case consisted of several files:

- a fourth-generation program that would be input to the interpreter/compiler
- ten input files to the fourth-generation program
- ten files containing the expected output of the fourth-generation program on the corresponding input file
- an MVS JCL file to compile the fourth-generation program, run it on each input file in turn, and compare the actual output with the expected output

4   A 3,000-line usage grammar was written by one person over three months to generate completely automatic, self-checking test cases to test the database services of a mainframe user interface product. The grammar was written to generate strange combinations of data base operations in order to find existing bugs in non-Cleanroom code that evolved over decades. The grammar generated a single REXX file that contained commands to create and initialize a data base, execute data base operations, and check the results in real time.

5   Statistical testing was performed for a GUI product that runs on AIX and OS/2. The generated test cases were partially self-checking. For more information, see Experience Report 1.

6   A grammar was written to aid in the testing of a compiler. For more information, see Experience Report 2.

Please note the following:

- The experience reports below include advantages and disadvantages of the STGF.
- Before writing a UDL grammar, planning must be done to decide:
  - what kind of testing (unit, coverage, statistical, etc.) the generated test cases will be used for
  - what files will be generated for each test case, the contents of each file, etc.
  - how complex the grammars should be based on resources available, the benefit and cost of a simple vs. complex grammar, etc.
- The UDL grammar is really a new code language. Nontechnical testers have written simple grammars on their own and more complex pieces of grammars under the guidance of a technical person.

EXPERIENCE REPORT 1

Statistical testing
This report was extracted from the paper, "Testing with Cleanroom Certification Assistant – experiences," presented at the IBM Software Testing Symposium in Boca, Florida in May 1994. Statistical testing was performed for software with a Graphical User Interface (GUI) that runs on AIX and OS/2. The UDL grammar was written to generate test cases that were partially self-checking.

Summary

Overall, the STGF tool is very powerful and can help automate testing, even if the Cleanroom Certification Model (CCM) or another reliability growth model is not used. If the Cleanroom Certification Model is used, then useful quality measurements can be obtained. This can help assess the readiness of the software and serve as a progress indicator.

Advantages

(1) *Test case maintenance is simpler.* It is necessary to maintain only the grammar file, not the generated test cases.
(2) *Test case execution is streamlined and less stressful.* The most challenging task is to develop the grammar. Once this is done, the remaining tasks are straightforward and very mechanical. During test execution this is a great advantage.
(3) *High degree of automation possible.* Depending on the software, it may be possible to batch together many test cases to be executed automatically.
(4) *Generated test cases tend to stress the software more thoroughly.* It was found that for many functional areas, the test cases presented a rich combination of inputs to the software. It would be very hard, and certainly tedious to have such combinations with hand-crafted test cases.
(5) *Forces close teamwork between development and test.* As the grammar demands that the software specification be known precisely, it is important for development and test to remove ambiguities in the functional specification early. If this is not done, the grammar may not generate valid test cases, and it is undesirable to have to modify the grammar after testing is already in progress.

Difficulties

(1) *Education.* It requires education and experience to write effective grammars.
(2) *Validating the grammar.* It is very important that the grammar generates expected test cases. It is not always easy to ensure that grammar is correct. There may be subtle logic errors which may not be detected or detected after the testing is already in progress.
(3) *Validating the usage profile.* The CCM model requires that test case generation follow the expected customer usage. In practice, such data is hard to obtain, especially for new software. In such cases,

assigning probabilities based upon consensus among the team members is the only feasible approach.

(4)   *Setting up test data.* Many test cases require elaborate setup before they can be executed. It can become a challenging task to generate the test data as well as the test command so that they match. Obviously, the complexity depends upon the software, and this problem exists in any form of testing.

(5)   *Self-checking is nontrivial.* Another difficult area which hampers automation is verification of the test case execution. Depending on the software, it may be difficult or impossible to generate self-checking logic.

Conclusion

Provided one invests the required effort into developing a valid grammar, the STGF can prove to be very useful. Otherwise, advantages cited will not be realized.

Finally, the grammar can become too complex if it is designed to generate all test cases. Some testing is best done in the traditional, and manual way. For example:

• test cases to test software with invalid data
• very special and unique situations

It may be a good idea, depending on the software, to do 20% of the testing manually to cover these situations.

EXPERIENCE REPORT 2

Testing a compiler
This is a personal report from a non-IBM tester who used the STGF to aid in the testing of a compiler.

Summary

I used the Statistical Test Case Generation Facility (STGF) to generate random instances of a specific code language. The grammar file which the STGF translated was modeled after the grammar for the language itself. The output of the STGF was a file containing compliable code, which was used to test the integrity of the compiler. The code that the sᴛɢF produced also contained self-checks, so that during execution-time, proper behavior was monitored.

The process revealed many bugs in our compiler in only the short time that it was run. I wrote a shell script to generate a new code file, compile it, and finally execute the binary. Errors were detected in the compiler both at compile-time and execution-time. It was planned that this process would run continuously overnight while the cᴘᴜ was idle; however this was seldom the case. Also, we generated enough work in fixing what the sᴛɢF showed up that we eventually stopped running it all together.

Advantages

(1) *Easy to translate* ʙɴF *grammar to* ᴜᴅʟ *format.* The grammar file which the sᴛɢF translated was modeled after the grammar for the language itself. With very few notation changes, I was able to use the ʙɴF grammar for the language with the sᴛɢF. The major changes were adding < >'s around each terminal, and assigning probabilities to choices.

(2) *Dynamic data structures of* ᴜᴅʟ *are very useful.* The more involved work came from inserting semantic information about the language into the grammar file. It was very helpful to have dynamic data structures such as maps and lists (not described in this chapter) to aid in this task.

(3) *Use of* sᴛɢF *improved our testing.* What I was able to produce using the sᴛɢF over the course of a few weeks was far more advanced than any other prior efforts to do the same task.

(4) *Overall.* The sᴛɢF was easy to use, easy to improve on, and produced results quickly.

Difficulties

(1) *Documentation.* I would suggest that if the user's guide contained a few more simple examples, it would help a new user get acquainted quicker and better with all of the functionality of the sᴛɢF.

Conclusion

It would take a good deal of time and effort to fully implement all the syntactic and semantic features of the language, but what I was able to produce using the sᴛɢF over the course of a few weeks was far more advanced than any other prior efforts to do the same task. Also, the sᴛɢF implies a natural framework which makes additions to the current state of the gram- mar easy. I was able to create a solid foundation and then steadily improve the grammar file to cover more and more features of the language as time permitted.

Overall I was very pleased with the STGF. It was easy to use, easy to improve on, and produced results quickly.

References

1   Currit, P. A., M. Dyer and H. D. Mills, Certifying the reliability of software, *IEEE Transactions on Software Engineering*, January 1986, Vol. SE-12, No. 1, pp. 3–11.
2   Whittaker, J. A. and J. H. Poore, Markov Analysis of Software Specifications, *ACM Transactions on Software Engineering and Methodology*, Vol. 2, No. 1, January 1993, pp. 93–106.
3   Musa, J. D., Operational Profiles in Software-Reliability Engineering, *IEEE Software*, March 1993, pp. 14–32.
4   Hopcroft, J. E. and J. D. Ullman, *Introduction to Automata Theory, Languages, and Computation*, Addison-Wesley, Reading, Mass., 1979.
5   Allen, Arnold O., *Probability, Statistics, and Queueing Theory: with Computer Science Applications*, Academic Press, Orlando, 1978 See p. 74.

13 Markov Analysis of Software Specifications

J. A. WHITTAKER AND J. H. POORE

1 MARKOV CHAINS AS MODELS FOR SOFTWARE USAGE

Cleanroom software engineering[6] results in a certification of the reliability of a software system based on the Certification Model.[2] The Certification Model is itself based on statistical testing,[11] which requires random selection of test cases from the input domain of a software system according to the intended usage distribution. Two key aspects of this form of software testing are the usage distribution and the generation of test cases. Previous applications of Cleanroom have used stochastic grammars[5] as the basis for statistical testing. In this chapter we explore the closely related idea of Markov analysis[12] of the specification of a software system as the basis for constructing the usage distribution and for generating random test cases based on that distribution.

Cleanroom software engineering produces software systems in a series of increments under statistical quality control.[8] These increments are organized based on information gleaned from a Box Structure[7] analysis and design. This results in a black box view of the system as depicted in figure 13.1. Stated differently, the black box view of the system expresses the specification in terms of carefully detailed stimuli, responses, and transition rules. Specifications in this form are amenable to usage modeling of the system so specified. The point of this chapter is to demonstrate that the Markov chain is useful in defining the underlying probability system of software usage and in guiding the statistical test.

© 1993 Association for Computing Machinery, Inc. Reprinted, with permission, from *ACM Transactions on Software Engineering and Methodology*, vol. 2, no. 1, January 1993, pp. 93–106.

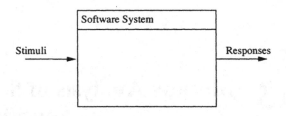

Figure 13.1   Black box view of a software system.

Statistical software testing is a random experiment, and as such requires the complete characterization of the sample space and its associated probability distribution, the definition of the appropriate event space, and a method of computing properties of descriptive random variables.[3] The sample space is the input domain of the software as indicated by the enumeration of stimuli in the specification document. The selection of points from the sample space is governed by some unknown probability distribution. In statistical testing the events of interest are *sequences* of stimuli that represent an execution of the software. These sequences constitute the event space of the specified software and are obtained by defining an ordering on the points in the sample space. It is the sequences that are ultimately the important attribute of the random experiment, for they represent the test cases for the software. Statistical descriptions of the sequences are desirable in order to gain insight into the makeup of the test cases and of how many are necessary to certify the software. These descriptions are obtained by defining random variables that describe the profile of the entire set of sequences that will be used to certify the software.

The nature of the statistical testing experiment is centered around sequences of events, and as such can be modeled by a stochastic process. Thus, we define a stochastic model to guide test case generation and to compute pertinent usage statistics. In this chapter we explore the use of the finite state, discrete parameter Markov chain to model software usage and to conduct statistical testing. The states of the Markov chain represent entries from the input domain of the software. The arcs of the chain define an ordering that determines the event space, or sequences, of the experiment. Furthermore, the ergodic nature of the chain induces a probability distribution on the sample space (i.e., the usage distribution) and facilitates the computation of pertinent random variables that describe the underlying statistics of the experiment.

The Markov chain proves to be a good model for several reasons. From the software engineering point of view, definitions and properties of the model ensure the testability of the software. Once a model has been built, any number of statistically typical test cases can be obtained from the model. From an analytical point of view, this is a tractable stochastic process and a good basis for statistical testing. There is a rich body of theory, analytical results, and computational algorithms. As will be shown, standard analytical results for Markov chains have important interpretations for software development. Furthermore, the work is based upon an analysis of the specification, which means that all of the information provided by the model, including the usage distribution and test cases, is available before a line of code is written.

2 MARKOV ANALYSIS OF SOFTWARE SPECIFICATIONS

The fundamental step in the Markov analysis of a software specification is to define the underlying probability law for the usage of the software under consideration. This analysis of the specification, performed prior to design and coding, yields an irreducible Markov chain[3] which we call the *usage Markov chain*. This chain has a unique start state S_0 (which represents invocation of the software) a unique final state S_F (which represents termination of the software) and a set of intermediate usage states $\{S_i\}$. Each usage state is labeled with a stimulus from the input domain of the software. The state set $S = \{S_0, \{S_i\}, S_F\}$ is ordered by the probabilistic transition relation ($S \times [0,1] \times S$). For each arc defined by this relation, the next state is independent of all past states given the present state. This is called the *Markov property*. A chain that possesses this property is said to be a *first order* chain. The usage Markov chain has a two-phase construction. In the *structural phase* the states and arcs of the chain are established, and in the *statistical phase* the transition probabilities are assigned.

At the highest level, software usage can be described by the three-state transition diagram depicted in figure 13.2. For application software, the software is invoked, a cycle of usage ensues, and eventually the software is terminated and control is returned to the operating system. (An analogous statement can be made for real-time software using "power on" and "power off".) The usage state is expanded by consulting the specification for all possible actions immediately following invocation. A new state is created for each action with an arc from the invocation state as its incoming arc. Exit arcs from the newly created states are established by determining (from the specification) which actions can be performed following the state in question. These arcs can be directed to preexisting states or they can lead to the creation of new states in the same manner. This method of creating states yields a directed graph whose states are labeled with entries drawn from the input domain of the software. The arcs of the graph define an ordering that the inputs must obey.

As an example, consider the window pictured in figure 13.3 and specified in table 13.1. Although this is an abbreviated specification, it is sufficient to describe the functionality for the purpose of this example. Invoking the software causes the window to be displayed; thus a state labeled *Window* is created as a neighbor of the invocation state. In order to determine the exit arcs from this new state, each possible action from the *Window* state is considered; *Maximize* (▲), *Minimize* (▼), *Move*, *Size*, and *Close*. The creation of these states yields the transition diagram of figure 13.4. Each of these states is analyzed in turn to determine the placement of their respective exit arcs. The state labeled *Maximize* simply returns the user to a fully functional window. Thus, the single exit arc from this state is back to the preexisting *Window* state. The state labeled *Minimize* requires another

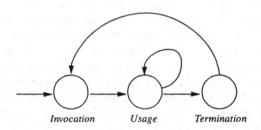

Invocation   Usage   Termination

Figure 13.2   Top level view of software usage.

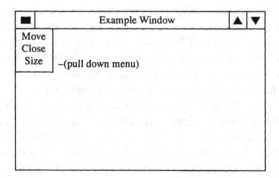

Figure 13.3   An example window.

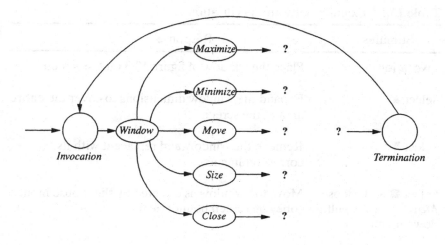

Figure 13.4 Expansion of the top level usage diagram.

series of states to be created to model the icon behavior. Establishing the state *Icon* as a neighbor of *Minimize*, we note that only one action is specified from the *Icon* state, namely *Restore* (which simply returns the user to the window). Thus the series, on single transitions with probability one, is *Window, Minimize, Icon, Restore,* and *Window. Move* and *Size* require mouse activity to be modeled. When either is selected, a directive to drag the mouse (*Drag Mouse*) is given, followed by the direction (if more detail is desired, a distance could also be supplied). Since the user may choose to change the direction of the mouse movement, the exit arcs from the direction states return to *Drag Mouse* in order to allow continued and varied movement. When all movement is complete, the window is restored (marked by a return to the *Window* state). Finally, the state labeled *Close* simply terminates the window. Thus its single exit arc is to the termination state. The complete transition diagram appears in figure 13.5.

It is necessary to note that the construction of the usage chain is a creative *design step* and not an algorithm. Formal, mathematical specification documents lend themselves to more systematic model construction than natural language specification. Good engineering practices are emerging to guide the design of a usage chain from a formal specification.

The structural phase is complete when usage (as defined by the specification) is completely modeled. At this stage the assignment of transition probabilities is the last step toward completion of the chain. This step constitutes the statistical phase of the usage model construction. There are three approaches to the statistical phase.

Table 13.1   Example software specification

Stimulus	Response
Invocation	Place the window of figure 13.3 on the screen
Select ▲	Expand the window dimensions to cover the entire area of the screen
Select ▼	Remove the window and replace it with its corresponding icon
Select ■ and choose *Move* from the pull down menu	Move the window as directed by the mouse input (obeying screen boundaries)
Select ■ and choose *Size* from the pull down menu	Size the window as directed by the mouse input (obeying minimum and maximum limits)
Select ■ and choose *Close* from the pull down menu	Remove the window from the screen
Select the icon and release	Remove the icon from the screen and restore the window

The first is called the *uninformed* approach. It consists of assigning a uniform probability distribution across the exit arcs for each state. This approach, which maximizes the entropy[1] across the exit arcs, produces a unique model and is useful when no information is available to allow a more informed choice.

The second approach, called the *informed* approach, can produce many models, and is used when some actual user sequences are available. These sequences could be captured inputs from a prototype or prior version of the software. Each sequence represents a path through the usage chain that takes the chain from the uninvoked state to the terminate state. Thus a set of structurally complete sequences establishes frequency counts for each arc traversed in the sequence set. The resulting relative frequencies can be used to estimate the transition probabilities in the usage chain. The informed approach is driven by field data.

The third approach, called the *intended* approach, is similar to the

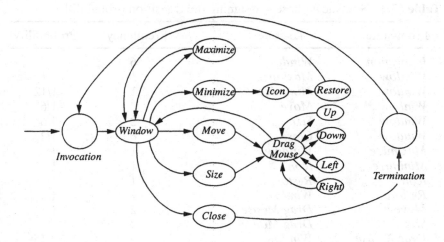

Figure 13.5 Structural phase – constructing the usage Markov chain.

informed approach in that it can lead to many models, but the sequences are obtained by hypothesizing runs of the software by a careful and reasonable user. Relative frequency estimates of the transition probabilities are computed from the symbol transition counts as in the informed approach. An example of the counting technique appears in table 13.2.

We offer three approaches in order to cover all situations. The informed approach with known sequences for one or more classes of users is best. Next best is the intended approach where general knowledge not supported by field data can be used. As a last resort we use the uninformed approach. The uninformed approach can produce anomalous results in the light of knowledge or intuition. For example, universally accessible "help" leads to an artificially high probability of occurrence. Either of the other two approaches will mitigate such problems.

The structure of the usage chain induces a probability distribution (the usage distribution) on the input domain of the software. That is, each state *i* has steady-state probability π_i, which can be computed analytically and is a direct consequence of the structure and statistics of the usage Markov chain. Even the uniformed method of assigning transition probabilities induces, in general, a nonuniform usage distribution on the input domain. The usage distribution is given, along with several other analytical results, in the next section.

Table 13.2   Statistical phase – assigning the transition probabilities

From-state	To-state	Frequency	Probability
Invocation	*Window*	6	1
Window	*Maximize*	1	1/12
Window	*Minimize*	1	1/12
Window	*Move*	2	1/6
Window	*Size*	2	1/6
Window	*Close*	6	1/2
Maximize	*Window*	1	1
Minimize	*Icon*	1	1
Icon	*Restore*	1	1
Restore	*Window*	1	1
Move	*Drag Mouse*	2	1
Size	*Drag Mouse*	2	1
Drag Mouse	*Window*	4	4/15
Drag Mouse	*Up*	1	1/15
Drag Mouse	*Down*	5	1/3
Drag Mouse	*Left*	3	1/5
Drag Mouse	*Right*	2	2/15
Up	*Drag Mouse*	1	1
Down	*Drag Mouse*	5	1
Left	*Drag Mouse*	3	1
Right	*Drag Mouse*	2	1
Close	*Termination*	6	1
Termination	*Invocation*	—	1

Captured or hypothesized sequences:

1. *<Invocation> <Window> <Maximize> <Window> <Close> <Termination>*
2. *<Invocation> <Window> <Minimize> <Icon> <Restore> <Window> <Close> <Termination>*
3. *<Invocation> <Window> <Move> <Drag Mouse> <Down> <Drag Mouse> <Right> <Drag Mouse> <Down> <Drag Mouse> <Window> <Close> <Termination>*
4. *<Invocation> <Window> <Size> <Drag Mouse> <Left> <Drag Mouse> <Up> <Drag Mouse> <Left> <Drag Mouse> <Window> <Close> <Termination>*
5. *<Invocation> <Window> <Move> <Drag Mouse> <Down> <Drag Mouse> <Left> <Drag Mouse> <Down> <Drag Mouse> <Window> <Close> <Termination>*
6. *<Invocation> <Window> <Size> <Drag Mouse> <Down> <Drag Mouse> <Right> <Drag Mouse> <Window> <Close> <Termination>*

3 TEST CASE GENERATION AND ANALYTICAL RESULTS

The usage Markov chain is the source of test sequences for the software. A *statistical test case* is any connected state sequence of the usage chain that begins with the invocation state and ends with the termination state. The process of generating statistical test cases is easily automated using a random number generator and any high-level language. One has simply to step through the states of the chain based upon the transition probabilities. The sequence of states visited becomes the test case. Any number of test cases can be obtained automatically from the model.

A major advantage of using the Markov chain as the stochastic model of software usage is that analytical descriptions of the set of test cases can be acquired before any testing begins. One such description is the *usage distribution*, denoted π, of the usage chain. This vector is computed by solving the system of equations

$$\pi = \pi P \tag{1}$$

where P is the *transition matrix* of the usage chain. (The state transition diagram of a Markov chain can be encoded as a 2-D matrix with the state labels as indices and the arc probabilities as entries. Note that the transition matrix is square and each of its rows sums to one.) The strong law of large numbers allows us to interpret each entry π_i as the expected appearance rate of state i in the long run. In terms of the test cases, this is the expected appearance rate of state i asymptotically. Since each state is ultimately associated with some part of the actual software, this information allows testers to determine which parts of the software will get the most attention from the test cases. Furthermore, the entries in the usage distribution for states related in some manner (for example, states in the same window) can be summed to obtain a long-run value for that group of states. This enables the comparison of the usage of subsections of the software that involve multiple states.

Properties of other random variables of interest to software testers may be derived from the usage distribution. An interesting statistic for testers is the number of states necessary until one can expect to generate state i. This value, denoted x_i, is computed by

$$x_i \pi_i = 1.$$

Solving for x yields

$$x_i = \frac{1}{\pi_i}. \tag{2}$$

When the value of x_i is computed for i equal to the termination state, the result is the expected number of states until termination of the software. For software testers, this translates to the *expected test case length* for the usage model.

The expected number of *sequences* necessary until state i occurs can be derived as

$$s_i = \frac{x_i}{x_{TERM}} = \frac{\pi_{TERM}}{\pi_i}. \tag{3}$$

The largest entry in the vector s identifies the amount of expected testing until all usage states are encountered at least once. The values for π, x, and s, computed using the informed probabilities, appear in table 13.3 for the example.

The mean first passage times are useful in many applications. These values are computed by

$$m_{jk} = 1 + \sum_{i \neq k} p_{ji} m_{ik}. \tag{4}$$

Each m_{jk} is interpreted as the expected number of usage states encountered from state j until the first occurrence of state k. This indicates the extent to which states j and k are encountered within the same sequence.

Table 13.3   Analytical results for the example usage model

State	π	x	s
Invocation	0.093750	10.7	1
Window	0.187500	5.3	0.5
Maximize	0.015625	64	6
Minimize	0.015625	64	6
Icon	0.015625	64	6
Restore	0.015625	64	6
Move	0.031250	32	3
Size	0.031250	32	3
Drag Mouse	0.234375	4.3	0.4
Up	0.015635	64	6
Down	0.078125	12.8	1.2
Left	0.046875	21.3	2
Right	0.031250	32	3
Close	0.093759	10.7	1
Termination	0.093750	10.7	1

For example, if m_{jk} is greater than the expected test case length, then the implication is that the occurrence of state j followed by state k is expected to require multiple sequences. The mean first passage values appear in figure 13.6 for the previous example. Note that the vector x is the diagonal of this matrix, the mean first passage from a state back to itself.

The last result discussed in this chapter is the source entropy of the usage chain. Intuitively, the source entropy quantifies the uncertainty present in a stochastic source. This value is computed by [1]

$$H = -\sum_i \pi_i \sum_j p_{ij} \log p_{ij}. \qquad (5)$$

where π is the usage distribution and the p_{ij} values are the transition probabilities. This single number is related (exponentially) to the number of sequences that are "statistically typical" of the Markov chain. That is, a Markov chain has a set of *typical sequences* whose ensemble statistics closely match the statistics of the chain. Thus, higher source entropy implies an exponentially greater number of typical sequences, i.e., more sequences exist because of the uncertainty present in the model.

The implication of a high source entropy in applications where a Markov chain is used as a sequence generator is that more sequences must be generated in order to accurately describe the Markov source. One can see from equation (5) that low entropy can be attributed to a biased usage

	Invocation	Window	Maximize	Minimize	Icon	Restore	Move	Size	Drag Mouse	Up	Down	Left	Right	Close	Term.
Invocation	11	1	64	62	63	64	26	26	11	74	22	31	42	9	10
Window	10	5	63	61	62	63	25	25	10	73	21	30	41	8	9
Maximize	11	1	64	62	63	64	26	26	11	74	22	31	42	9	10
Minimize	13	3	66	64	1	2	28	28	13	76	24	33	44	11	12
Icon	12	2	65	63	64	1	27	27	12	75	23	32	43	10	11
Restore	11	1	64	62	63	64	26	26	11	74	22	31	42	9	10
Move	17	8	71	69	70	71	32	32	1	64	13	21	32	15	16
Size	17	8	71	69	70	71	32	32	1	64	13	21	32	15	16
Drag Mouse	16	7	70	68	69	70	31	31	4	63	12	20	31	14	15
Up	17	8	71	69	70	71	32	32	1	64	13	21	32	15	16
Down	17	8	71	69	70	71	32	32	1	64	13	21	32	15	16
Left	17	8	71	69	70	71	32	32	1	64	13	21	32	15	16
Right	17	8	71	69	70	71	32	32	1	64	13	21	32	15	16
Close	2	3	66	64	65	66	28	28	13	76	24	33	44	11	1
Termination	1	2	65	63	64	65	27	27	12	75	23	32	43	10	11

Figure 13.6 The mean first passage matrix for the example usage model (entries are rounded).

distribution or from uneven distributions over the exit arcs of the states of the chain.

The source entropy serves as a comparative measure for usage chains with the same structure but different transition probabilities. For example, suppose one develops usage chains U_1 and U_2 using the same structural analysis and assigns U_1's transition probabilities using the uninformed statistical analysis and U_2's using the informed statistical analysis. Let H_1 and H_2 be the source entropies for U_1 and U_2, respectively. As explained earlier, when $H_1 > H_2$ one should expect to generate an exponentially greater number of sequences using U_1 to obtain asymptotic behavior than using U^2. U_1 often serves as a good basis for determining how much the informed approach has biased the usage chain. The values for the example are $H_1 = 1.0884$ bits for the uninformed chain and $H_2 = 0.8711$ bits for the informed chain. Thus the U_2 source will require fewer sequences to reach asymptotics than U_1.

The analytical results obtained from the usage chain serve to give testers advance knowledge of the time and resources it will take to conduct pre-scribed testing for the software in question.

4 INITIAL FIELD EXPERIENCE

In this section we give an overview of the experience we have had in building and analyzing Markov usage models. Each project presents new challenges, each of which must be met within theoretical constraints. These solutions might be characterized fairly as arcane technical details. While we do not catalog tips to the practitioner here, we touch on the practical lessons learned for each project mentioned below.

The method of usage modeling and statistical testing described in this paper has been used with success in a demonstration project.[9] The demonstration was to show how Cleanroom ideas could be applied in an environment[10] of mixing reuse of existing code units with newly developed units to achieve planned reliability levels. A system was designed to interact with the user through five screens in a spreadsheet style. One screen managed project files, another managed data entry and editing, and all others provided for parameter set-up, initiation, and display of results for curve-fitting, matrix calculations, and similar mathematical chores. The certification aspect of the demonstration project was based on Markov usage modeling as described here. This project involved approximately 24,000 lines of Ada, new and reused, and was developed and certified in four increments. A Markov chain that modeled the entire system was developed and subsets were extracted for the certification of each increment (the increments were cumulative so that the parts of the model used in testing grew at each subsequent increment). The entire Markov chain had 90 states and 237 arcs (3% nonzero cells in the transition matrix). A "blunder state" was created from each state to model illegal usage. Whenever this state appeared in a test case, a random keystroke or series of keystrokes was applied to the software. Similarly, the model also contained states that represent data values. For each data value, two states were installed in the chain for legal and illegal configurations of the data, respectively. The appearance of a data state that modeled, for example, a string of characters, caused the generation of an appropriate set of data. In the case of a filename, this data would consist of a string of 1–8 randomly selected alphanumeric characters. In this case study the data values were generated beforehand and then used when directed by the Markov chain. In retrospect, it would have been just as easy to incorporate the additional states into the Markov chain. Thus, we were able to randomize both the control flow through the software and the data that was entered.

We are using Markov chains to generate test cases and certify a comprehensive Cleanroom CASE tool[4] that is under development at the University of Tennessee with IBM sponsorship. These tools are being developed for the OS/2 environment in C. Tools for building, editing, and analyzing Markov models are included. Since the inception of the project in 1989, eight increments have been completed in more than 20,000 lines of C, and work continues. Two separate usage models have been built by two different persons. Just as two programmers can write two very different programs to meet one and the same specification, so too can different Markov usage models be constructed that model one specification. The first model, evolved over seven increments, had reached some 400 states, and as a result of the pressures of complexity and computation time, new insights led to an improved model with fewer than 350 states and a better way to manage the subtleties involved with the multitasking features of the software.

A Markov usage model has been constructed for IBM's DB2 software product; however, the model has not yet been used in statistical testing. The model has approximately 2,000 states. In the course of building this model we created a special notation for representing large models, complete with macros. This, in turn, has presented the concept of translating models expressed in this special notation into the usual arc-probability representation in order to facilitate working with large models.

We know of about 20 Cleanroom projects that are under way in several companies and government agencies. Markov usage models are being used to support certification in three or more of them. The environments range from real-time, embedded code on a bare machine to sophisticated software engineering environments. Code-size estimations range from 75,000 lines of C to 40,000 lines of Ada. These are small systems, but well beyond the scale of academic exercises.

We do not yet have field experience with every class of software. However, we have become relaxed about several issues. First, building usage models is not essentially more difficult than writing specifications or designing code. As an activity that improves specifications, gives an analytical description of the specification, and quantifies the testing costs, it is well worth the effort. Constructing models is a creative process, but good engineering practices are emerging to constrain the process.

Second, the size of the model is a function of the usage states and arcs implicit in the specification and not of the input space. Just as a small program can have an enormous input space or an enormous internal program state space, a small usage model can be the source for a very complex stochastic process.

Third, we are not concerned about computation time for model analysis. Matrices for large models are inherently very sparse and have the property that each row sums to one. These insure that we can use certain iterative sparse matrix techniques which will keep computation time modest even for models with thousands of states (should we encounter such large models).

5   CONCLUSIONS AND FUTURE WORK

We are currently investigating Markov chains to model the execution of the test cases. We hypothesize that it is possible to develop a Markov chain that will "evolve" as the testing process unfolds. The chain must model software failures as well as software usage. Such a model will lead to analytical stopping criteria and a data-driven, discrete software reliability model. We are also working toward a reliability prediction model.

Engineering process is being developed as well as theoretical understanding. This includes the process of model construction, techniques for handling special situations, representation of complex models in simplified form, transformation from one model to an equivalent model, expansion of states to submodels, compression of submodels to states, tools for writing and editing models, computation tools for analysis, and comparison and evaluation of models.

Usage modeling focuses attention and resources on understanding the customer and the product: What will the user likely do with the software? What is the software to be capable of doing? Once an acceptable usage model is in hand, there are no further assumptions. Everything flows analytically and probabilistically from the model. Changes to specifications can be accommodated by structural changes to the model. Furthermore, as new information is learned about users or classes of users, it can be reflected in the parameters of the model. Statistical testing for software certification is supported directly.

Acknowledgements

The authors acknowledge the helpful conversations and interactions with several persons, including H. D. Mills, Software Engineering Technology, Inc., J. Hudepohl, Northern Telecom, Inc., R. Drake, R. C. Linger, and M. Pleszkoch, IBM, and M. G. Thomason, University of Tennessee. We also appreciate the assistance of E. Ploedereder and the anonymous referees.

References

1　Ash, R., *Information Theory*, Wiley, New York, 1966.
2　Currit, P. A., Dyer, M., and Mills, H. D., Certifying the reliability of software. *IEEE Trans. Software Engng*, SE-12, 1 (Jan. 1986), 3–11.
3　Feller, W., *An Introduction to Probability Theory and its Applications*. Vol. 1, Wiley, New York, 1950.
4　Fuhrer, D., Mao, H., and Poore, J. H., OS/2 Cleanroom environment: a progress report on a Cleanroom tools development project. In *Proceedings of the 25th Hawaii International Conference on Systems Science*, IEEE Computer Society Press, Vol. 2, 1992, pp. 449–458.
5　Linger, R. C., and Mills, H. D., A case study in Cleanroom software engineering: The IBM Cobol restructuring facility. In *Proceedings of COMPSAC '88*, IEEE, 1988.
6　Mills, H. D., Dyer, M., and Linger, R. C., Cleanroom software engineering. *IEEE Software* (Sept. 1987), 19–24.
7　Mills, H. D., Linger, R. C., and Hevner, A. R., Box structured information systems. *IBM Systems J.* **26** (1987).
8　Mills, H. D., and Poore, J. H., Bringing software under statistical quality control. *Quality Progress* (Nov. 1988), 52–55.
9　Poore, J. H., Mills, H. D., Hopkins, S. L., and Whittaker, J. A., Cleanroom reliability manager: A case study using Cleanroom with box structures ADL. Software Engineering Technology, Inc., IBM STARS CDRL 1940, May 1990.
10　Poore, J. H., Mutchler, D., and Mills, H. D., STARS-Cleanroom reliability: Cleanroom ideas in the STARS environment. Software Engineering Technology, Inc., IBM STARS CDRL 1710, Sept. 1989.
11　Sexton, B. C., Statistical testing of software, Master's thesis, Department of Computer Science, University of Tennessee, 1988.
12　Thomason, M. G., Generating functions for stochastic context-free grammars. *Int. J. Pattern Recogn. Artif. Intell.* **4**, 4 (April 1990), 553–572.

14 A Markov Chain Model for Statistical Software Testing

J. A. WHITTAKER AND M. G. THOMASON

I INTRODUCTION

The *black box approach*[19,28] to the software testing process unfolds as follows. Given a program P with intended function f and input domain d, the objective is to select a sequence of entries from d, apply them to P, and compare the response with the expected outcome indicated by f. Any deviation from the intended function is designated as a failure. It is assumed that f is well defined and completely specified, so that any deviation is unambiguously detected and a failure is explicitly noted. The history of the test at some time n is a sequence of inputs $d_0 d_1 d_2 \ldots d_{n-1}$ and a corresponding sequence of zero or more failures, each of which is uniquely identified with the particular input d_i at which the failure was observed.

Statistical testing follows the black box model with two important extensions. First, sequences from d are stochastically generated based on a probability distribution that represents a profile of actual or anticipated use of the software. Second, a statistical analysis is performed on the test history that enables the measurement of various probabilistic aspects of the testing process. Thus, one can view statistical testing as a sequence generation and analysis problem. A solution to the problem is achieved by constructing a generator to obtain the test input sequences and by developing an informative analysis of the test history.

This chapter describes a sequence generation and analysis technique for statistical testing using Markov chains. We discuss the construction of a Markov chain as a sequence generator for statistical testing and show how analytical results associated with Markov chains can aid in test planning.

© 1994 IEEE. Reprinted, with permission, from IEEE *Transactions on Software Engineering*, vol. 20, no. 10, pp. 812–24, October 1994.

An innovative aspect of this method is that the test sequences generated and applied to the software are used to create a second Markov chain to encapsulate the history of the test, including any observed failure information. The influence of the failures is assessed through analytical computations on this chain. We also derive a stopping criterion for the testing process based on a comparison of the sequence generating properties of the two chains.

II   A STATISTICAL TESTING MODEL FOR SOFTWARE

The need for testing methods and reliability models that are specific to software has been discussed in various forms in the technical literature.[3,10,11,20] Statistical testing for software is one such method. The main benefit of statistical testing is that it allows the use of statistical inference techniques to compute probabilistic aspects of the testing process, such as reliability,[3,10,16,20] mean time to failure (MTTF),[4,22] and mean time between failures (MTBF).[18]

Current statistical testing techniques model software usage by assigning a single, unconditional probability distribution to individual inputs (or groups of inputs) from the software's input domain.[4,7,8,11,16,19] This distribution represents the best estimate of the operational frequency of use for each input. Input sequences are obtained by sampling from the distribution with or without replacement (depending on the application). Obviously, this model is insufficient for many types of software, because the probability of applying an input can change as the software is executed. As software processes inputs, it moves from one *state* or *mode* to the next, depending on any or all prior inputs received. Thus, the probability of an input can change depending on the mode of the software.[20] It is necessary, therefore, to maintain multiple probability distributions for each such mode of a software system.

This chapter proposes that statistical testing be carried out with a stochastic model of software usage. We define a stochastic model that is capable of modeling multiple probability distributions corresponding to pertinent software modes and is tractable for the computation of properties of informative random variables that describe its sequence generating capabilities. Ideally, the parameters of the model are established using information obtained from various sources, including the software's intended function and usage patterns of prior versions or prototypes of the software. However, it is often the case that complete information about the probabilities that describe usage is not available from any source; in this case, the stochastic model is based on estimated usage patterns.[27]

This *usage model* consists of elements from d, the domain of the intended function, and a probablistic relationship defined on these elements. A test input is a finite sequence of inputs from domain d probabilistically generated from the usage model. The statistical properties of the model lend insight into the expected makeup of the sequences for test planning purposes.

As the test sequences are applied to the software, the results are incorporated into a second model. This *testing model* consists of the inputs executed in the test sequences, plus any failures discovered while applying the sequences to the software P. In other words, it is a model of what has occurred during testing. The testing model also allows analysis of the test data in terms of random variables appropriate for the application. For example, we may measure the evolution of the testing model and decide to stop testing when it has reached some suitable "steady state."

This chapter explores the use of finite state, discrete parameter, time homogeneous Markov chains as the software usage and testing models for program P. For the usage model, the state space of the Markov chain is defined by externally visible modes of the software that affect the application of inputs. The state transition arcs are labeled with elements from the input domain d of the software (as described by the intended function f). Transition probabilities are uniform (across exit arcs from each state) if no usage information is available, but may be nonuniform if usage patterns are known. This model is called the *usage Markov chain*. For the testing model, the state space of the Markov chain is initially the same as the usage chain, but additional states are added to mark each individual failure. This model is called the *testing Markov chain*.

III   THE USAGE MARKOV CHAIN

A usage chain for a software system consists of states, i.e., externally visible modes of operation that must be maintained in order to predict the application of all system inputs, and state transitions that are labeled with system inputs and transition probabilities. To determine the state set, one must consider each input and the information necessary to apply that input. It may be that certain software modes cause an input to become more or less probable (or even illegal). Such a mode represents a state or set of states in the usage chain. Once the states are identified, we establish a start state, a terminate state (for bookkeeping purposes), and draw a state transition diagram by considering the effect of each input from each of the identified states. The Markov chain is completely defined when transition probabilities are established that represent the best estimate of real usage.

Consider the simple selection menu pictured in figure 14.1. The input domain consists of the up-arrow key and the down-arrow key, which move the cursor to the desired menu item, and the "Enter" key, which selects the item. The cursor moves from one item to the next, and wraps from top to bottom on an up-arrow and from bottom to top on a down-arrow. The first item, "Select Project," is used to define a project (the semantics of which are not described here for simplicity). The project name then appears in the upper-right corner of the screen. Once a project is defined, the next three items, Enter Data, Analyze Data, and Print Report, can be selected to perform their respective functions. (These additional screens are also not described.) If no project is defined, selecting these items gives no response.

In this example, there are two items of interest when applying inputs. First, the current cursor location must be maintained to determine the behavior of the "Enter" key. Second, whether a project has been defined must be known to determine which of the menu items are available.

These two items of information are organized as the following *usage variables*:

(1)   *cursor location* (which is abbreviated CL and takes on values "Sel," "Ent," "Anl," "Prt," or "Ext" for each respective menu item), and
(2)   *project defined* (which is abbreviated PD and takes on the values "Yes" or "No").

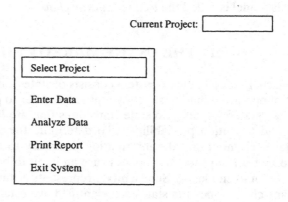

Arrow Keys to Move Cursor   Enter to Select

Figure 14.1   An example software system.

The state set therefore consists of the following: {(CL = Sel, PD = No), (CL = Ent, PD = No), (CL = Anl, PD = No), (CL = Prt, PD = No), (CL = Ext, PD = No), (CL = Sel, PD = Yes), (CL = Ent, PD = Yes), (CL = Anl, PD = Yes), (CL = Prt, PD = Yes), (CL = Ext, PD = Yes)}. In addition, we include states that represents placeholders for the other system screens, as well as start and end states that represent the software in its "not invoked" mode. The state transitions are depicted in figure 14.2 in a graphical format.

This state transition diagram defines the possible input sequences for the software in a formal and concise model. A path, or connected state/arc sequence, from the initial "Uninvoked" state to the final "Terminated" state, represents a single execution of the software. A set of such sequences are used as test cases for the software. Since loops and cycles exist in the model, an infinite number of sequences are possible. In order to generate sequences statistically, probability distributions are established over the exit arcs at each state that simulates expected field usage. The assignment of these probabilities is discussed below.

Sequences are generated from the model by stepping through state transitions (according to the transition probabilities), from "Uninvoked" to "Terminated," and recording the sequence of inputs on the path tra-

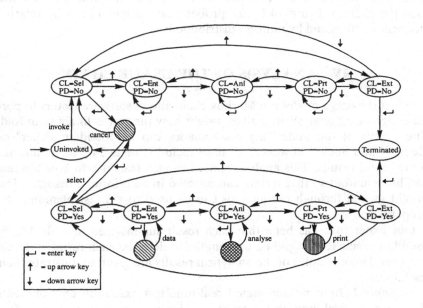

Figure 14.2 Usage chain (structure) for the example.

versed. A sample input sequence from the model of figure 14.2 is: **invoke** ⏎ **select** ↓↓⏎ **analyze** ↓↓⏎. It is readily apparent that the generation of sequences can be automated using a good random number generator and any high-level programming language. Thus, a large number of input sequences can be obtained once a usage chain is constructed.

The construction of the transition diagram identifies the probabilities that need to be estimated, i.e., the state transition probabilities. An investigation into usage patterns of the software should focus on obtaining information about these probabilities. Sequences of use from a prototype or prior version of the software, for example, may be used to estimate these probabilities. These usage sequences, captured as inputs (keystrokes, mouse clicks, bus commands, buffered data, and so forth) from the user, are mapped to states and arcs in the model in order to obtain frequency counts that correspond to state transitions. Normalizing the frequency counts establishes relative frequency estimates of the transition probabilities and completes the definition of the Markov chain.

In the event that no sequences are available to aid in the estimation of the transition probabilities, all probabilities can be distributed uniformly across the exit arcs at each state. In this case, the model building process amounts to establishing only the *structure* of usage sequences without developing any informed statistics. Table 14.1 lists each transition for the example chain in figure 14.1 with probabilities assigned both by relative frequency counts and by uniform distributions.

IV   ANALYSIS OF THE USAGE CHAIN

The fact the usage model is a Markov chain allows software testers to perform significant analysis that gives insight how the test is likely to unfold. The details of the underlying mathematics can be found in Feller[9] or Kemeny and Snell;[14] however, we have included table 14.2 to summarize some useful results. This analysis is used to gain insight into how the test will likely unfold so that testers can proceed in an informed manner. The insight gained through the analysis can be used to aid test planning and preparation.

Our experience has been that each result summarized in table 14.2 is useful in practice. It would be too lengthy to describe each result in detail; however, two examples of the analytical results are given to illustrate their usefulness.

Example 1. In some automated real-time test execution environments there is a physical limit on the number of inputs in a single test case.[1] It is useful, therefore, to know the "expected length and standard deviation of

Table 14.1 Transition probabilities for the example usage model

From state	Transition stimuli	To state	Unif. prob.	Est. prob.
Uninvoked	invoke	{CL = Sel, PD = No}	1	1
{CL = Sel, PD = No}	→	{CL = Ent, PD = No}	1/3	1/10
	←	{CL = Ext, PD = No}	1/3	1/10
	⌐	{CL = Sel, PD = No}	1/3	8/10
{CL = Ent, PD = No}	→	{CL = Anl, PD = No}	1/3	1/3
	←	{CL = Sel, PD = No}	1/3	1/3
	⌐	{CL = Ent, PD = No}	1/3	1/3
{CL = Anl, PD = No}	→	{CL = Prt, PD = No}	1/3	1/3
	←	{CL = Ent, PD = No}	1/3	1/3
	⌐	{CL = Anl, PD = No}	1/3	1/3
{CL = Prt, PD = No}	→	{CL = Ext, PD = No}	1/3	1/3
	←	{CL = Anl, PD = No}	1/3	1/3
	⌐	{CL = Prt, PD = No}	1/3	1/3
{CL = Ext, PD = No}	→	{CL = Sel, PD = No}	1/3	1/3
	←	{CL = Prt, PD = No}	1/3	1/3
	⌐	Terminated	1/3	1/3
{CL = Sel, PD = Yes}	→	{CL = Ent, PD = Yes}	1/3	5/9

Table 14.1 – *continued*

From state	Transition stimuli	To state	Unif. prob.	Est. prob.
	←	{CL = Ext, PD = Yes} Select Project	1/3	3/9
	¬		1/3	1/9
{CL = Ent, PD = Yes}	→	{CL = Anl, PD = Yes}	1/3	4/7
	←	{CL = Sel, PD = Yes}	1/3	1/7
	¬	Enter Data	1/3	2/7
{CL = Anl, PD = Yes}	→	{CL = Prt, PD = Yes}	1/3	3/6
	←	{CL = Ent, PD = Yes}	1/3	1/6
	¬	Analyze Data	1/3	2/6
{CL = Prt, PD = Yes}	→	{CL = Ext, PD = Yes}	1/3	2/6
	←	{CL = Anl, PD = Yes}	1/3	1/6
	¬	Print Report	1/3	3/6
{CL = Ext, PD = Yes}	→	{CL = Sel, PD = Yes}	1/3	1/6
	←	{CL = Prt, PD = Yes}	1/3	2/6
	¬	Terminated	1/3	3/6
Select Project	cancel	{CL = Sel, PD = No}	1/2	1/8
	select	{CL = Sel, PD = Yes}	1/2	7/8
Enter Data	data	{CL = Ent, PD = Yes}	1	1

Analyze Data	analyze	{CL = Anl, PD = Yes}	1
Print Report	print	{CL = Prt, PD = Yes}	1
Terminated	null	Uninvoked	1

V. THE TESTING MARKOV CHAIN

the input sequences," so that overloading the test execution environment can be controlled. Using (4) with i = Uninvoked and j = Terminated, this expectation for the example chain with relative frequency estimated probabilities is 20.1, with standard deviation of 15.8. If these results were unacceptable (i.e., outside the range of the test environment), then modification of the transition probabilities would be necessary to obtain more suitable results.

Example 2. In practice, software testers are often concerned with the *coverage* of some specific attribute of the software under test. For example, Myers[19] relates coverage criteria concerning the percentage of source code executed by a set of test cases. When testing is performed from the black box point of view, coverage of elements of the input domain is often of interest.[19]

Equations (6) and (8) are used to estimate the coverage of usage chain states and arcs. This measure goes beyond input domain coverage, because the software modes are represented (i.e., as states) as well as inputs (i.e., as arcs). The information is organized into percentages of states and arcs in table 14.3. For example, table 14.3 indicates that 81.25% of the states have expectation of seven sequences or less until they appear in the test sequences.

The information from each of these examples is used to make the following estimates of expected effort to achieve full coverage (each result is rounded up to the nearest integer). Suppose testers determine that it takes 5 s, on average, to apply an input to the example selection menu software. An average sequence will then take $21 \times 5 = 105$ s (1 min, 45 s) to execute. Further, it will take $12 \times 105 = 1260$ s (21 min), on average, to execute enough sequences so that every state is covered and $36 \times 105 = 3780$ s (1 hr, 3 min) so that every arc is covered. In addition to these results, each measure in table 14.2 has been used in practice to analyze some aspect of software usage or testing. More detail is presented elsewhere.[1,26]

V   THE TESTING MARKOV CHAIN

When the usage chain is complete, a series of input sequences is stochastically generated and applied to software P. The application of the test sequences can be manual or automatic, depending on the testing environment and the availability of suitable automated support. We assume the presence of an oracle that is capable of comparing the output of P with the intended behavior, f, and correctly classifying success or failure. Thus, the history of the test at some time n is a series of input sequences (and usage chain states) $d_0 d_1 \ldots d_{n-1}$ and a corresponding sequence of failures, each of

Table 14.2 Some standard analytical results for Markov chains*

Result	Equation for prob. or mean		Interpretation of mean
Recurrent chain Stationary distribution, π	$\pi_j = \sum_i \pi_i U_{ij}$	(1)	π_j is the asymptotic appearance rate of state j in a large number of sequences from U
Recurrence time for state j	$m_{jj} = \dfrac{1}{\pi_j}$	(2)	The mean number of state transitions between occurrences of state j in a large number of sequences from U
No. of occurrences of state i between occurrences of state j	$m_{jj}\pi_i = \dfrac{\pi_i}{\pi_j}$	(3)	The mean number of occurrences of state i between occurrences of state j
First passage times	$m_{ij} = 1 + \sum_{k \neq j} U_{ik} m_{kj}$	(4)	The mean number of state transitions until state j occurs from state i
Absorbing chain (for initial state i) Single sequence prob. for state j	$y_{ij} = U_{ij}^a + \sum_{k \in \tau} U_{ik}^a y_{kj}$	(5)	The probability that state j occurs in a single sequence (i.e., from the initial state to the absorbing state)

Table 14.2 – *continued*

Result	Equation for prob. or mean		Interpretation of mean
No. of sequences to occurrence of state j	$h_j = \dfrac{1}{y_{ij}}$	(6)	The mean number of sequences until state j occurs
Single sequence prob. for arc j,k	$z_{jk} = y_{ij} U_{jk}$	(7)	The probability that arc j,k occurs in a single sequence (i.e., from the initial state to the absorbing state)
No. of sequences to occurrence of arc j,k	$h_{jk} = \dfrac{1}{z_{jk}}$	(8)	The mean number of sequences until arc j,k occurs
No. of occurrences of state j in a single sequence	$m(j\|i)$ $= \sum\limits_{k \in \tau} U_{ik}^{a} m(j\|k) + \begin{array}{l} 1 \quad \text{if } i = j \\ 0 \quad \text{if } i \neq j \end{array}$	(9)	of state j in a single sequence The mean number of occurrences

*Each measure in this table is based on the usage model encoded as a *transition matrix*, U, with states as indices and transition probabilities as entries. U is called the *recurrent model* because the arc from Terminated to Uninvoked occurs with probability 1, causing a new sequence to begin each time the previous sequence ends. The *absorbing model*, U, is achieved by redirecting the arc from Terminated to Uninvoked back to Terminated; thus, this is a model representing only single executions of the software. In this case, the state Terminated is called *absorbing*, and the other states are called *transient*. (The set of transient states is denoted τ.)

which is uniquely identified with the particular sequence and specific input d_i with which the failure was observed.

As failures are discovered and the software's internal faults repaired, the software evolves, becoming more or less reliable, depending on the success of the fixes. Each change to the software creates a new software version. Corresponding to each such version is a subset of the test history that represents the testing experience for that particular version. Thus, if one is interested in quantifying the behavior of a specific, homogeneous software version, then the applicable data to use as a basis for measuring this is the corresponding subset of the test history.[20] In addition, if one is interested in studying the rate at which failures are identified and how this rate varies during the complete testing process, then the applicable data are the entire test history over successive software versions. Although the entire test history pertains to no specific software version, it does represent the entire testing experience for a software project and can be helpful in analyzing the underlying software process used to create the software. The following discussion applies to either view of the testing history. In fact, both analyses can be performed simultaneously for any given project.

Table 14.3 Expectations for state and arc coverage from the example usage chain

No. of input sequences	Expected percentage of states covered	Expected percentage of arcs covered
1	18.75	86.32
2	62.50	87.89
3	68.75	89.45
4	75.00	91.01
5	75.00	91.79
6	75.00	92.18
7	81.25	92.57
8	87.50	92.57
9	87.50	93.35
10	87.50	94.92
11	87.50	95.31
12–19	100.00	95.31
20–22	100.00	96.48
23–33	100.00	97.65
34–35	100.00	98.82
36	100.00	100.00

The test history (or any meaningful subset thereof) is a realization of a stochastic process and is appropriately analyzed by a stochastic model. In this paper, we use a stochastic model of a test history to identify the length of the test sequence that will be a suitable stopping point for testing the software, and to analyze the effect of the failures on the testing stochastic process. For these purposes, the test history is encoded as another Markov chain, the *testing Markov chain*, *T*. This section describes construction of the testing chain from a test history and derives an analytical stopping criterion. In addition, analytical results associated with Markov chain theory are used to quantify the impact of the failures on the testing process.

A set of test input sequences is a realization of the usage chain *U* and has certain characteristics imposed by *U*; e.g., states and transitions appear with known probabilities in the long run. The development of these characteristics occurs probabilistically; i.e., given a new random seed, a different set of sequences could be obtained in which states and arcs are generated in a different order. Detailed analysis of the testing process therefore requires a model that itself evolves as specific testing is carried out.

A Constructing the testing chain

Usage chain *U* has stationary transition probabilities; i.e., they do not change throughout the test. However, probabilities in testing chain *T* are updated, and tracking *T*'s evolution is an inherent part of monitoring the statistical testing process. Let $s_1, s_2, ..., s_m$ denote the set of test sequences in the order generated by *U* and applied to software *P*. The corresponding series of testing chains $T_0, T_1, ..., T_m$ describes the evolution of *T* during testing and is constructed as follows.

Before any sequence is input to *P*, the test history is empty. The initial chain T_0 is a copy of usage chain *U*, with all arc probabilities set to 0. Assume first that no software failures occur. T_1 is obtained from T_0 by incrementing arc frequencies along the path of states from "Uninvoked" to "Terminated" in s_1. Similarly, T_2 is obtained from T_1 by sequence s_2, and, in general, T_i is obtained from T_{i-1} by sequence s_i. In this way, frequency counts on arcs in T_i are always obtained from specific sequences applied to software *P*. These arc frequencies are converted to relative frequency probabilities whenever computation with T_i's state transition probabilities is required.

The testing chain's arc counts are reset when fixes are applied to *P*. Thus, as the software changes, a new testing chain is created to model only the sequences applied on that version. In this manner, the testing chain remains an accurate model of the testing experience of the current software version. An additional formulation is to maintain a testing chain that is not reset between fixes and incorporates testing experience across different software versions. This latter testing chain is really a model of the *process* of error discovery and fault removal, whereas the former series of chains represents each successive version of the software *product*. Either interpretation can provide valuable feedback about software development activity.

What can be said about the series $T_0, T_1, \ldots, T_m$? If no failures are detected, the evolution of T is dictated solely by sequences from U. The Strong Law of Large Numbers for Markov chains[6] guarantees (with probability 1) that these sequences $s_1, \ldots, s_m$ will become statistically typical of U when enough are generated. This means that convergence of T to U is certain, because the relative frequencies on T's arcs will converge to the probabilities on U's arcs. A key point is that the test history T is statistically typical of the usage chain U if and only if convergence is achieved.

In other words, U is a fixed reference toward which T_i evolves at an expected rate with statistical variation that depends on factors such as the source entropy of U.[26] This evolution is well controlled and predictable in statistical terms.

B Incorporating failure data

Suppose now that failures do occur and that the jth failure f_j is detected during input of sequence s_i to P. To incorporate this failure event into the test history, a new state labeled f_j is placed in Markov chain T_i exactly as it was ordered in s_i. The arcs to and from the new state f_j have frequency count 1. If f_j is a catastrophic failure, then the run of software P is aborted, and the arc from f_j goes to "Terminated"; otherwise, the test sequence can continue, and the arc from f_j goes to the next state in s_i. In this way, T_i is maintained as a Markov chain that incorporates both the underlying structure of the source of test sequences, U, and the frequency count history of sequences-plus-failures as testing evolves.

Convergence of T to U is adversely affected by failures of software P during testing. To achieve convergence when failures have been observed, the relative frequency probabilities on arcs to failure states in T_i must approach 0. In this way, the probabilities on the nonfailure arcs are still forced to converge to the corresponding (nonzero) values in U. If even one failure occurs, this can be accomplished only when P responds to more test sequences without exhibiting failures. Thus, failures automatically impose additional testing to overcome their adverse impact on the convergence of T to U.

When no failures occur in the test history, convergence will ultimately be achieved. Intuitively, comparison of the actual evolution of T (including failures) with its expected evolution (without failures) supports statistical estimation of *P*'s characteristics based on the software's actual performance. At any point in the testing process, the most recent test history T_i is available for analysis. Because T_i itself is a well-defined Markov chain, computations are based on the theory of Markov chains.

The testing chain, *T*, is a model of the current test history and is useful for computing properties of descriptive random variables as shown in the next section. An alternative would be to obtain statistics directly from the set of sequences executed; however, *T* incorporates explicitly the *structure* of the usage chain, which is only implicit in the sequences. In other words, each sequence is accorded different status according its specific attributes; e.g., sequences can vary in length and probability, and thus contribute a different amount of information to the statistical testing experiment. The testing chain incorporates each event of each sequence, recognizing the probabilistic relationship between states and arcs established in the usage chain. Any computation based on *T* incorporates this information as well. Thus, *T* is an important model for the identification and derivation of measures that describe the statistical testing process. See [26] for proofs concerning specific attributes of testing chains.

To illustrate testing chain construction, consider the example usage chain of figure 14.2. The initial testing chain, before any sequences are executed, is a copy of this chain, with each arc frequency initialized at zero. A randomly generated sequence is then obtained and executed against the software. The testing chain is updated to reflect the states and arcs traversed in that sequence. For example, the following sequence causes the corresponding transition arcs in the testing chain to be updated (states are included in the sequence for reference; individual inputs are indented):

Uninvoked
    invoke   update transition: (Uninvoked,
    {CL = Sel, PD = No})   {CL = Sel, PD = No}
                          from 0 to 1
    Enter key   update transition: ({CL = Sel,
                          PD = No}, Select Project)
                          from 0 to 1
Select Project Screen
    select   update transition: (Select Project,
                          {CL = Sel, PD = Yes})
                          from 0 to 1
{CL = Sel, PD = Yes}
    Dn Arrow key   update transition:

                                ([CL = Sel, PD = Yes},
                                {CL = Ent, PD = Yes})
                                from 0 to 1

{CL = Ent, PD = Yes}
   Dn Arrow key   update transition:
                                ([CL = Ent, PD = Yes},
                                {CL = Anl, PD = Yes})
                                from 0 to 1

{CL = Anl, PD = Yes}
   Dn Arrow key   update transition:
                                ([CL = Anl, PD = Yes},
                                {CL = Prt, PD = Yes})
                                from 0 to 1

{CL = Prt, PD = Yes}
   Enter key   update transition:
                                ([CL = Prt, PD = Yes}, Print
                                Report) from 0 to 1

Print Report Screen
   print   update transition: (Print Report,
                                {CL = Prt, PD = Yes})
                                from 0 to 1

{CL = Prt, PD = Yes}
   Enter Key   update transition: ([CL = Prt,
                                PD = Yes}, Print Report)
                                from 1 to 2

Print Report Screen
   print   update transition: (Print Report,
                                {CL = Prt, PD = Yes})
                                from 1 to 2

{CL = Prt, PD = Yes}
   Dn Arrow key   update transition:
                                ([CL = Prt, PD = Yes},
                                {CL = Ext, PD = Yes})
                                from 0 to 1

{CL = Ext, PD = Yes}
   Enter key   update transition:
                                ([CL = Ext, PD = Yes},
                                Terminated) from 0 to 1

Terminated   update transition: (Terminated,
                                Uninvoked) from 0 to 1

Suppose now that a failure appeared during printing that caused the system to halt execution. This same sequence, under these circumstances, would achieve the following updates in the testing chain:

Uninvoked
    invoke   update transition: (Uninvoked,
                                {CL = Sel, PD = No})
                                from 0 to 1

CL = Sel, PD = No
    Enter key   update transition:
                                ({CL = Sel, PD = No},
                                Select Project) from 0 to 1

Select Project Screen
    select   update transition: (Select Project,
                                  {CL = Sel, PD = Yes})
                                from 0 to 1

{CL = Sel, PD = Yes}
    Dn Arrow key   update transition:
                                ({CL = Sel, PD = Yes},
                                {CL = Ent, PD = Yes})
                                from 0 to 1

{CL = Ent, PD = Yes}
    Dn Arrow key   update transition:
                                ({CL = Ent, PD = Yes},
                                {CL = Anl, PD = Yes})
                                from 0 to 1

{CL = Anl, PD = Yes}
    Dn Arrow key   update transition:
                                ({CL = Anl, PD = Yes},
                                {CL = Prt, PD = Yes})
                                from 0 to 1

{CL = Prt, PD = Yes}
    Enter key   update transition:
                                  ({CL = Prt, PD = Yes},
                                Print Report) from 0 to 1

Print Report Screen
    print   add state: Failure State *j*
                                update transition: (Print Report,
                                Failure State *j*) from 0 to 1

Failure State *i*   update transition: (Failure State
                                j, Terminated) from 0 to 1

Terminated   update transition: (Terminated,
                                Uninvoked) from 0 to 1

Thus, the testing chain is updated with frequency counts that reflect the actual events that occurred when the sequence was executed. If the failure had not caused the system to halt, then the testing chain would be updated with the failure state followed by the remaining sequence parts. Whenever computation is desired, the frequency counts are normalized to probabilities.

VI ANALYTICAL RESULTS FOR THE TESTING CHAIN

In this section, the testing chain, T, is used to obtain analytical results to answer two questions. First, at what point does the test history become representative of usage (as defined by U)? Second, how does each failure impact the testing process?

A An analytical stopping criterion

Stopping criteria for statistical software testing can be as simple as choosing some target reliability,[3,4,10,18,20,22,24] and testing until the estimate of the reliability meets or exceeds the target. However, the usage-to-testing-chain approach suggests an analytic stopping criterion based directly on the statistical properties of the usage and testing chains. The usage chain is a model of ideal testing of the software; i.e., each arc probability is established with the best estimate of actual usage, and no failure states are present. The testing chain, on the other hand, is a model of a specific test history, including failure data. Thus, the usage chain represents what *would* occur in the statistical test in the absence of failures, and the testing chain represents what *has* occurred. Dissimilarity between the two models is therefore a useful measure of the progress of testing. When the dissimilarity is small, the test history is an accurate picture of the usage model.

Failure states are introduced into the testing chain by actual observations of software failure during testing. Since the usage chain does not have these failure states, they have an implied long-run probability of zero in U. In order to match the stochastic characteristics of the testing chain T in which the failure states may exist, enough nonfailure sequences from U must end in correct termination to push the long-run occupancy of all failure states in T close to zero. Thus, failures observed during testing tend to increase the number of sequences that must be applied to P.

Regardless of whether failures are encountered, we are seeking to identify the point at which the stochastic properties of the usage chain and the testing chain are indistinguishable within some acceptable tolerance. In order to measure this, one could compute, for example, the stationary distribution of each chain and use a goodness of fit criterion (e.g., Chi-squared[5]) to measure their similarity. However, this approach takes into account only a single (albeit very important) attribute of the two models. If we want to measure the difference of the ensemble characteristics of each chain, then another approach is desirable.

Consider each chain as an ergodic stochastic source. Each chain has a set of typical sequences that accurately characterize it as a sequence generator. If both chains have the same set of typical sequences, we may draw the conclusion that the two chains are indistinguishable as sequence generators. Stated differently, it should be extremely difficult, if not impossible, to determine whether a long concatenation of sequences $d_0 d_1 \ldots d_{n-1}$ was generated by U or T.

The *log likelihood ratio*[15] is a fundamental computation in measuring the evidence an observation provides for or against a hypothesis. In this case, the hypothesis is "stochastic process U is equivalent to stochastic process T," and an observation is a large number of sequences generated by recurrent chain U. We define a measure for two stochastic processes as the expected value of the log likelihood ratio, called the *discriminant*.[15] This value is computed for two arbitrary ergodic stochastic processes λ_0 and λ_1[13] as follows:

$$D(\lambda_0,\lambda_1) = \lim_{n \to \infty} \frac{1}{n} [\log_2 p(d_0,d_1 \ldots d_{n-1}|\lambda_0) - \log_2 p(d_0,d_1 \ldots d_{n-1}|\lambda_1)], \quad (10)$$

where $p(d \ldots |\lambda)$ denotes the probability with which stochastic process λ generates sequence d. Although $D(\lambda_0,\lambda_1)$ cannot be directly computed for arbitrary processes λ_0 and λ_1, it can be computed for Markov chains U and T[26] as follows:

$$D(U,T) = \sum_{ij} \pi_i p_{ij} \log_2 \frac{p_{ij}}{\hat{p}_{ij}}, \quad (11)$$

where π is the stationary distribution of U, p_{ij} is the probability of a transition from i to j in U, and $\hat{p}_{ij}$ is the corresponding probability in T. Each $\hat{p}_{ij}$ that corresponds to a nonzero p_{ij} must be greater than zero in order for $D(U,T)$ to be defined. $D(U,T)$ is nonnegative and equal to zero if and only if $p_{ij} = \hat{p}_{ij}$ for all i,j.[15]

The two sources U and T are likely to generate a similar set of typical sequences only if the value for $D(U,T)$ is very small. A value of $D(U,T)$ approaching zero has several implications for software testing. First, it ensures that each usage state appears in the test history in the correct proportion, as computed in the stationary distribution of U, and that the sequencing properties of the test history closely match those of U. Second, it forces the probability of occurrence of the failure states in T to be pushed toward zero. This means that confidence must be gained in every path through the testing chain before $D(U,T)$ will be acceptably small. Third, it recognizes the limitations of the usage chain for testing the software. When the statistics of the testing chain and usage chain match, the usage chain is unlikely to generate a sequence that adds any additional information to the statistical testing experiment.

To monitor the testing process, $D(U,T)$ can be computed with each sequence applied to the software after T becomes fully defined. A downward trend in the values of $D(U,T)$ signifies growing similarity of the two models. Usage chain U never changes; however, $D(U,T)$ reflects the impact of each additional sequence on the stochastic characteristics of the testing chain. $D(U,T)$, for example, can rise when no failures are observed if a sequence reinforces some low-probability event. Of course, a rise is expected when a failure occurs. When the discrimination drops below some predefined threshold and experiences little change for an extended period, it is implied that additional test sequences will not significantly impact the statistics of the testing model, and testing can stop.

Figure 14.3 shows two plots of $D(U,T)$ that depict typical behavior of

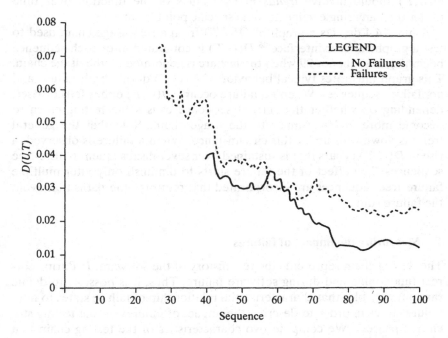

Figure 14.3 Two plots of $D(U, T)$ for the example usage chain.

the function. Each plot represents a separate series of sequences from the example usage chain with relative frequency estimated transition probabilities. The solid line depicts behavior of $D(U,T)$ with no failures. The dotted line depicts a sequence with three failure states. There are several interesting features of this figure. First, note that $D(U,T)$ becomes computable at sequence 40 for the first plot and at sequence 26 for the second plot. Since $D(U,T)$ is computable only when every arc in T has been initialized (i.e., generated by U and applied to the software), its first occurrence is a random variable and depends on the specific sequences generated by U. Second, the failure states cause T to converge to U more slowly than without failures. The general trend of the failure-free plot is toward significantly smaller values than the plot with failures. Third, the fluctuation of $D(U,T)$, even in the absence of failures, can be seen in both plots. When states and arcs occur in a sequence which reinforces low probability events, $D(U,T)$ can rise significantly. This is made explicit in the plot at sequence 56, where the failure-free plot rises significantly and even surpasses the plot with failures temporarily. The general trend of both curves is downward; however, each is affected by the appearance of atypical events in the sequences. It is important to stress that analysis of $D(U,T)$ should involve *trends* in the values of the function over time rather than any single value at some specific point in time.

Figure 14.4 depicts a graph of $D(U,T)$ from a real usage chain used to test a graphical user interface.[26] $D(U,T)$ is computed after each sequence beginning at sequence 29 when the last arc is generated by the usage chain. This graph illustrates typical behavior of $D(U,T)$ during both failure and nonfailure sequences. When no failure occurs, $D(U,T)$ either falls or rises, depending on whether the current sequence causes the testing chain to become more or less similar to the usage chain. Note that the general trend is downward under this circumstance. When a failure is observed, a rise in $D(U,T)$ occurs that is sustained over several subsequent failure-free sequences. The effect of the failure starts to diminish only after multiple failure-free sequences are incorporated that reinforce the paths that avoid the failure state.

B   Measuring the impact of failures

The testing chain represents the test history of the software, P, during correct functioning and during software failure. Thus, it is possible to define random variables that characterize the relationship of failure states to nonfailure states in order to describe the impact of failures on the testing stochastic process. We compute two characteristics of the testing chain that give insight into the effect of the failures. The first is the probability of a

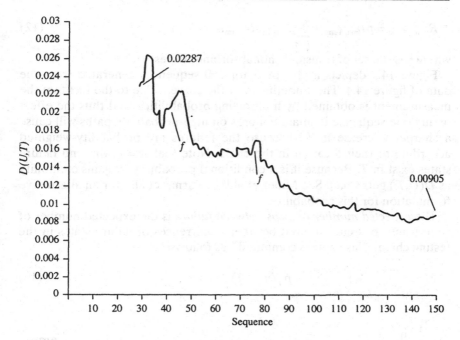

Figure 14.4 Plot of $D(U, T)$.

failure-free realization of the testing chain, denoted R, computed by using a standard result from Markov chain theory. The second is the expected number of steps between failure states, denoted M, which requires a new computation.

R and M can be computed directly from the testing chain T at any time during the testing of software P, even when only a single sequence has been input to P. It must be emphasized that R is a probability and M is an expected value *conditioned* on the test history encoded as T. These values gain credibility as statistical measures as the discrimination $D(U,T)$ becomes relatively small, for this indicates that T is becoming statistically typical of software P's response to the input sequences from usage chain U.

The *probability, R, of a failure-free realization* of the testing chain is the probability that a realization of T beginning with "Uninvoked" and ending with the first occurrence of "Terminated" will not contain a failure state. To compute R, each failure state and "Terminated" are made absorbing states. R is the probability that absorption occurs at "Terminated," given "Uninvoked" as the start state;[9,14] namely, as follows:

$$R_{\text{Unin, Term}} = \hat{p}_{\text{Unin, Term}} + \sum_{j \in \tau} \hat{p}_{\text{Unin}, j} R_{j, \text{Term}}, \tag{12}$$

where τ is the set of transient (nonabsorbing) states.

Figure 14.5 depicts a plot of R for 150 sequences generated from the data of figure 14.4. The smoothness of the curve is due to the fact that the measurement is obtained by multiplying probabilities, and thus the effect of any one sequence is small. Failures on high-probability paths will cause a sharper decrease in R, because the failures are probability-weighted according to their location in the chain. Note that $R = 1$ when no failure states exist in T. Because it is a conditional probability, R gains credibility as $D(U,T)$ gets small. See Miller et al.[16] or Parnas et al.[20] for an alternative formulation for this probability.

The *expected number of steps between failure* is the expected number of state transitions encountered between occurrences of failure states in the testing chain. This value is computed[26] as follows:

$$M = \sum_{i \in f_1, \ldots, f_m} v_i \left(\sum_{j \in u_1, \ldots, u_n} \hat{p}_{ij} (m_j + 1) \right), \tag{13}$$

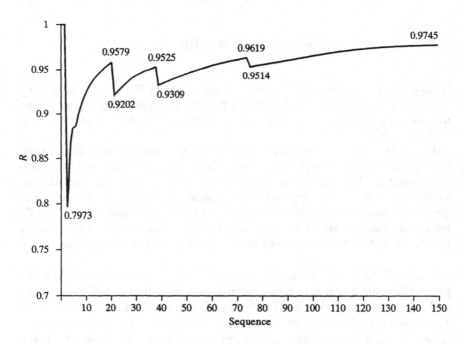

Figure 14.5   Plot of R.

where v_i is the conditional long-run probability for failure state f_i, given that the process is in a failure state, m_j is the mean number of steps until the first occurrence of any failure state from j, $u_1, \ldots, u_n$ is the set of usage chain states, and $f_1, \ldots f_m$ is the set of failure states.

Figure 14.6 is a plot of M for 150 sequences generated from the data of figure 14.4. Since M counts the number of steps between failure states, which could grow significantly when arcs are traversed for the first time, the increase tends to be more pronounced than the measure for R. Thus, when new paths are established by traversing arcs for the first time, the increase can be quite large. However, as the testing chain becomes complete, the changes are less dramatic.

The analytical results computed for the testing chain have several beneficial features. First, they are based on actual occurrences of failures. No assumptions about the distributions of failures are required in order to measure these quantities. Second, each state generated is accounted for in the computations. Each sequence of states contributes to the model in proportion to its length and probability of occurrence. The computations on the model take into account the facts that the sequences are not equally

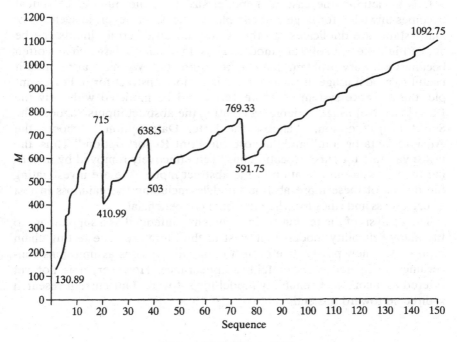

Figure 14.6   Plot of M.

likely and that some have more impact than others. Third, each failure is probability weighted according to its location in the testing chain. Failures attached to relatively high-probability paths will impact the testing stochastic process more than failures attached to lower-probability paths. Thus, the testing chain delivers results that are based on the usage patterns described in the usage model.

VII CONCLUSIONS AND PROSPECTS FOR FUTURE WORK

The finite state, discrete parameter, time homogeneous Markov chain represents a practical option for software test engineers in the development and analysis of usage models and automatic test input generation. There have been several successful applications of Markov chain usage models to date[1,27] involving both real-time embedded systems and user-oriented applications. Our experience has shown that Markov chain usage models can be constructed in a diverse set of application domains, and are useful for driving statistical tests.

It is sometimes the case that model size (i.e., the number of states) becomes unwieldy for large and complex systems. However, in such cases, many states are duplicates of other states, because certain inputs can be applied in different software modes. Thus, maintaining large chains often becomes a library problem that can be automated. We have also found it useful to model usage of such systems in a more abstract form. For example, the software system of figure 14.1 could be modeled with only the PD = {Yes, No} usage variable by creating the abstract inputs "choose the Select Project option," "choose the Enter Data option," "choose the Analyze Data option," and "choose the Print Report option." Thus, the usage variable for cursor location has been effectively removed by including the necessary information in the abstract inputs. We are investigating the details of these more abstract models, including the gain/loss in test effectiveness and rules for when it is or is not beneficial.

The analysis of the testing chain is currently intended as a supplement to the many reliability models that exist in the literature. The testing chain represents a new perspective on test data and bypasses assumptions concerning anticipated rates of failure appearance. However, it is not yet offered as a complete reliability model for software. Our current research is directed toward this end.

References

1 K. Agrawal and J. A. Whittaker, "Experiences in applying statistical testing to a real-time embedded software system," *Proc. Pacific Northwest Software Quality Conf.*, 1993, pp. 154–170.
2 R. Ash, *Information Theory and Coding*. New York: McGraw-Hill, 1963.
3 R. C. Cheung, "A user-oriented software reliability model," *IEEE Trans. Software Eng.*, vol. SE-6, Mar. 1980.
4 P. A. Currit, M. Dyer, and H. D. Mills, "Certifying the correctness of software," *IEEE Trans. Software Eng.*, vol. SE-12, no. 1, pp. 3–11, Jan. 1986.
5 H. Cramer, *The Elements of Probability Theory*. Huntington, NY: Robert E. Krieger, 1955.
6 J. L. Doob, *Stochastic Processes*. New York: Wiley, 1953.
7 J. W. Duran and S. C. Ntafos, "An evaluation of random testing," *IEEE Trans. Software Eng.*, vol. SE-10, no. 4, pp. 438–444, July 1984.
8 J. W. Duran and J. J. Wiorkowski, "Quantifying software validity by sampling," *IEEE Trans. Reliability*, vol. R-29, no. 2, pp. 141–144, June 1980.
9 W. Feller, *An Introduction to Probability Theory and Its Applications*, vol. 1. New York: Wiley, 1950.
10 R. Hamlet, "Testing software for software reliability," Tech. Rep. TR-91-2, rev. 1, Dept. of Comput. Sci., Portland State Univ., Portland, OR, USA, Mar. 1992.
11 R. Hamlet and R. Taylor, "Partition testing does not inspire confidence," *IEEE Trans. Software Eng.*, vol. 16, pp. 1402–1411, Dec. 1990.
12 J. E. Hopcroft and J. D. Ullman, *Introduction to Automata Theory*. Reading, MA: Addison-Wesley, 1979.
13 B. H. Juang and L. R. Rabiner, "A probabilistic distance measure for hidden Markov models," *AT&T Tech. J.*, vol. 64, no. 2, pp. 391–408, Feb. 1985.
14 J. G. Kemeny and J. L. Snell, *Finite Markov Chains*. New York: Springer-Verlag, 1976.
15 S. Kullback, *Information Theory and Statistics*. New York: Wiley, 1958.
16 K. W. Miller, L. J. Morrell, R. E. Noonan, S. K. Park, D. M. Nicol, B. W. Murrill, and J. M. Voas, "Estimating the probability of failure when testing reveals no failures," *IEEE Trans. Software Eng.*, vol. 18, pp. 33–43, Jan. 1992.
17 H. D. Mills, "The new math of computer programming," *Commun. ACM*, vol. 18, no. 1, pp. 43–48, Jan. 1975.
18 J. D. Musa, "A theory of software reliability and its application," *IEEE Trans. Software Eng.*, vol. SE-1, pp. 312–321, Aug. 1975.
19 G. J. Myers, *The Art of Software Testing*. New York: Wiley, 1979.
20 D. L. Parnas, A. J. Van Schouwen, and S. P. Kwan, "An evaluation of safety-critical software," *Commun. ACM*, vol. 23, pp. 636–648, June 1990.
21 E. Parzen, *Stochastic Processes*. San Francisco, CA: Holden-Day, 1962.
22 M. L. Shooman, *Software Engineering: Design, Reliability, and Management*. New York: McGraw-Hill, 1983.
23 C. E. Shannon, "A mathematical theory of communication," *Bell Syst. Tech. J.*, vol. 27, pp. 379–423, 623–656, 1948.

24   K. Siegrist, "Reliability of systems with Markov transfer of control," *IEEE Trans. Software Eng.*, vol. 14, pp. 1049–1053, July 1988.
25   M. G. Thomason, "Generating functions for stochastic context-free grammars," *Int. J. Patt. Recognition Art. Intell.*, vol. 4, pp. 553–572, Apr. 1990.
26   J. A. Whittaker, "Markov chain techniques for software testing and reliability analysis," Ph.D. dissertation, Dept. of Comput. Sci., Univ. of Tennessee, Knoxville, USA, 1992.
27   J. A. Whittaker and J. H. Poore, "Markov analysis of software specifications," *ACM Trans. Software Eng. Methodology*, vol. 2, pp. 93–106, Jan. 1993.
28   D. M. Woit, "Realistic expectations of random testing," CRL Rep. 246, McMaster Univ., Hamilton, ON, Canada, May 1992.

15 Statistical Testing of Software Based on a Usage Model

G. H. WALTON, J. H. POORE, AND C. J. TRAMMELL

INTRODUCTION

Some amount of time and money will be devoted to testing software before it is released to field use or shipped as a product. Because test budgets have upper bounds for both time and money, it is important to determine the most efficient use of the test budget. There is considerable diversity of opinion concerning the efficacy of various testing technologies. General approaches to software testing include the following:

(a) functional testing – test all user functions of the software;
(b) coverage testing – test all paths through the software;
(c) partition testing – divide the software's input domain according to homogeneous classes, and test each class;
(d) statistical testing – use a formal experimental paradigm for random testing according to a usage model of the software.

JUSTIFICATION FOR STATISTICAL TESTING BASED ON A USAGE MODEL

Reliability of a software system is generally defined as the probability that the software will not fail during operational use. A "failure" occurs when

© 1995 John Wiley & Sons, Ltd. Reprinted, with permission, from *Software – Practice and Experience*, vol. 25, no. 1, January 1995, pp. 97–108.

the software does not perform according to its specification. Predicting software reliability requires:

(a)   a model of the expected operational use of the software;
(b)   a test environment that simulates the operational environment; and
(c)   a protocol for analyzing the test data and making statistically valid inferences about reliability.

In statistical testing, a model is developed to characterize the population of uses of the software, and the model is used to generate a statistically correct sample of all possible uses of the software. Performance on the sample is used as a basis for conclusions about general operational reliability. Mills[1] points out that testing with selected test cases can provide nothing but anecdotal evidence; statistical testing is needed to scientifically certify the reliability of software. Duran and Ntafos' results[2] indicate that random testing can be superior to partition testing and coverage testing, is more cost effective, and allows the tester to make "sound reliability estimates." However, they caution that random testing may not thoroughly test the software's ability to handle exceptional conditions. Hamlet and Taylor[3] concluded that partition testing should not be used to make inferences about reliability of the software in use.

A software "usage model" characterizes operational use of a software system. "Operational use" is the intended use of the software in the intended environment, i.e., the population from which a statistically correct sample of test cases will be drawn.

The usage model is based on the functional specification and usage specification for the software. Thus, all the information required to develop the model should be available before a line of code is written. This allows independence of the software development and usage modeling efforts. It allows test planning to occur in parallel with the software development, thus shortening the elapsed time required to develop and deliver software. The model provides information to developers concerning the importance (in terms of probability of use) of each function, provides the information required by testers to construct effective and informative test cases and, with statistical testing, provides a basis from which inferences of software reliability may be made.

Upon analyzing the software failure history data from nine large IBM software products, Adams[4] demonstrated that a relatively small proportion of errors in the software account for the vast majority of reported failures in the field. Further, the Adams report demonstrated that these frequently reported failures occur early in the operational life of the software. Thus, statistical testing based on a software usage model ensures that the failures that will occur most frequently in operational use will be found early in the test cycle. Musa[5] reports a benefit-to-cost ratio of 10 or greater in developing and using operational usage models. These benefits indicate that, apart from certain anecdotal tests that are justified on legal, moral, ethical, or political grounds, the most cost effective way to spend the test budget is on statistical testing based on a usage model.

METHODOLOGY FOR CREATING A USAGE MODEL

(1) Review and clarify the software specification.
(2) Identify expected users of the software, expected uses of the software, and expected system environment.
(3) Define a stratification of user and environment parameters.
(4) Determine the desired levels of usage model granularity.
(5) Iteratively develop usage model structure.
(6) Verify the correctness of the structure against the specification.
(7) Iteratively develop a probability distribution for the model.
(8) Verify the correctness of the probability distribution against any information available concerning intended usage of the software.

Usage modeling is an iterative process. Any changes to the software specification or to the expected use of the software must be accompanied by review and appropriate modifications to the usage model.

Review and clarify the software specification

The usage model mirrors intended use of the software, as defined by the specification. Thus, prior to developing the usage model, the specification must be reviewed and clarified to ensure that it provides complete functional specifications and a description of the intended use of the software in its intended environment.

Identity expected users, uses, and environment

Software is "used" by a "user" in some "environment." The definitions of user, use, and environment will specify the operational environment to which certification of the software applies.

User
A "user" is any entity that interacts with the software (i.e., that applies stimuli and receives a response). For example, a user may be other soft-

ware, a human, or a hardware device. Some parameters to classify human users might include:

(a)   job descriptions (operator versus data entry, etc.);
(b)   access privileges to various system resources;
(c)   experience in the usage environment (e.g., naïve user, occasional user, experienced user);
(d)   knowledge of the usage domain (i.e., technical knowledge of the subject area supported by the software).

Some parameters to characterize hardware users might include:

(a)   physical properties of the hardware base;
(b)   properties of the software configuration (e.g., operating system, communication software);
(c)   usage properties of the traffic being handled by the hardware.

Use
A "use" of the software may be a keystroke, work session, transaction, completed telephone call, or any other unit of performance appropriate to the service the software is intended to perform. The use is further defined by the way it is processed. For example, for a particular software tool a user's view may be identical whether the tool is used by the single user or is shared by multiple concurrent users. Thus, testing of single-user access and multi-user access to the tool will be required to ensure that the software operates correctly for both types of processing. Types of processing include:

(a)   menu-driven versus *ad hoc* query system;
(b)   interactive versus batch processing;
(c)   information system versus real-time; and
(d)   multi-user versus single user.

Environment
A usage "environment" can be characterized by a wide variety of factors such as:

(a)   interactions with other systems (software, databases, I/O devices, etc.);
(b)   computer system load (memory, CPU, network load, etc.);
(c)   integrity of externally provided data; and
(d)   need for simultaneous access of data.

Stratify user and environment parameters

There can be a very large number of practical combinations of values for the parameters that define usage, including multiple stimuli applied simultaneously. The usage modeler must define a stratification of user and environment parameters that will be sufficient to satisfy the conflicting goals of (1) providing an adequate characterization of the entire system and (2) developing a usage model that is simple enough to allow for effective verification of the usage model and cost-effective statistical testing and certification of software reliability based on the model.

After partitioning usage into classes, the usage modeler must determine how to represent the classes in the usage model and how to ensure that testing based on the model will be conducted in an environment that corresponds to the assumptions for the class being tested. There are at least two approaches to modeling classes of usage: (1) develop a separate usage model for each user class, or (2) develop a single usage model with different "paths" as appropriate for each user class, making informed judgments about the total population's distribution of users in each class.

Any inferences made from statistical testing based on a usage model are qualified by assumptions that were made to cluster usage types and assumptions that were made to model usage based on these clusters. For example, consider an on-line software tool's usage model that clusters users by experience in the usage environment. First-time naïve users access on-line help 80 percent of the times they visit a particular state, but this access frequency decreases with each subsequent use of the tool by that user until that user becomes an experienced user. On the average, on-line help is accessed from this state in 30 percent of the uses by naïve users. If the usage model defines transition probabilities according to average uses by average users for each usage class, it would include in the naïve users' cluster model a transition probability of 30 percent from the state in question to on-line help. Statistical testing based on this usage model can be used to make inferences about the reliability of the software tool for a large amount of use for a large number of naïve users. However, it cannot be used to make inferences about the reliability of the software for the first use of the tool by a naïve user.

Determine desired levels of granularity

The cost of developing and maintaining a usage model tends to increase as the granularity of the model increases. To determine appropriate levels of granularity, the modeler should periodically analyze the cost of development and maintenance of a more detailed model versus the benefit of improved testing that such a model provides.

Specification granularity often increases throughout the development cycle. Greater model abstraction can facilitate development of the model earlier in the development cycle and enable easier modification later on. Greater abstraction in the usage model also provides a model that is easier to develop and modify. However, greater detail in usage model structure can allow more precise modeling of actual operation of the software. Assuming that the model is correct, greater model detail should increase the correspondence between reliability estimates derived from random testing using the usage model and reliability of the software in actual operation.

It may be the case that the granularity of the usage model need not be uniform throughout the model. For example, the modeler could consider modeling critical software features or new software in more detail, and noncritical features or mature software in less detail. Other factors that influence the level of model granularity are the extent to which the input space is partitioned and the extent to which error sequences are modeled. Testing and certification requirements may take the form of reliability estimation procedures, categories of uses, users, and environments, number of test cases that must be run, available budget and schedule, etc. Metrics concerning the size of usage models may take the form of number of states, number of arcs, etc. With experience, the relationship between such requirements, metrics, and costs of development and maintenance of each model will provide assistance concerning the optimal level of granularity. An approach to cost–benefit analysis using mathematical programming has been developed[6] and is currently being field tested.

Develop the structure of the usage model

The usage model structure provides a model of events and transitions between events, where events may be concrete stimuli (inputs from the user or from the environment) or abstract placeholders (indicating a state of use of the software). The usage model structure is based on the specification and is developed by iterative refinement. In addition to the stimuli entered directly by the user, it must include any external stimuli that affect system operation (for example, input from an external system or a file). The structure will evolve as the software matures and as more knowledge is gained concerning operational use of the software.

The usage model structure can be represented by a graph, a formal grammar, or a Markov chain. These three methods to represent a usage model are demonstrated below for a simple interactive system with two screens: a Main Menu with two choices (Display Screen or Termination) and a Display Screen that always returns to the Main Menu. The usage

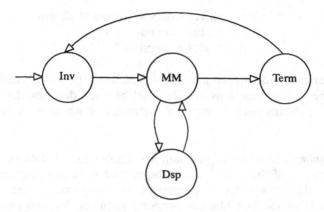

Figure 15.1 Graph of a simple interactive system.

model for this system might contain four states-of-use: Invocation (Inv), Main Menu (MM), Display Screen (Dsp), and Termination (Term).

Graphs
A usage model can be represented as a graph, defined as a set of nodes and arcs where the nodes are the usage states and the arcs define ordered transitions between states. Graphs are often quite useful in verification of the usage model, because they provide a representation that is easily understood by customers and potential users of the software. Figure 15.1 provides a graph for this simple system.

Formal grammars
Formal grammars can be used to precisely specify usage. Formal grammars consist of:

(a) a finite set of terminals;
(b) a finite set of nonterminals described recursively in terms of each other and terminals;
(c) the rules (called productions) relating the terminals and nonterminals.

The simple interactive system can be specified by a formal grammar as follows:

```
<Random usage>  →   <Inv><Use> <Term>
<Inv>           →   "invoke main menu"
<Use>           →   <MM> {<Dsp> <MM>}
```

<MM>	→	"invoke display screen" | <Term>
<Dsp>	→	"return to main menu"
<Term>	→	"exit from system"

In this grammar, the nonterminals are enclosed by < >; terminals are enclosed by " "; productions are denoted by →; \| denotes the Boolean OR; and {...} means zero or more occurrences of whatever is inside the brackets.

Markov chain. A Markov usage chain has a unique start state (that represents invocation of the software), a unique final state (that represents termination of the software), a set of intermediate usage states, and transition arcs between states. The Markov property requires that the next state is independent of all past states given the present state. Whittaker and Poore[7] demonstrated the applicability of the Markov chain for modeling software use and defined the procedure for modeling software usage with a finite state, discrete parameter Markov chain.

The state transitions of a Markov chain can be represented as a two-dimensional matrix with the state labels as indices and the arc probabilities as entries. To take advantage of known long-run properties of irreducible Markov chains one must ensure that every state has a next state (the next state for the termination state is invocation) and that exit arcs for each state have probabilities that sum to one. The transition matrix is square and each of its rows sums to one. For the example system, Inv is the unique start state, Term is the unique final state, and MM and Dsp are intermediate usage states. Table 15.1 gives the transition matrix for this example. An X in cell (i,j) of the transition matrix represents the probability of a transition from state i to state j.

Table 15.1   State transitions

	Inv	MM	Dsp	Term
Inv		X		
MM			X	X
Dsp		X		
Term	X			

Verify the correctness of the structure

The usage model structure must be verified against the specification before the process continues. Any decisions concerning the expected system operating environment, user classes, critical functions of the system, or other parameters that may affect the structure must be made and verified at this point.

Develop a probability distribution for the model

The next phase involves assigning probabilities to each transition in the usage structure. The set of transition probabilities defines a probability distribution (the usage distribution) over the input domain of the software. This usage distribution is the basis from which statistical testing of the software can be performed.

Transition probabilities are based on expected use of the software. Whittaker and Poore[7] describe three approaches to defining usage distributions: (1) transition probabilities can be assigned based on field data, (2) transition probabilities can be assigned based on informed assumptions about expected use, or (3) if no information is available concerning expected use of the software, uniform probabilities can be assigned across the exit arcs for each state.

The Markov property requires that the next state depends only on the present state. Thus, for any state that can be invoked more than once during a particular run, if the probability of invoking that state differs for different invocations, the modeler must choose between modeling the "average" probability or creating separate states for each invocation type. The choice may dictate a change in the usage model structure. For example, consider again the simple interactive system from the example above and assume that for any ten uses of the system, the state sequences are distributed as indicated in table 15.2.

If the usage probabilities were developed without considering whether or not inputs are independent, probabilities would be assigned as indicated in table 15.3.

The structure of this model corresponds to the graph given in figure 15.1. However, close examination of the usage data in table 15.2 indicates that the probability of transition from the Main Menu to Termination

Table 15.2 State sequences

State sequences	Frequency
Inv, MM, Dsp, MM, Term	8
Inv, MM, Dsp, MM, Dsp, MM, Term	1
Inv, MM, Term	1

Table 15.3   State transitions and probabilities, first model

From state	To state	Frequency	Probability
Inv	MM	10	1.0
MM	Dsp	10	0.5
MM	Term	10	0.5
Dsp	MM	10	1.0

depends on whether or not the Display Screen has been invoked previously. To provide a more accurate representation of actual usage, MM can be split into two states: MM0 to represent initial invocation of the Main Menu and MM1 to represent all subsequent invocations of the Main Menu. The structure of the new model corresponds to the graph given in figure 15.2. The usage distribution is given in table 15.4.

Although the new model accurately represents the observed state sequences, it should be noted that only one of the observed sequences included multiple invocations of the Display Screen. The model assumes that there can be a infinite number of such invocations. Further, the model assumes that after the first invocation of the Display Screen and subsequent return to the Main Menu, the probability of a transition from the Main Menu to the Display Screen is a constant.

A more accurate model of general operational use for this system might have specified the probability of a specific invocation of the Display Screen to be less than the probability of each previous invocation. To address this issue one could continue to split the MM states, but there is a

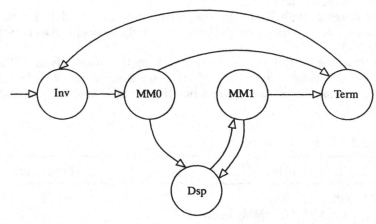

Figure 15.2   Alternative graph of a simple interactive system.

Table 15.4 State transitions and probabilities, second model

From state	To state	Frequency	Probability
Inv	MM0	10	1.0
MM0	Dsp	9	0.9
MM0	Term	1	0.1
MM1	Dsp	1	0.1
MM1	Term	9	0.9
Dsp	MM1	9	1.0

trade-off between the gains from greater detail in the usage model and the cost to develop and maintain a large model.

Verify correctness of probability distribution

The correctness of the probability distribution must be verified against any information available concerning intended usage of the software. The distribution should evolve as the software matures and more knowledge is gained about operational use of the software.

USAGE MODELING ISSUES

Random testing based on usage distributions ensures that on average the most frequently used operations receive the most testing. It is often important, however, to ensure the exercise of specific operations of the software irrespective of their usage probabilities. Two examples are operations of high criticality due to potential impacts of a failure, and operations implemented by new software.

Critical functions in large models

Three options for handling the testing of critical operations are:

(1) Develop a separate usage model for each category of infrequent, critical operation and test based on these models.
(2) Use coverage testing or anecdotal testing to conduct separate tests for infrequent, critical operations. (No scientific inference about reliability can be made from such tests, however.)
(3) Adjust the usage distribution to ensure that critical operations are tested more frequently. (This usage distribution would not be an

accurate model of the expected usage population, and that would limit inferences about operational reliability.)

Dilution effect with incremental software development

New software added to a mature base will be represented as a new portion of an existing usage model. As the software system becomes larger over several increments, certification of the reliability of the system could result in progressively less testing of the newest code because this code represents a progressively smaller portion of the software as a whole. Three possible approaches to this problem are

(1)   Create a separate usage model for the new software.
(2)   "Prune" the usage model by adjusting granularity throughout the model. The older operations would be modeled more abstractly whereas the newer operations would be modeled with a higher level of detail.
(3)   Adjust the usage distribution to ensure that less mature software is tested more frequently. (This usage distribution would not be an accurate model of the expected usage population, and that would limit inferences about operational reliability.)

USE OF THE USAGE MODEL

The following steps define the procedure for statistical test planning and software certification:

(1)   Perform cost–benefit analyses of the usage distribution with respect to the defined test environment.
(2)   Plan and implement the defined system environment.
(3)   Determine stopping criteria for testing.
(4)   Generate random test cases from the usage model. Where the test case includes a class of input variables, randomly generate input stimuli for the test case from the class of input variables.
(5)   Establish how each event of each test case will be evaluated to determine that it meets the specification.
(6)   Perform statistical testing of the software. Record any observed failure (i.e., any deviation from the specifications).
(7)   Analyze the test results using a reliability model to provide a basis for statistical inference of reliability of the software during operational use.

Inferences from statistical testing based on a usage model must be understood in the context of assumptions that were made about the specifications, assumptions that were made to cluster usage types, assumptions that were made to model usage based on these clusters, and assumptions that were made during the testing process.

RECENT ADVANCES IN USAGE MODEL APPLICATION

The Markov approach to usage modeling provides procedures to make the testing process more efficient. Whittaker and Poore[7] describe procedures for using analytical results known for Markov processes to provide insight into testing and for using Markov chains to generate random test cases, conduct statistical tests, and determine stopping criteria. They use Markov calculations to generate the following information:

(a) expected test case length (can be used to help estimate resources required for testing);

(b) expected number of test cases required to cover all states in the usage model (can be used to identify the amount of testing required to guarantee that each usage state was visited at least once in testing);

(c) expected proportion of time spent in each state in testing (can be used to identify which usage functions will get the most attention from the test cases);

(d) expected number of test cases to first occurrence of each state (can be used to identify states that are seldom visited);

(e) entropy (a measure of uncertainty) of the usage model (can be used to compare usage models)

This information allows the certification team to perform cost–benefit analyses on the planned testing based on the usage model. For example, if the number of test cases required is too high, cost reductions can be achieved by reducing the scope of the usage environment. Such scope reductions require careful consideration because the result is a constraint on inferences that can be made from testing.

CONCLUSIONS AND RECOMMENDATIONS

Statistical testing of software based on a usage model provides the most cost-effective use of the testing budget and the only direct statistical method for making inferences concerning reliability of software in operational use. Usage modeling has been demonstrated to be an activity that improves specifications, gives an analytical description of the specification, quantifies the testing costs and, with statistical testing, provides a basis from which inferences of software reliability may be made.

Experience in statistical testing of software and in building, analyzing, and applying Markov usage models is accumulating. Projects have been completed successfully in several companies and government agencies.[8-10] The environments range from real-time, embedded code on a bare machine to sophisticated software engineering environments.

Whittaker and Poore's work with Markov models[7] shows that the use of a Markov model as the source of random sequences gives access to a wealth of useful information about the testing process. This work provides the basis for discovery of further efficiencies in model design, test case generation, and testing work load. Research continues in the areas of usage modeling, testing technology, and reliability estimation. It is expected that new methods will be discovered to lower testing costs by orders of magnitude and increase by orders of magnitude the level at which scientific model-based certification statements can be made.

References

1   H. D. Mills, "Certifying the correctness of software," *Proc. Hawaii International Conference on System Sciences, Vol. II, Software Technology,* 1992, pp. 373–381.
2   J. W. Duran and S. C. Ntafos, "An evaluation of random testing," *IEEE Trans. Software Engineering,* **10**, (4) 438–444 (1984).
3   D. Hamlet and R. Taylor, "Partition testing does not inspire confidence," *IEEE Trans. Software Engineering,* **16**, (1), 1402–1411 (1990).
4   E. N. Adams, "Optimizing preventive service of software products," *IBM Journal for Research and Development,* **28**, (1), 3–14 (1984).
5   J. D. Musa, "Operational profiles in software-reliability engineering," *IEEE Software,* March 1993, pp. 14–32.
6   J. H. Poore, G. H. Walton and J. A. Whittaker, "A mathematical programming approach to the representation and optimization of software usage models," In review, May 1994.
7   J. A. Whittaker and J. H. Poore, "Markov analysis of software specifications," *ACM Trans. Software Engineering and Methodology,* **2**, (2), 93–106 (1993).
8   K. Agrawal and J. A. Whittaker, "Experience in applying statistical testing to a real-time, embedded software system," *Proc. Pacific Northwest Software Quality Conference,* 1994.
9   J. A. Whittaker and K. Agrawal, "A case study in software reliability measurement," *Proc. Quality Week '94,* May, 1994.
10 C. Wohlin and P. Runeson, "Certification of software components," *IEEE Trans. Software Engineering,* **20**, (6), 494–499 (1994).

16 Certification of Software Components

C. WOHLIN AND P. RUNESON

I INTRODUCTION

Interest in software reliability engineering is growing rapidly with particular focus being set on usage testing[1] or operational profile testing.[2] An important issue in software engineering is reuse, which seems to be one of the key factors in coping with the cost and quality of software systems.[3] To fulfil the objective of reuse, it is necessary to have reliable reusable components. The reliability of the components can be certified with usage testing by developing usage models, applying usage profiles and finally applying a certification model to show the level of confidence in them. This chapter focuses on combining experience from usage testing with the need for reliability engineering in the reuse community.

The basis for reuse is the reliability of the components intended for reuse and the gains achieved through its application. This means that the components developed for reuse must have a quality stamp concerning, for example, reliability and performance. This is achieved by continuous evaluation, in parallel with the development process for reuse. The process must include methods and models for quantifying the characteristics of the reusable components. In particular, one important issue is to establish methods of certification, i.e., both to certify a component being developed, as well as being able to rely on a reusable component. The development of new software components to be reused is referred to as development for reuse, whilst the development reusing components stored in the repository is referred to as development with reuse. The term component is used in a generic sense. A component may be, for example, a system, subsystem or system service.

The focus in this chapter is on usage modelling, usage profiles and the certification of components by applying a hypothesis certification model. A more detailed version of this chapter is available from the authors.[4]

II   CERTIFICATION AND REUSE

A   Introduction

Object-oriented techniques make it possible to develop components in general, and to develop reusable components in particular. These components must be certified regarding their properties, for example their reliability.

A component developed for reuse must have reliability measures attached to it, based on one or several usage profiles. The objective of the certification method discussed below is to provide a basis for obtaining a reliability measure of components. The reliability measure may either be the actual reliability or an indirect measure of reliability such as MTBF (Mean Time Between Failures).

During development for reuse, a usage model must be constructed in parallel with the development of the component. The usage model is a structural model of the external view of the component. The probabilities of different events are added to the model, creating a usage profile, which describes the actual probabilities of these events. The objective is that the components developed will be certified before being put into the repository. The component is stored together with its characteristics, usage model and usage profile. The reliability measure stored should be connected to the usage profile, since another profile will probably give a different perceived reliability of the component altogether.

Development with reuse involves retrieving components from the repository, and at the retrieval stage it is necessary to examine the reliability of the components being reused. The components have been certified using the specific profiles stored, and if they are to be reused in a different environment with another usage profile, they must then be certified with this new usage profile.

A method of certification can be described in the following steps:

(1)   modelling of software usage;
(2)   derivation of usage profile;
(3)   generation of test cases;
(4)   execution of test cases and collection of failure data; and
(5)   certification of reliability and prediction of future reliability.

The method can be applied to certification of components as well as to system certification.

B Component certification

The components must be certified from an external view, i.e., the actual implementation of the component must not influence the certification process. The estimation of usage probabilities must be as accurate as possible. It may in many cases, be impossible to exactly determine the usage profile for a component. This will be problematic, especially when the individual component is indirectly influenced by the external users of the system. It must, however, be emphasized that the most important issue is to find probabilities that are reasonable relative to each other, instead of aiming at the "true" probabilities, i.e., as they will be during operation.

The reuse of components also means that the usage model of the component can be reused, since the usage model describes the possible usage of a component (without probability estimates of events being assigned). This implies that the structural description of the usage can be reused, even if the actual usage profile can not. The problems of component reuse and model reuse for different cases are further discussed in section III-E. Component certification is also discussed by Poore et al.[5]

III USAGE MODELLING

A Introduction

This section discusses usage models and usage profiles for software systems as a whole, as well as for individual components, and an illustration is given in section V by means of a simple telecommunication example. A system may be seen as consisting of a number of components. A component is an arbitrary element which handles coherent functionality.

Usage models are intended to model the external view of the usage of the component. The user behavior should be described and not the component behavior. The users may be humans or other components. Modelling usage of software components includes problems which do not arise when modelling the usage for systems as a whole. The primary users of a component are those in the immediate vicinity, for example other components. But in most cases there are other users involved, for example end-users, which indirectly affect the use of actual components. Therefore, the usage of a component may have to be derived from an external user of the system, even if the user does not communicate directly with the component.

It is assumed that the usage models are created in accordance with the system structure to support reuse. The view is still external, but the objective is to create usage model parts which conform to the structure of the system. The reuse of components also means that it will be possible to reuse the usage model describing the external usage of that particular component. The usage models of the components may combine in a way similar to the components combination within a system, providing services to an external user.

Different usage profiles may be attached to one usage model.

B   Usage model

Markov chains as a means of modelling usage are discussed by Whittaker and Poore.[6] The use of Markov chains has several advantages, including well-known theories. A main disadvantage is, however, that the chain grows very large when applying it to large multi-user software systems.[7] The objective or the usage model is to determine the next event, based on the probabilities in the Markov chain. The chain is used to generate the next event without taking the time between events into consideration, which means that the times between events are handled separately and an arbitrary time distribution can be used.

A hierarchical Markov model is introduced, the State Hierarchy model (SHY), to cope with this disadvantage, known as the state explosion problem.[7]. The SHY model can describe different types of users, i.e., human users, other systems, system parts, and multiple combinations and instances of the user types. During the development of the usage model the user types are handled and constructed separately, and they are composed into a usage model for the system as a whole. The model, being modular, is therefore suitable for reuse, since the objective is to ensure a conformity between the usage model and the system structure; see section III-A.

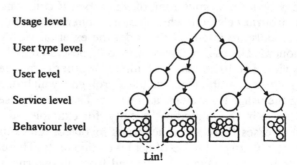

Usage level

User type level

User level

Service level

Behaviour level

Lin!

Figure 16.1   The State Hierarchy model.

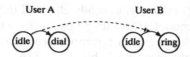

Figure 16.2 Link example: A dials B.

System configurations, for example, in different markets may differ in terms of user types and services available. Therefore, usage models for different system configurations, may be constructed, by combining the SHY models of the reusable components, and SHY models of the configuration-specific parts, hence obtaining SHY models for different system configuration. In particular, different services are one of the key component types to be reused. This implies that the certification is often related to the services potentially provided by the system.

The general principles behind the SHY model are shown in figure 16.1.

The usage is divided into a hierarchy, where each part represents an aspect of the usage:

(1) The usage level is a state which represents the complete usage.
(2) The user type level contains user types or categories.
(3) The user level represents the individual users.
(4) The service level represents the usage of the services which are available to the user. The service usage description is instantiated for different users.
(5) The behavior level describes the detailed usage of a single service as a normal Markov chain.

The interaction between different services is modelled as "links", meaning a transition in one Markov chain on the behavior level, causing a transition in another chain on the behavior level. An example, A dials B, is shown in figure 16.2, where the transition from "idle" to "dial" for user A leads to a transition from "idle" to "ring" for user B.

The model is discussed in more detail by Wohlin and Runeson[4,7] and it is also used in the example in section V; see in particular section V-B.

C Usage profile

The usage model is complemented with a usage profile, which assigns probabilities to every branch in the hierarchy, together with every transition on the behavior level. The probabilities must be derived based on experience from earlier systems and expected changes concerning the actual system or expected usage of the system as it is marketed.

The probabilities in the hierarchy can be assigned static values, as in the example in section V, or be dynamically changed depending on the states of the users in the model. The latter approach is needed to be able to model the fact that some events are more probable under special conditions. It is, for example, more probable that a user who has recently lifted a receiver will dial a digit, than that a specific user will lift the receiver. The user of dynamic probabilities in the hierarchy are further discussed by Runeson and Wohlin.[7]

Test cases are selected by running through the SHY model. First, a user type is selected by random controlled selection, then a specific user is chosen, after which a service, available to the selected user, is drawn. Finally, a transition in the Markov chain on the behavior level for the actual service is selected. This transition corresponds to a specific stimulus which is appended to the test script, and the model is run through again, beginning from the usage level; see figure 16.1 and section V–D. The generation of a specific stimulus also means generating the data being put into the system as parameters to the stimulus; hence data is taken into account.

D   Usage profile and reuse

A component developed for reuse is certified with a particular usage profile for its initial usage and is stored in a repository for future reuse. The component is stored together with its characteristics, usage model and usage profile.

The reliability measure is attached to the actual usage profile used during certification, and since it is based on this particular profile it is not valid for arbitrary usage. The parts of the components, most frequently used in operation, are those tested most frequently, which is the key objective of usage testing. These parts are less erroneous, since failures found during the certification are assumed to be corrected. Another usage profile relating to other parts of the component, will probably give a lower reliability measure.

When developing with reuse of software components, it is necessary to compare the certified usage profiles with the environment in which the component is to be reused. If a similar profile is found, the next step is to assess whether the reliability measure stored with the component is good enough for the system being developed. If the component has not been certified for the usage profile of the new system, a new certification must be performed. The usage model stored with the component is used for the certification. After certification the new profile and the new certified reliability are stored in the repository with the component.

Objective measures of reliability for an arbitrary usage profile would be of interest in development with reuse. It is, however, impossible to record such measures, since the definition of reliability is: the probability of a device performing its purpose adequately for the period of time intended, under the operating conditions encountered. The component has therefore to be re-certified if it is reused under other operational conditions than initially profiled.

E   Reuse of the usage model

The proposed usage model itself can easily be reused. The extent of model reuse and how the model is reused depends on how the system or components of the system are reused. Some different reuse scenarios are presented for component certification, together with those in a system context.

Component certification:

(1)   Reuse with the same usage model and usage profile: The usage model and usage profile for a component can be reused without modification, if the component has been certified before being stored in the repository.

(2)   Reuse of the usage model with an adjusted usage profile: The usage model for a component can be reused, if the component is to be certified individually with a new usage profile. The certification can be obtained with the same model by applying the new usage profile. This gives a new reliability measure of the component, based upon the new expected usage.

(3)   Reuse with adjustments in both the usage model and the usage profile: Adjustments in the structural usage of a component are made if the component is changed in order to be reused. The usage model must therefore be updated accordingly and a new certification must be made.

Reuse of components in a system context:

(1)   Reuse of a component without modification: The objective is to derive the usage model of the system, from the usage models of the components, when a system is composed of a set of components. This can, in particular, be achieved when the structural usage of the component is unchanged, but the probabilities in the usage profile are changed. It should be further investigated whether it is possible to derive system reliability measures from the reliability measures of the components, when the usage profiles for the components are unchanged. The main problem is the probable interdependence

between components, which has not been assessed during component certification. This is an area for further research.

(2)   Reuse of a component with modification: The change in the usage
model is a result of the change or adaptation of the component.
Therefore, the usage model of the individual component must be
changed, thereby changing the usage model of the system. The system has either to be certified with the expected usage profile of the
system, or the reliability of the system must be derived from the
components. This problem is further addressed in reference 5.

(3)   Changes to the existing system: If an element of the system is
changed, for example a component is replaced with another which
has different functionality, the usage of the affected component is
changed in the existing usage model. A new certification must then
be obtained based on the new usage model.

Two factors concerning the SHY usage model make it suitable for reuse.
First, the distinction between the usage model and the usage profile is
important, since it facilitates the use of the same model, with different profiles, without changes. Second, the modularity of the usage model, and the
traceability between the constituents in the usage model and components
in the system, are essential from the reuse point of view.

F   Evaluation of the SHY model

Important aspects of the SHY model are the following:

(1)   Intuitive: The conformity between model parts and system constituents makes it natural to develop the model. This is particularly
the case when a system constituent provides a specific service for the
external user.

(2)   Size: The model size increases only linearly with the increasing numbers of users.[7]

(3)   Degrees of detail: The model supports different levels of detail. The
actual degree of detail is determined based on the system, the size of
the components and the application domain.

(4)   Dependencies: Functional dependencies are included in the model
through the "link" concept.

(5)   Reuse support: The model supports reuse, as stated in section III-E,
through its modularity and conformity to system constituents.

(6)   Assignment of probabilities: The structure of the model helps to partition the problem into smaller parts, hence making it easier to derive
transition probabilities.

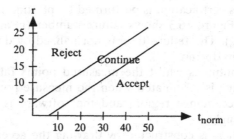

Figure 16.3   Control chart for hypothesis certification of the reliability.

(7)   Calculations: It is theoretically possible to make calculations on the hierarchical model, by transforming it into a normal Markov model. However this is impossible practically due to the size of the normal model. Work is in progress to allow calculations to be performed directly on the SHY model.

(8)   Generation of test cases: Test cases can be generated automatically from the model.

IV   CERTIFICATION OF COMPONENTS

A   Theoretical basis

In the book by Musa et al.[8] a model for reliability demonstration testing is described. The model is a form of hypothesis certification, which determines if a specific MTBF requirement is met with a given degree of confidence or not. A hypothesis is proposed and the testing is aimed at providing a basis for acceptance or rejection of the hypothesis. The procedure is based on the use of a correct operational profile during testing and faults not being corrected. The primary objective is, however, to certify that the MTBF requirement is fulfilled at the end of the certification, hence corrections during the certification process ought to be allowed. A relaxation of the assumption in the model of no correction after failure is discussed below. The hypothesis certification model is based on an adaptation of a sampling technique used for acceptance or rejection of products in general.

The hypothesis is that the MTBF is greater than a predetermined requirement. The hypothesis is rejected if the objective is not met with the required confidence and accepted if it is. If the hypothesis is neither accepted nor rejected, the testing must continue until the required confidence in the decision is achieved.

The hypothesis certification is performed by plotting the failure data in a control chart. Figure 16.3 shows failure number (r) against normalized failure time (t_{norm}). The failure time is normalized by dividing the failure time by the required MTBF.

The testing continues whilst the measured points fall in the continue region. The testing is terminated when the measure points fall in the rejection or the acceptance region, and the software is then rejected or accepted accordingly.

The control chart is constructed by drawing the acceptance and rejection lines. They are based on the accepted risks taken for acceptance of a bad product and rejection of a good product. The calculations are described by Musa et al.[8]

Correction of software faults can be introduced by resetting the control chart at the correction times. It is not practical to reset the control chart after every failure, so the chart is reset after a number of failures has occurred. The reason for resetting the chart is mainly that after the correction, the software can be viewed as a new product.

It can be concluded that the hypothesis certification model is easy to understand and use. The hypothesis certification model provides support for decisions of acceptance or rejection of software products at specified levels of confidence.

If different failure types are monitored, for example with different severities, the failure data for each type can be plotted in a diagram and related to a required MTBF for specific types. The overall criterion for acceptance should be that the software is accepted after being accepted for all failure types.

The hypothesis certification model does not give any predictions of the future reliability growth. The certification can, however, be complemented with a software reliability growth model for that purpose.

B   Practical application

The hypothesis certification model is very suitable for use for certification of both newly developed and reusable software components. A major advantage with the model is that it does not require a certain number of

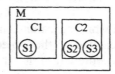

Figure 16.4   Module to be certified.

failures to occur before obtaining results from the model. It works even if no failure occurs at all, since a certain failure-free execution time makes it possible to state that the MTBF, with a given degree of confidence, is greater than a predetermined value. Therefore, the MTBF is a realistic measure, even if a particular software component may be fault free. The model does not assume any particular failure distribution. Most available software reliability growth models require the occurrence of many failures before predictions can be made about component reliability. A normal figure would be in the region of 20–40 failures. Hopefully, this is not a realistic failure expectation figure for a software component.

It is also anticipated that as the popularity of reuse develops, the quality of software systems will improve, since the reusable components will have been tested more thoroughly and certified to a specific reliability level for different usage profiles. Therefore implying, that when performing systems development with reuse, the number of faults in a component will be exceptionally low. The proposed hypothesis certification model can still be applied.

V A SIMPLE EXAMPLE

A General description

The objective in this section is to summarize and explain the models presented in the sections above in a thorough but simple manner using an example from the telecommunication domain. The example follows the steps outlined in section II-A and the basic concept of the usage model presented in figure 16.1.

A model M is to be certified. The module is composed of two components, C1 and C2. The module itself can be seen as a component. C1 is a reused component found in a repository and C2 is reused with extensive adjustments. C1 offers service S1 to the user, whereas C2 originally offered S2. In the reused component version, S2 is changed to S2', and a further service is added, S3. The module is shown in figure 16.4.

The reused component, C1, has been certified before but with a usage profile other than the profile expected when using C1 in module M. It must therefore be re-certified.

B Modelling of software usage

The SHY usage model for module M is developed according to the structure in figure 16.1. Two different user types use the module, namely UT1 and

UT2. There are two users of the first type, i.e. U11 and U12, and one user of the second type, U21. The three upper levels of the SHY model usage level, user type level and user level are illustrated in figure 16.5.

Three services are available for the users of the module. The first service, S1 and C1, is reused without adjustment. Therefore, the behavior level usage model for the service can also be reused without adjustment. The usage profile for S1 has, however, changed and a new profile must be derived. Service S2 in C2 has changed to S2', which results in the addition of two new states to the original usage model of S2. For service S3 in C2, a new behavior level usage model must be developed, since the service is new. The behavior level usage models for the services are illustrated in figure 16.6. The shaded areas are changed or new.

Now the entire usage model can be composed using the structure in figure 16.5, together with the usage models for each service in figure 16.6. The users of type 1 have access to service S1. For each user of user type 1, an instance of the usage model of service S1 is connected. The user of type 2 has access to services S2' and S3, and hence one instance of each usage model is connected to the user of type 2. If the services are interdependent, links between services would be added, hence modelling the dependence between services used by the external users.

The entire usage model for the module is shown in figure 16.7.

C   Derivation of usage profile

The usage profile is derived, i.e., probabilities are assigned to the different transitions in the usage model. Static probabilities are used in this example

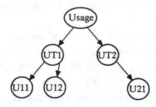

Figure 16.5   Upper levels of the usage model for the module.

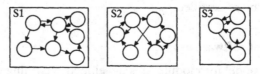

Figure 16.6   Usage models for S1 (reused), S2' (modified), and S3 (new).

(see section III-C). First the probabilities for the different user types are determined, followed by the assignment of probabilities for the users of each type. The probabilities for selection of the services available for each user are determined. Finally, the transition probabilities within the behavior level model for the services are assigned.

The usage profile can be derived bottom-up, if it is more suitable for the application in question. The strength of the modelling concept is that only one level need be dealt with at a time.

A possible usage profile for the usage model is shown in figure 16.8, though without probabilities for S2' and S3.

Unfortunately, it is impossible to go through the example in detail in this chapter, and in particular to discuss the links in more depth. For a more detailed presentation, see references 4–7.

D Generation of test cases

Initially, the usage model starts in a well-defined initial state, i.e., each of the behavior level models are in their defined initial states. The selection

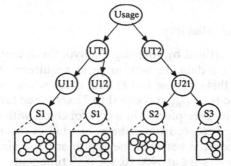

Figure 16.7 Usage model for the module.

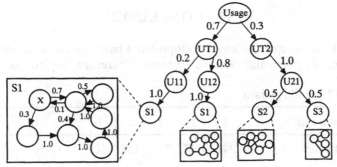

Figure 16.8 Usage profile for the module.

starts in the usage state, where a random number is drawn, for example 0.534 selecting UT1, since 0.534 < 0.7 see figure 16.8. Another random number is drawn, for example 0.107 selecting U11, and for selection of its service no random number is needed. The actual state of the service usage model is denoted "X". A transition is then selected and performed. The stimulus connected to that transition is appended to the test script and the SHY model is run through again beginning from the usage state.

Several test cases or one long test case can be generated, depending on the application.

E   Execution of test cases and collection of failure data

The test cases generated are executed as in other types of tests and the failure times are recorded. Failure times can be measured in terms of execution time or calendar time, depending on the application. An example of failure data is shown in table 16.1. Times between failures are given in an undefined time unit. The failure data are constructed to illustrate the example.

F   Certification of reliability

The reliability is certified by applying the hypothesis certification model to the collected failure data. In fact, an MTBF requirement is certified. The MTBF objective in this example is 800 time units, which means that the first normalized failure time (t_{norm}) is equal to 320/800; see table 16.1 and figure 16.9. The data points are plotted in a control chart, with the module under certification being accepted when the points fall in the acceptance region. The module is accepted between the eighth and the ninth failure and the time for acceptance is about 5400 (6.8 × 800) time units.

VI   CONCLUSIONS

Reuse will be one of the key developmental issues in software systems in the future, in particular reliable systems. Therefore, the reused compo-

Table 16.1   Failure data

Failure number	1	2	3	4	5	6	7	8	9	10
Time between failures	320	241	847	732	138	475	851	923	1664	1160

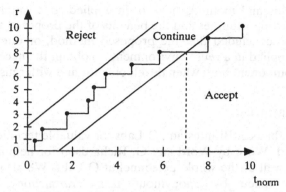

Figure 16.9 Control chart for certification.

nents must be reliable. Component reliability can be achieved by applying sound development methods, implementing fault tolerance and finally, by adapting methods to ensure and certify the reliability and other quality attributes of the components both when developing for and with reuse.

Usage testing or operational profile testing has already shown its superiority over traditional testing techniques from a reliability perspective. A higher perceived reliability during operation can be obtained by usage testing, than with coverage testing, with less effort and cost. The gains in applying usage testing have been presented by, for example, Musa.[2]

This article has concentrated on the certification of software components. The other issues (development of reliable software and fault tolerance) are equally important, although not discussed here.

The proposed method of usage modelling, i.e., the State Hierarchy (SHY) model, is shown to be a valuable abstraction of the fundamental problem concerning components and their reuse. The model in itself is divided into levels and the services are modelled as independently as possible, therefore supporting the reuse objective. The area of certification of software components is quite new. Some ideas and capabilities have been presented, but more research and, of course, application are needed.

The reliability certification model discussed is well established in other disciplines and it can also be adapted and used in the software community. The model is simple to understand and apply.

It has been emphasized that the usage models developed and the reliability measures with a given usage profile can be reused together with the components. The division into a structural usage model and different usage profiles makes it possible to reuse the usage model, and to apply new profiles, as a new environment has a behavior different to that considered earlier.

The models and methods have been applied to a simple example to illustrate the opportunities and the benefits of the proposed scheme. It can therefore be concluded that the proposed method, or one similar to it, should be applied in a reuse environment, to obtain the necessary reliability in the component both when developing for and with reuse.

Acknowledgements

We wish to thank J. Brantestam, Q-Labs for valuable technical comments, H. Sheppard, Word by Word and G. Richardson for helping us with the English, as well as the whole personnel at Q-Labs. We also acknowledge suggestions made by anonymous *IEEE Transactions on Software Engineering* referees.

References

1   H. D. Mills, M. Dyer, and R. C. Linger, "Cleanroom software engineering," *IEEE Software*, pp. 19–24, Sept. 1987.
2   J. D. Musa, "Operational profiles in software reliability engineering," *IEEE Software*, pp. 14–32, Mar. 1993.
3   W. Tracz (ed.), *Software Reuse: Emerging Technology*. Washington, DC: IEEE Computer Society Press, 1989.
4   C. Wohlin and P. Runeson, "Certification of software components" (long version), REBOOT-ESPRIT Project 7808, Tech. Rep., REBOOT-8213-1, 1993.
5   J. H. Poore, H. D. Mills, and D. Mutchler, "Planning and certifying software system reliability," *IEEE Software*, pp. 88–99, Jan, 1993.
6   J. A. Whittaker and J. H. Poore, "Markov analysis of software specifications," *ACM Trans. Software Eng. Methodol.*, vol. 2, pp. 93–106, Jan. 1993.
7   P. Runeson and C. Wohlin, "Usage modelling: The basis for statistical quality control," in *Proc. 10th Ann. Software Rel. Symp.*, 1992, pp. 77–84.
8   J. D. Musa, A. Iannino, and K. Okumoto, *Software Reliability: Measurement, Prediction, Application*. New York: McGraw-Hill, 1987, pp. 201–203.

17 Experimental Control in Software Reliability Certification

C. J. TRAMMELL AND J. H. POORE

INTRODUCTION

There is growing interest in software "certification," i.e., confirmation that software has performed satisfactorily under a defined certification protocol. Regulatory agencies, customers, and prospective reusers all want assurance that a defined product standard has been met.

In other industries, products are typically certified under protocols in which random samples of the product are drawn, tests characteristic of operational use are applied, analytical or statistical inferences are made, and products meeting a standard are "certified" as fit for use. A warranty statement is often issued upon satisfactory completion of a certification protocol.

The statistical principles that underlie such product protocols have long been advocated by Mills and colleagues[1-4] and Musa and colleagues[5-7] as the basis for software reliability certification. The terminology used by Mills and Musa differs slightly, but their ideas are similarly drawn from scientific approaches to product certification in mature engineering disciplines. The terminology of Mills will be used in this chapter.

"Statistical testing" was conceived by Mills and has been advanced by his colleagues at IBM, Software Engineering Technology Inc., and the University of Tennessee. In statistical testing:

(1)   expected operational use is represented in a usage model of the software;
(2)   test cases are randomly generated from the usage model;

This contribution is reprinted from the *Proceedings of the Seventeenth Annual NASA/Goddard Software Engineering Workshop*, held in Greenbelt, Maryland, on November 30–December 1, 1994.

(3)   test cases are executed in an environment that simulates the operational environment; and

(4)   failure data are interpreted according to mathematical and statistical models.

Methods for the construction of usage models[8,9] and the interpretation of failure data[10] have been given. Usage models are developed *before* testing, and interpretation of failure data occurs *after* testing. Proper experimental control *during* testing is critical to the integrity of the protocol, however, and has not previously been addressed.

This chapter outlines specific engineering practices that must be used to preserve the validity of the statistical certification testing protocol. The assumptions associated with a statistical experiment are given, and their implications for statistical testing of software are described. The ideas in this chapter have evolved from experience in 15 Cleanroom projects conducted in the Software Quality Research Laboratory at the University of Tennessee.

THE SLIPPERY SLOPE

It was a typical day in the testing phase of a software development project at ACME *Software.*

Jane had been testing for hours, and her mind was drifting. She took a break. When she returned and ran the next test case, she noticed something unexpected, but she knew this unexpected event had to have been happening all along. She realized she had been too tired to observe it when it first occurred. She didn't know when it had first shown up.

John and Mary were both running test cases. John saw a screen event and thought it was expected behavior. Mary saw the same event and recorded it as unexpected behavior.

Joe suddenly realized that there was an error in his part of the code, and he was anxious to fix it. He waited until testers had stopped for the day, made the change, and recompiled. The testers would continue their work the next day using his new version. He knew he had made the change and recompiled properly, so there was no need to bother the test team about this.

Michael looked over the stack of test cases and saw that they varied greatly in length. He knew that they had been randomly generated, so he assumed that they were all equally usable test cases. He rifled through the stack and picked the shortest ones so he could run the most cases in the least time.

Deborah was a new hire assigned to take the place of a certification engineer who left the company abruptly. She worked with the experienced engineer for a day, and then started testing on her own. She couldn't really read the spec to check the details of correct output, so she decided to just use her best judgment and not bother the others unless she was really confused.

Bill had an extremely long test case. In the middle of the test case, the prescribed events led him back to the Main Menu. Ordinarily, a test case would end at this point, but this case called for a second major scenario. Bill decided the case was unreasonably long, and counted the second major scenario as a new test case.

These very common events are threats to the integrity of a statistical approach to software testing. Statistical software testing, as a scientific endeavor in the real world, inevitably requires some compromises in methodological purity, and it is important to understand the nature of the slippery slope. The assumptions underlying a statistical experiment must be understood, the practical threats to experimental integrity must be recognized, and a strategy for experimental control must be employed.

SOFTWARE TESTING AS A STATISTICAL EXPERIMENT

In statistical certification testing, software testing is viewed as a statistical experiment. A subset of all possible uses of the software is generated, and performance on the subset is used as a basis for conclusions about general operational reliability. In standard experimental parlance, a "sample" is used to draw conclusions about a "population." Figure 17.1 shows the parallel between a classical statistical experiment and statistical software testing. Under a testing protocol that is faithful to the principles of applied statistics, a scientifically valid statement can be made about the expected operational performance of the software based on its test performance.

The premise that must be accepted as a starting point in this analogy is that it is not possible to test *all* ways in which software may be used. This is apparently not a premise that can be assumed as obvious. In a discussion of software testing with the top software manager in a large aerospace corporation, the infeasibility of testing all possible usage scenarios was cited as the motivation for statistical testing. "But we *have* to test every possible use of the software," he said. "The kind of software we develop could cause deaths if it is not tested completely."

Software with an unbounded input sequence length has a theoretically infinite number of possible usage scenarios. For software with only two user inputs, A and B, the possible scenarios of use are A, B, AA, AB, BB,

BA, AAA, AAB, ABA, BAA, and so on. Software with a bounded but large input sequence length has a finite but astronomical number of possible usage scenarios.

The functional testing community measures test coverage in terms of function coverage. But testing every function is not the same as testing every combination of functions. And testing every combination of functions is not the same as testing every possible sequence of functions.

The structural testing community measures test coverage in terms of code coverage. But testing every line of code is not the same as testing every path. And testing every path is not the same as testing every possible sequence of paths.

There is really no question about whether all possible scenarios of use will be tested. They will not. The only questions are how the population of uses will be characterized, and how a subset of test cases will be drawn. A random sample of test cases from a properly characterized population, if applied to the software with proper experimental control, will allow scientific generalization of conclusions from testing to operational use. Any other set of test cases, no matter how thoughtfully constructed, will not.

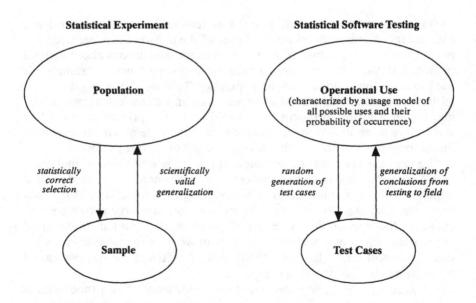

Figure 17.1   Software testing as a statistical experiment.

ASSUMPTIONS IN A STATISTICAL EXPERIMENT

In a statistical experiment, a well-defined procedure is performed under specified conditions, and produces one of two or more possible outcomes. Each performance of the procedure is called a "trial" of the experiment. The outcome data from successive trials of the experiment can be used to estimate the probability of each of the outcomes. Figure 17.2 portrays the general structure of a statistical experiment.

Several assumptions underlie the validity of inferences from a statistical experiment, however. The assumptions are as follows:

(1)   Each trial is performed under the same conditions.
(2)   There is one outcome per trial.
(3)   All outcomes are possible in each trial.
(4)   Trials are independent.

The implications of these assumptions for the testing protocol must be understood. Proper experimental control in statistical certification testing is essential to the validity of the claims that result.

MEETING THE ASSUMPTIONS OF A STATISTICAL EXPERIMENT IN STATISTICAL TESTING OF SOFTWARE

In statistical testing, a trial is ordinarily considered to be a test case. A test case generated from the usage model is a complete usage scenario beginning with some appropriate initial event (e.g., invocation, switchhook up,

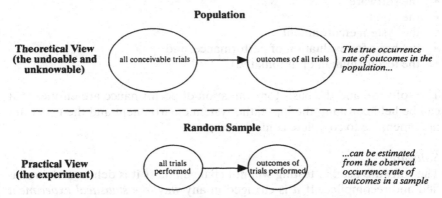

Figure 17.2   Structure of a statistical experiment.

power on) and ending with some appropriate final event (e.g., termination, switchhook down, power off). Other definitions of a trial are possible, however, such as a single transaction or some other set of transactions. The certifier defines a trial in a manner that is appropriate for the application, and must do so in conjunction with the form of generalization the certifier wants to make about the population.

A statistical test case results in one outcome from a specified set of possible outcomes. The possible outcomes of a test case, for example, may be defined as {success, failure}. Under another design, the possible outcomes might be {success, cosmetic failure, serious nonblocking failure, blocking failure, crash}. Another design still may entail outcomes of {0 failures, 1 failure, 2 failures, ... 10 or more failures}. The challenges in experimental control grow with the complexity of the design since more granular judgments are required.

Regardless of the design of the statistical experiment – i.e., the definition of a trial and the specified set of possible outcomes – the foregoing assumptions about a statistical experiment must be met in the way trials are conducted and evaluated.

The implications of each of the foregoing assumptions is considered next. In the following discussion, a trial will be regarded as a test case that has been randomly generated from the usage model, and the possible outcomes of the test case will be regarded as success and failure.

Assumption 1: each trial is performed under the same conditions

What "conditions" are relevant to the conduct of a test case? The entities associated with a test case are, at a minimum:

- the software
- the input
- the system environment
- the basis for evaluation of performance, and
- the tester (human or automated)

The software and the basis for evaluation of performance are entities that can be held constant; the input, the system environment and the tester are not amenable to complete control.

Software
The software used in testing will not change unless it is deliberately modified and recompiled. If it is changed in any way, *the statistical experiment must begin anew*. One may not amass data over several versions of soft-

ware and treat them as a simple statistical experiment. Such data may be applied to reliability *growth* models that predict growth as a function of performance history and *changes* in the software, but may not be used to estimate parameters of a specific version of the software. Testing of each version of the software is a separate statistical experiment.

Input

To the extent that input varies with classes of usage – e.g., novice vs. expert, literary vs. mathematical subject matter, new vs. mature database – separate statistical experiments may be desirable. Otherwise, input (regardless of its origin in the system under test or another source) may be directly incorporated in the usage model structure and randomized via the usage probability distribution (e.g., percentage access of short and long files). The latter strategy effectively removes input from the set of conditions to which Assumption 1 applies by making it part of the trial rather than part of the background. This strategy also eliminates the distortion that could result from tester bias toward the shortest test cases, the "easiest" ones, the most subjectively interesting ones, etc.

System environment

The system environment is perhaps the most illusive of the conditions to be controlled. Variability of background will be a feature of the real operational environment, however, so the experimental task is to simulate a test environment with variability that is typical of the actual environment. Concurrent activity, system load, interrupt schedules, etc., make for a constantly changing background. Again, key variables may be directly incorporated in the usage model structure and randomized via the usage probability distribution.

Basis for evaluation

The basis for evaluation of a test case may be the specification, an independent "oracle," or both. It is not uncommon for a specification to change at any stage of development, including testing. Consistent evaluation criteria must be applied within a testing experiment, however. Behavior that is regarded as correct (or incorrect) in one test case must be evaluated the same way in any other test case applied to that version of the software.

Tester

A given human tester may vary in the way he or she conducts and evaluates test cases, and the performance of any two testers may vary. Training, alertness, motivation, perception, and any number of other variables may affect the performance of human testers. While complete control over these factors is impossible, most of the variability can be eliminated through:

- coordination of all test activities by a chief certification engineer
- thorough tester training
- explicit policies about test materials, session length, and data collection
- documented guidance about issues on which the "test script" is not explicit
- periodic "recalibration" of testers through paired performance of test cases with the chief certification engineer, and
- timely communication among testing team members with regard to observations and decisions that may affect test judgment

Assumption 2: there is one outcome per trial

If the specified set of outcomes (i.e., elementary events) is {success, failure}, then the outcome of a test case is either one success or one failure; it is not both, not two successes, *and not two (or more) failures*. A success is a test case in which the software performs correctly on all inputs in the test case; otherwise, the test case is counted as a failure.

In the strictest sense, then, counting of successes and failures is a simple matter. The number of successes plus the number of failures equal the number of test cases run.

The implication of one-outcome-per-trial is that a test case must be counted as a failure as soon as a failure on any input occurs. This is an unpopular policy, however, because a minor but unavoidable failure that occurs early in every test case will drive the measured reliability of the version to zero even though the software does most everything correctly.

An organization using statistical certification testing must develop a testing policy that accommodates the assumption of one-outcome-per-trial, yet allows testing to proceed in the presence of minor failures. Policy options may be politically difficult (e.g., counting every failure, with the result that status reports show declining reliability) or scientifically suspect (e.g., not counting recurrences of a failure, such that a correct fix and independence of failures must be assumed). Policies each have their advantages and disadvantages. A reasoned policy must be reached and used, however, so that the implications for the integrity of the statistical experiment are understood.

Assumption 3: all outcomes are possible in each trial

All possible scenarios of usage must be candidates for selection in each trial, such that all the ways the software could succeed and all the ways it could fail are potentially observable.

In addition, this assumption implies that testing must not proceed in the presence of "blocking" failures. If a portion of the test script cannot be applied due to a blocking failure that is "not counted" upon recurrence, then success or failure that would result from the input cannot be observed. The detection of a blocking failure is grounds for stopping the testing process and creating a new version of the software.

Assumption 4: trials are independent

Trials are independent if the occurrence of one trial has absolutely no connection with the occurrence of any subsequent trial. For software, trials (i.e., test cases) are independent if the inputs and outcomes of one test case have no bearing on the inputs and outcomes of any subsequent test case.

It may be argued that this assumption cannot be met since programs build up state information over successive runs. Since state data is the encapsulation of input history, the input in one trial may result in a change in state, and the new state may increase the probability of exposing a program defect – i.e., producing a failure – in a subsequent trial.

The only certain way to avoid dependency between failures is to fix each fault and corresponding state data after a failure, and restart testing with the new version of the software.

Alternatively, it may be possible to either avoid or randomize state data. Two types of state information exist: internal variables and external files. Internal variables exist for the duration of an execution. A test case that ends in termination, therefore, will not carry over internal state data to the next run. External files persist from one execution to the next, of course, but it is often not necessary to use them in sequential runs; their use may be randomized. Test cases for word processing software, for example, may randomly access one of a number of files (e.g., no file; short and long files; narrative and equation-filled files; etc.) according to an expected usage distribution.

Regression testing is a violation of the assumptions of statistical experiments. If previously used test cases are run on a new version of the software, they should not be counted as new trials.

Independence of trials in statistical software testing is defensible, but requires a deliberate strategy – either fixing failures as they are found, avoiding the carryover of state data, or randomizing state data according to an expected usage distribution.

THE SLIPPERY SLOPE REVISITED

ACME *Software improved control over its software testing process by establishing a documented testing protocol and training the project team. Things were different in the next project.*

Before testing began, the testing team reviewed the specification, the test script, and other reference materials in detail. The group executed the first several test cases together, with each person taking a turn as the tester. The group reconvened at several points in testing for brief "recalibration" sessions. John and Mary's evaluations of test cases were much more consistent this time.

As prescribed by the protocol, Jane took a short break after each testing hour to review her annotations on the test script, update the chief certification engineer on her progress, and confer with other testers. She was much more alert and attentive to detail as a result.

Joe now understood that the product reliability claim would only be valid if engineering changes were made in a controlled way. Everyone understood that any deviation from the protocol was to be discussed by the team so that the impact on the integrity of the testing process could be determined.

Michael and Bill both now understood the "selection bias" that could result from picking and choosing among test cases, subdividing test cases, or otherwise altering the randomly generated sample of test cases. They now executed test cases in the order in which the test cases were generated.

Testers recorded all choices and observations as notes on the test script. Anyone with points of uncertainty – such as new hires – could later go over the specifics with the chief certification engineer to ensure the correctness of evaluations.

THE ENGINEERING PRACTICE OF STATISTICAL RELIABILITY CERTIFICATION

If test team members are aware of the threats to experimental integrity, they can approach the innumerable decisions that must be made during testing with an eye toward preserving the validity of results. Recommendations for control over the testing process in the foregoing discussion are summarized here.

Test preparation

- Define a test case as a usage scenario that is a longer period than the software can retain internal state data (e.g., invocation-to-termination).

- Randomize external state data via the usage probability distribution.
- Define the system environment(s), and either establish different usage models for different environments or sustain the conditions in a given environment throughout testing.
- Train test staff to ensure a common understanding of all test materials and policies, and monitor performance to prevent "drift."

Test case execution and evaluation

- Hold the specification and independent oracle constant for each version of the software that is tested.
- Assign each test case one outcome from the specified set of possible outcomes.
- Run test cases in the order in which they are generated. Do not pick and choose.
- If previously used test cases are rerun on a new version, they should be performed for peace-of-mind only and not counted as new random trials.
- If it is not possible to execute a portion of a test case (due, e.g., to a blocking failure), stop and create a new version.
- If a failure occurs which could conceivably cause a subsequent failure, stop and create a new version.
- Schedule regular communication between test team members for discussion of matters that may affect test judgment.

SURVIVING THE COMPROMISES OF EVERYDAY PRACTICE

A sound testing strategy may be compromised in practice if the rationale for the strategy is not well understood, is not embodied in a documented process, or is not practiced as documented. Indeed, "the difference between theory and practice in practice is greater than the difference between theory and practice in theory."

The threats to validity in certification testing can largely be controlled through understanding the assumptions in a statistical experiment, establishing explicit policies to meet them, and monitoring adherence to the policies in practice. Such experimental control is necessary to sound footing on the slippery slope of applied science.

References

1 Currit, P. A., M. Dyer, and H. D. Mills. "Certifying the reliability of software." *IEEE Transactions on Software Engineering*, Vol. SE-12, No. 1, January 1986.

2   Mills, H. D., M. Dyer, and R. C. Linger. "Cleanroom software engineering." *IEEE Software*, September, 1987, pp. 19–24.
3   Mills, H. D. and J. H. Poore. "Bringing software under statistical quality control." *Quality Progress*, November 1988.
4   Cobb, R. H. and H. D. Mills. "Engineering software under statistical quality control." *IEEE Software*, November 1990.
5   Musa, J. D., A. Iannino, and K. Okumoto. *Software Reliability: Measurement, Prediction, Application*. McGraw-Hill: New York, 1987.
6   Musa, J. D. and W. W. Everett. "Software-reliability engineering: technology for the 1990s." *IEEE Software*, November 1990.
7   Musa, J. D. "Operational profiles in software-reliability engineering." *IEEE Software*, March 1993.
8   Whittaker, J. A. and J. H. Poore. "Markov analysis of software specifications." *ACM Transactions on Software Engineering and Methodology*, January 1993.
9   Walton, G. H., J. H. Poore and C. J. Trammell. "Software usage modeling." *Software Practice and Experience*, January 1995.
10 Poore, J. H., H. D. Mills, and D. Mutchler. "Planning and certifying software system reliability." *IEEE Software*, January 1993.

Evolving Practice in Cleanroom Certification

OPTIMIZATION

The fundamental benefit of using a tractable stochastic process – the Markov chain – to treat specification analysis and testing is the wealth of research that relates this model to operations research techniques. Highly promising results have emerged from the application of operations research techniques to optimize usage models for specified test management objectives.

- "Representation and optimization of software usage models using mathematical programming" (J. H. Poore, G. H. Walton, and J. A. Whittaker, 1994, in review) outlines the basic process for representing models as systems of mathematical constraints. This makes possible the automatic generation of the transition probabilities representing the intended usage environment as the solution to a mathematical programming problem. Rather than maintain a file of perhaps thousands of state transition arcs and their probabilities, it is possible to maintain a system of constraints and generate a transition matrix on demand.
- "Measuring complexity and coverage of software specifications" (Walton and Poore, 1995, in review) introduces a new complexity measure for Markov chain usage models and identifies some useful basic constraints and objective functions for use in model optimization. Since usage models are derived from specifications, the complexity of specifications can be measured by these modeling methods. Model complexity is measured in terms of statisti-cally typical paths through the model, and maximum complexity cor-responds to the least unbiased model that satisfies all constraints.

OTHER APPROACHES TO STATISTICAL TESTING

- "Operational profile specification, test case generation, and reliability estimation for modules" (D. M. Woit, Ph.D. dissertation, McMaster University, 1994) gives a method for specifying operational profiles based on input histories. An algorithm is given for generating test cases from operational profiles specified in this manner, as well as a check that a set of test cases is statistically typical of the profile. Reliability estimation is based on statistical hypothesis testing.

Appendix A Training and Consultation

CLEANROOM SOFTWARE TECHNOLOGY CENTER

IBM Corporation,
6710 Rockledge Drive,
Bethesda, MD 20817, USA
Telephone 301-803-2684
Fax 301-803-2769

The IBM Cleanroom Software Technology Center (CSTC) was established in 1990 to provide technology transfer services (education and consultation) to customers initiating Cleanroom team operations. The CSTC has offered more than 5000 student days of training to clients in the USA, Europe, Japan, Australia, and New Zealand. In addition to developing a comprehensive training and consulting program, the CSTC has developed three software products using the methodology, including the IBM COBOL Structuring Facility, the first complete product built using the Cleanroom method. Customers include IBM software laboratories, and commercial and governmental organizations, including the financial, insurance, and telecommunications industries. The CSTC has helped client teams achieve 2–10× improvements in quality and 1–5× improvements in productivity. Cleanroom has been identified as one of 12 Good Programming Practices within IBM.

QUALITY LABORATORIES (Q-LABS)

Quality Laboratories Sweden AB,
IDEON Research Park,
S-223 70 Lund, Sweden
Telephone 46 46 182980
Fax 46 46 152880

Q-Labs Software Engineering GmbH,
Technopark I,
D-67661 Kaiserslautern, Siegelbach, Germany
Telephone 49 630 170360
Fax 49 630 170377

Q-Labs was founded in 1989 by the current president, Geir Fagerhus, and some key software engineering researchers in IDEON Research Park in Lund, Sweden. From the outset, the business concept of the company has been state-of-the-art mapping (QSAM) in the software engineering field. In the company's search for state-of-the-art technologies for industrial software development, the potential of Harlan D. Mills' work and the Cleanroom concept was identified in 1990. Since then the Cleanroom philosophy and techniques have been utilized in combination with other influences to perform process improvement in the European software industry. Q-Labs' Cleanroom speciality is application in large real-time systems in the telecommunications domain. The foremost user of Cleanroom in Europe is the Ericsson corporation, and Q-Labs has supported all technology transfer projects in the corporation involving Cleanroom. Other application domains supported by Q-Labs are the medical instrumentation industry, the automotive industry, and the defense industry. Since 1991 Q-Labs has operated the first Cleanroom Competency Centre in Europe (QCCC).

Q-Labs is also involved with a number of research activities, the largest being the PERFECT project (Process Enhancement for the Reduction of software deFECTs) funded by the European Commission through the ESPRIT program. Q-Labs has close research relationships with Lund Institute of Technology and the University of Kaiserslautern. Current research and development in Cleanroom at Q-Labs involves reuse, re-engineering, usage models and profiles for large real-time systems, and combination with maturity model assessments, specifically CMM.

SOFTWARE ENGINEERING TECHNOLOGY, INC.

Corporate Office,
·2770 Indian River Boulevard,
Vero Beach, FL 32960, USA
Telephone 423-637-1333
Fax 423-637-0802
SET Laboratory, Mills Building,
Suite 304, 2200 Sutherland Avenue, Knoxville, TN 37919, USA

Telephone 423-637-1333
Fax 423-637-0802

SET was founded by Harlan D. Mills in 1987 following his retirement from
IBM. From its inception, SET's only business has been the development
and commercialization of Cleanroom. SET is focused on the defining principles and practices of Cleanroom, and has a business base comprised of:

- R&D to extend the science base and engineering practices of
  Cleanroom
- contract software development using SET's Cleanroom process
- development of CASE tools to support Cleanroom practice
- teaching and coaching of others in the use of Cleanroom software engineering

SET has played a major role in the Department of Defense STARS
(Software Technology for Adaptable, Reliable Systems) program, and
has introduced Cleanroom to the armed services. SET has helped private
industry to produce software-intensive products that have proved to be of
exceptionally high quality in field use. In 1993 SET joined with the EP
Consulting Group (an Ericsson company) to become a minority stock-
holder in Q-Labs of Lund, Sweden, to be its source of Cleanroom technology, and to support Q-Labs' introduction of Cleanroom in Europe.
In 1994, SET Laboratory was established in Knoxville, Tennessee, to
facilitate interaction with the Cleanroom research program at the
University of Tennessee and to be SET's base for Cleanroom technology
development.

SOFTWARE QUALITY RESEARCH LABORATORY

Department of Computer Science,
107 Ayres Hall,
University of Tennessee, Knoxville, TN 37996, USA
Telephone 423-974-5784
Fax 423-974-4404

The University of Tennessee Software Quality Research Laboratory
undertakes applied research and development in software engineering.
Industrial and governmental sponsors support software quality research,
demonstration, and technology transfer activities by a staff of software
engineering students and professionals. The Laboratory's primary areas of
work are as follows:

- precise methods of software specification, design, and verification
- scientific methods of software reliability assessment
- improvements in management, development, and certification technologies for Cleanroom software engineering
- tool support for the Cleanroom method

The Laboratory works with industrial partners on software process improvement and with federal government agencies on software policy. The Cleanroom method is used in all the Laboratory's development work, and continuous improvement of the Cleanroom process is an objective in all projects.

Appendix B Tools

CLEANROOM CERTIFICATION ASSISTANT

Cleanroom Software Technology Center, IBM Corporation,
6710 Rockledge Drive,
Bethesda, MD 20817, USA
Telephone 301-803-2684
Fax 301-803-2769

The IBM CSTC Cleanroom Certification Assistant automates elements of the Cleanroom Certification (statistical usage testing) process. It automatically generates test cases from usage probability distributions and carries out statistical analysis of test results. The Cleanroom Certification Assistant is composed of two major components, the Statistical Test Case Generation Facility and the Cleanroom Certification Model.

Statistical Test Case Generation Facility

The Statistical Test Case Generation Facility contains a Usage Distribution Language (UDL) Translator that accepts a usage probability distribution written in UDL, and generates a compilable C program (the Statistical Test Case Generator) that will produce any required number of test cases randomized in proportion to the given usage distribution. The UDL is a grammar that allows specification of format and content of all test cases and the frequency with which to generate them.

By appropriately constructing the usage grammars, generated test cases can reflect statistical customer usage testing or traditional testing techniques such as coverage testing, regression testing, functional verification testing, and/or stress testing of the product. An advanced programming capability in usage grammars enables the creation of self-checking test cases. In association with test automation tools such as the IBM Workstation Interactive Test Tool, the STGF can provide total test automation.

In this mode, the usage grammar specifies test cases formatted for input to the test automation tool.

Cleanroom Certification Model

The *Cleanroom Certification Model* is implemented as a PC-based, graphical tool that automates the analysis of statistical usage testing results for the reliability certification process. CCM takes as input the run times between failures in testing product versions resulting from different engineering changes during test. The output is the projected MTTF for the next engineering change. The CCM computes MTTF estimates reflecting the increase in system reliability as errors are fixed. These statistical reliability measurements computed by the CCM can be used to assess and improve product quality. The time units for MTTF can be defined by the user (e.g., run time or the number of transactions processed).

toolSET

Software Engineering Technology, Inc.

Corporate Office,
2770 Indian River Boulevard,
Vero Beach, FL 32960, USA
Telephone 407-569-3722
Fax 407-569-9303

SET Laboratory,
Mills Building,
Suite 304, 2200 Sutherland Avenue, Knoxville, TN 37919, USA
Telephone 423-637-1333
Fax 423-637-0802

Software Engineering Technology, Inc., has introduced the first in its set of planned Cleanroom tools. The collection is called toolSET, and the first is a certification tool called toolSET_*Certify*.

Certify supports SET's treatment of software testing as a stochastic process based on a Markov chain usage model. This approach enables modeling and quantitative analysis of software specifications, quantitative test planning and evaluation of plans, and conducting testing as a scientific experiment. Use of the Markov chain model makes available a wealth of established techniques in operations research and quantitative decision-making.

Certify is used through a graphical user interface, and supports the three phases of statistical testing: model development, model analysis and test planning, and certification testing:

- Model development provides features for developing new models, editing models, importing models, generating model reports, and managing files of models. Model development and editing features support the entry, deletion, and editing of states, arcs, and probabilities.
- Model analysis checks a model for mathematical integrity and structural errors, if they exist. Test planning is supported by an analysis that reports number of states, number of arcs, source entropy, expected sequence length, lower bound state coverage expectation, lower bound transition coverage expectation, long run probability of each state (sometimes called the usage profile), number of events until first occurrence of a state, probability of state occurrence in a test case, and the mean number of state occurrences in a test case. This information is used in test planning and its evaluation leads to cycles of model refinement and re-evaluation.
- Testing is supported by generating random test cases, producing a statistical summary of test cases, maintaining a log of reported failures, and maintaining a certification report as testing progresses. The statistical summary for a set of test cases includes sequence length and percentage of states and arcs covered. The certification report includes a reliability measure with confidence limits, and two stopping criteria. The stopping criteria are based on comparison of the Markov chain usage model with a Markov chain constructed from the testing experience. One stopping criterion is an information-theoretic discriminant and the other is a measure of the Euclidean distance between the two chains.

Certify is currently available on SunOS, Solaris and IBM RISC 6000 machines. The API is available.